This book is a theoretical investigation of the influence of human learning on the development through time of a 'pure labour' economy. The theory proposed is a simple one, but aims to grasp essential features of the industrial economies. Economists have long known that two basic phenomena lie at the root of long-term economic movements in industrial societies: capital accumulation and technical progress, but attention has generally been concentrated on the former. In this book, by contrast, technical progress is assigned the central role. Within a multi-sector framework, the author examines the structural dynamics of prices, production, and employment (implied by differentiated rates of productivity growth and of expansion of demand) against a background of 'natural' relations. He also considers a number of problems that arise at the institutional level. Individuals' and social learning, know-how, and the diffusion of knowledge emerge as the decisive factors accounting for the success and failure of industrial societies.

Structural economic dynamics

Structural economic dynamics

A theory of the economic consequences
of human learning

LUIGI L. PASINETTI

CAMBRIDGE
UNIVERSITY PRESS

Published by the Press Syndicate of the University of Cambridge
The Pitt Building, Trumpington Street, Cambridge CB2 1RP
40 West 20th Street, New York, NY 10011-4211, USA
10 Stamford Road, Oakleigh, Victoria 3166, Australia

First published 1993

Printed in Great Britain at the University Press, Cambridge

A catalogue record for this book is available from the British Library

Library of Congress cataloguing in publication data

Pasinetti, Luigi L.
    Structural economic dynamics: a theory of the economic consequences of
human learning / Luigi L. Pasinetti.
        p.   cm.
    Includes bibliographical references and index.
    ISBN 0 521 43282 0 (hardback)
    1. Technological innovations – Economic aspects.   2. Diffusion of
knowledge.   3. Production (Economic theory).   4. Economic
development.   5. Labour productivity.   I. Title.
HC79.T4P37   1993
338'.064–dc20   92-13438   CIP
ISBN 0 521 43282 0 hardback

Contents

Preface

The present work is a theoretical investigation on the development through time, as a consequence of human learning, of a 'pure labour' economy, i.e., an economy in which production activity is carried out by labour alone – labour unassisted by any intermediate commodity. The theoretical scheme of a pure labour economy is obviously an abstraction, yet it is aimed at grasping basic features of the industrial economies of our time.

Economists have long since discovered that the long-term movements of industrial economies have at their roots two basic phenomena – capital accumulation and technical progress. But a sort of privileged position has always been given to capital accumulation. For decades, economic theories have been elaborated concerning a process of capital accumulation that takes place *without* technical progress; the idea being that technical change could be introduced later. But this later introduction of technical change has never been easy, and has given rise to endless difficulties.

In the present work, I am taking a reversal of this approach. I am assigning technical progress the central rôle, leaving the introduction of capital accumulation to later investigation.

The main justification is of course analytical – to take advantage of the full potential of a new approach, without at the outset facing too many complications. But other, subsidiary, justifications reinforce the main one. Capital accumulation seems to have lost recently that pre-eminent and absolutely crucial rôle that it played in the early stages of industrialization. At the same time, technological innovations and know-how have been emerging with ever increasing importance. It may also be of some interest to be able to carry out economic investigations, at a fundamental level, without having to face immediately such emotion-stirring issues as those of income distribution and class conflict.

The basic theoretical scheme was already in the background of earlier works of mine (Pasinetti, 1962, 1963, 1965, 1981), and on many occasions

(Pasinetti, 1980–81, 1987) I actually used it explicitly as a simplifying device. Those readers who find it difficult to follow the abstraction of a world without capital goods might still regard it in that light. I had long thought myself that even a simple production model should always envisage the use of both labour and capital (however simplified the way in which they are considered; which is what I did in most of my previous works). But as I went along to present my elaborations in seminars and lectures, I was startled to find how many typical features of the structural dynamics of a production system could be conveyed by a simple model of production with labour alone. Indeed I soon realized that the pure labour model, though no doubt simple, is by no means 'simplified'. I realized that a pure labour economy constitutes in fact the really fundamental core of a whole family of models, and basically of that whole stream of economic thought that, starting with classical economics, was in this century resumed by Keynesian and post-Keynesian economic theory. In the end, I became convinced that indeed the 'pure labour economy' takes in classical and Keynesian economics the place that the 'pure exchange economy' has taken in Walrasian (or more generally, using a widespread though inappropriate term, in 'neo-classical') economic theory.

In this connection I recently argued, with reference to the theory of value (Pasinetti, 1986), that, in the historical evolution of economic ideas since the classics, all economic theories belong to either of two alternative broad paradigms – one focussing on exchange (and more fundamentally on utility) and subjective value, the other focussing on production (and more fundamentally on labour) and objective value.

In the 'exchange' paradigm, to which what has come to be called neo-classical economics belongs, the basic role is. played by a 'pure exchange (or pure utility) model', in which, given a set of original resources with which a community of individuals is supposed to be arbitrarily endowed, single individuals maximize their utilities by exchanging the resources they have been endowed with. Thereby they reach the unintended result of leading the economic system to a better (actually an optimum) allocation of the (at origin arbitrarily distributed) resources. All theorems, all elaborations, are normally developed first for this minimal model. Other features are introduced later, *after* theorems have been proved for that minimal pure exchange (utility) model. This model thereby emerges as absolutely essential, in the sense that it contains those analytical features, and *only* those features, which the theory cannot do without.

In a symmetric way, the 'pure labour (production) model' represents precisely that minimal and basic model that contains the very essential features of the 'production' paradigm, to which classical and Keynesian economics belongs. It contains those analytical features, and *only* those features, which classical and Keynesian economic theory cannot do without.

If this is so, the importance of the analysis of a pure labour economy goes far beyond the simple model investigated here.

There are evident symmetries between the two basic schemes. Each of them refers to a certain type of goods ('scarce' goods, and 'reproducible' goods, respectively), each of them concentrates on a specific problem (the optimum allocation of given resources, and the continually improving application of labour in the production of goods and services, respectively), and each of them is dominated by a basic general principle (individuals' maximizing behaviour in the one case, individual and social learning in production in the other).

At the same time however one should not push the symmetries so far as to make them artificial. Once the pure exchange (utility) model is singled out, one can see very clearly that its approach is indeed reconducible to what in the philosophy of science has been called 'methodological individualism'. All explanations are given in terms of decisions of single individuals. This is not the case with the pure labour model, which, besides not being reconducible to methodological individualism, is not reconducible to any symmetrical set of concepts either (such as 'methodological holism' or 'methodological collectivism'); the point being that it involves both individually based and socially based relations.

At a more immediate level, therefore, it seems more useful to accept, alongside the symmetries, a series of asymmetries also. The maximizing principle, so essential to the pure exchange (utility) model, in fact links it up with very specific micro-foundations (precisely the individual's maximizing behaviour), and to a very specific institutional set-up (that of a free market economy). The learning principle, which is at the root of the pure production (labour) model, goes down to a more profound level of investigation. The classical economists intuitively perceived the importance of moving down to this deeper level: they called it 'natural'. In the present work, the 'natural' relations emerge as having *pre-institutional* characteristics, and thus as being even more fundamental than in classical analysis. They are open in many directions – and in particular they are open to the absorption of alternative types of individual behaviour (and not only the maximizing one, though not excluding it either), and to the absorption of alternative types of institutional organizations (and not only those of a free market economy, though again not excluding them). These characteristics may incidentally turn out to be crucial in allowing the absorption into this approach even of investigations which have already, sometimes with difficulty, been carried out within other approaches.

Methodological issues, however, will not be attempted here. If, or when, a methodological discussion is going to be opened on this respect, it will have to go very deep indeed; and perhaps even require much of eonomic theory to be rewritten.

This makes it even more necessary to stress the limitations of the present short work, which is only concerned with the minimal model – the one containing those elements, and only those elements, which the theory cannot do without. More complex models, extending the analysis to the phenomena of capital accumulation and the use of natural resources, as well as to the explicit and detailed analysis of the typical institutions of industrialized societies, will have to come later.

But in order to underline the importance of the further steps to be taken, a substantial chapter (chapter VIII) will be devoted to major hints on the working of the institutions of industrialized economic systems. And a final chapter (chapter IX) will be devoted to basic implications concerning the relations among different economic systems, the plurality of which is shown to be a consequence of the institutional development that has taken place.

L.L.P.

Milan
December 1991

Acknowledgements

My thanks for this work go first of all to my students. It is for them that I originally started a transcription of my *Structural Change and Economic Growth* into the simpler terms of a pure labour economy. A deep metamorphosis thus began. It was the students' enthusiasm when clearer versions were achieved, their scepticism when simplicity did not go with relevance, their sense of bewilderment and persistent questioning, that forced me to the synthesis and essentiality which – I hope – is now a characteristic of the whole scheme.

What was meanwhile emerging became the basis of several lectures, talks and seminars, which I gave at the invitation of various universities and learned societies. To them I should like to express my thanks. I shall mention: the two Special Lectures at Manchester University, April 1986; the Solari Lecture at the University of Geneva, November 1986; the Special Lecture at the 7th Latin American Meeting of the Econometric Society, São Paulo, August 1987; the Inaugural Lecture at the 24th Annual Meeting of the Argentinian Economic Association, Rosario, November 1989; a seminar talk at the Siena meeting of the Editorial Board of 'Structural Change and Economic Dynamics', July 1990; and yet other, less formal, ones.

It was in fact after the Manchester Special Lectures – at the insistence of publishers who were pressing for a written text – that I decided I had to write the present book. It has taken much longer to complete than I thought. In the process, I have benefited from financial support for secretarial work from various institutions – Università Cattolica of Milan, the Italian Ministry of Education ('Fondi 60%'), Gonville and Caius College, Cambridge (where I held a Visiting Research Fellowship in Lent and Easter Term 1989), WIDER, the United Nations University World Institute for Development Economics Research, Helsinki (where, in May–June 1991, I could concentrate for a month, in splendid isolation, thanks to a MacDonnell Distinguished Scholars Fellowship). To all of them I express my gratitude.

I did not discuss the typescript with colleagues and friends (even resisting their insistence) until the very last stages before publication. At this late stage, I have received useful criticisms and suggestions from Mauro Baranzini, Heinrich Bortis, Michael Landesmann, Piercarlo Nicola, Roberto Scazzieri, Stefano Zamagni. I have also profited from the comments of Andrea Boitani, Antonio D'Agata, Siro Lombardini, Marco Martini, Andrea Salanti, Domenico Siniscalco, Ian Steedman, Paolo Varri. No one of them bears any responsibility, but I am very grateful to them all.

L.L.P.

Symbols

$Q_1, Q_2, \ldots, Q_m$	physical quantities of produced commodities
$q_1, q_2, \ldots, q_m$	per-capita physical quantities
Q_n	total quantity of employed labour
N	total population
$E_1, E_2, \ldots, E_m$	sectoral employment
$p_1, p_2, \ldots, p_m$	'natural' commodity prices
w	wage rate
$l_1, l_2, \ldots, l_m$	labour coefficients (labour per produced unit)
$c_1, c_2, \ldots, c_m$	consumption coefficients (per-capita physical quantities)
m	number of production sectors and commodities
n	$m+1$;
t	time
z	length of each time phase
θ	time elapsed since the beginning of the time phase
h	commodity chosen as numéraire of the price system
μ	proportion of active to total population
ν	proportion of working time to total time
δ_i	rate of workers' retirement in sector i
g	rate of growth of population
ρ	rate of (uniform) growth of labour productivity
ρ_i	rate of growth of labour productivity in sector i
ρ^*	'standard' rate of growth of labour productivity
r_i	rate of change of the consumption coefficient for commodity i
σ_w	rate of change of the wage rate
σ_i	rate of change of the price of commodity i
σ_M	rate of change of the price of the standard dynamic commodity, or rate of monetary inflation
α_i	weight coefficients (for a composite commodity)

λ_i	weight coefficients (for the rates of growth of productivity)
$\bar{w}^{(M)}(0)$	wage rate at time zero expressed in terms of the money unit
$\bar{w}^*(0)$	wage rate at time zero expressed in terms of the dynamic standard commodity
i_M	nominal rate of interest
i_h	rate of interest in terms of commodity h
i^*	'natural' rate of interest

I Economic theory and the neglect of structural change

1. Structural economic dynamics – definitions

The term 'structural economic dynamics' was, until a short time ago, practically unknown in the economic literature. Yet the phenomenon of structural dynamics is as old as the very problems of economic development themselves, to which it is intimately connected.

The evolution of modern economic systems, especially since the inception of the industrial revolution, shows that, as time goes by, the permanent changes in the absolute levels of basic macro-economic magnitudes (such as gross national product, total consumption, total investment, overall employment, etc.) are invariably associated with changes in their composition, that is, with the *dynamics* of their *structure*.

In the short run it is not always easy to see clearly a distinction between those changes that are purely transitory and reversible (as they reflect adjustments to temporary scarcities or to various accidental external shocks) and the genuine structural changes – the latter being defined as those changes in the composition that are permanent and irreversible. But in the long run, temporary deviations, in one direction or the other, cancel each other out, while the major basic trends emerge more and more distinctly as time goes on. It becomes therefore reasonable to try and discover the inter-relationships of the cumulative movements of the macro-economic magnitudes and the changes that take place within their structure.

With regard to these problems there has been a surprising lack of both awareness and attention on the part of theoretical economists.

2. From classical theory to von Neumann's 'proportional dynamics'

In the economic literature, the problems of long- and short-term economic dynamic (already anticipated by certain classical economists, such as Ricardo (1951) [1817], and Malthus (1820); as well as by Marx (1867, 1885, 1894)) have been analysed at length, especially in connection with business cycles. By contrast, the problems concerning long-term *structural* dynamics, despite the interest again shown since the time of classical economists, have been investigated far less frequently.

An accurate examination reveals that Smith, in his inquiry on the nature and causes of the wealth of nations, noticed that a process of continual expansion presupposes changes in the structure of employment, notably an increase in the share of 'productive' work (relative to 'unproductive' work).[1] Ricardo, on his part, starting from the statement that land and natural resources are available in limited quantities, pointed out that the growth of overall production brings about a continuous re-proportioning of the sectors of the economic system, along with well defined changes in income distribution.[2] An interest in long-term structural dynamics can also be found in the writings of Marx on the development of capitalist economies. In Marxian terminology, the tendency toward an increase in the ratio of 'constant' capital to 'total' capital (an increase in the 'organic composition of capital') brings about a series of changes in the proportions among the various commodities that are produced.[3]

It is curious that the classical economists, despite their insights into structural change, were never able to develop a sound analytical basis in this regard. In fact, it is just those parts of classical economic theory that were most fertile from a purely analytic point of view that also had recourse to the most drastic and unrealistic assumptions on the structure of the economic systems.

For example, Ricardo's labour theory of value is shown to be logically consistent only on the hypothesis of uniform proportions between capital and labour in all production sectors. Marx, for his part, faced a problem of the 'transformation of values into prices of production', which is shown to vanish only when once again the 'organic composition of capital' is uniform in all production sectors. It is therefore no coincidence that Marx made precisely this assumption for his entire analysis of volumes I and II of *Das Kapital*. Again it is no coincidence that Ricardo's labour theory of value, even while conceding all the necessary qualifications, avoids all difficulties only if one accepts the extremely restrictive assumption of uniform proportions between labour and capital in all production processes.

It would almost seem that, on strictly analytic ground, the most noteworthy contributions were obtained precisely by the imposition of the most restrictive assumptions on structural change, if not actually by the assumption that structural change does not occur at all.

The decline of classical political economy and the subsequent emergence, from the 1870s onward, of marginal economic theory – which brought to centre stage the problems concerning the optimal allocation of already

---

[1] See Smith (1904) [1776], book II, ch. 3.   [2] See Ricardo (1951) [1817], chs. 2, 5, 6.
[3] See Marx (1867, 1885, 1894).

existing resources – was accompanied by a gradual loss of interest in long-term economic dynamics and even more in structural change as such.

But when, more recently, the analysis and insights of the classical economists on long-term economic movements were taken up again, the same analytic features mentioned above re-emerged. Schumpeter (1934, 1939) was undoubtedly the economist who more than any other insisted on the economic relevance of those unpredictable breaks with the past that are due to technical innovations. This notwithstanding, he was never able to give his notable insights on economic dynamics any worthwhile analytic expression. When he wanted to rely on an analytic framework, he could do no better than refer to the static circular process of Walrasian economic theory, only to add that innovations would periodically upset it.

For brevity's sake, we may leave aside here that economic literature, between the two world wars and in the post-war period, which concerns formal models of business cycles; a literature that dealt with the problems of booms and depressions with mathematical models conceived in entirely aggregate terms, without making any room for structural change.

It is more interesting to note, as far as the theory of economic growth proper is concerned, that those economists, who were able to recapture the impetus of classical dynamics and give it the modern shape of an analytically satisfactory model of long-term economic growth (think of Roy Harrod (1939, 1948), and Evsey Domar (1946), and all the literature on macro-dynamic models that has followed them), were compelled to abandon any hypothesis of change in the structure.

But the most paradoxical and troubling example in this regard is the one offered by the growth model of John von Neumann (1937). This model, from a strictly analytic and mathematical point of view, is generally regarded as the most elegant of all models of economic growth that have been presented. Yet, it has been conceived with the extremely restrictive assumption that the structure of the economic system remains constant for all time – for all of the past and for all of the future. Von Neumann's model embodies a kind of long-term dynamics which will be called here 'proportional dynamics' – a dynamics according to which *all* sectors expand indefinitely over time, while maintaining exactly the same proportions. The contrast between this very elegant formalization and the economic reality of two centuries of industrialization is rather disconcerting.

3. The serious shortcomings of proportional dynamics

The most obvious objections to the models of proportional dynamics come spontaneously from observing economic reality.

To get an idea of the basic point which is meant here, it is enough to have a look at a few data which are here collected, tables 1 and 2, which show, for a few selected countries, figures concerning the proportions of gross domestic product (GDP) and the proportions of employment, respectively, which are attributable to the three main broad sectors – agriculture, industry, services – in the two years 1961 and 1981: a mere twenty-year interval.[4] The countries have been selected (from an almost complete set of countries, appearing in the *World Development Report* published yearly by the World Bank of Washington) so as to cover the wide range offered by the world situation, without loading it with too many details. Data are of course available on a much more disaggregated basis, but there is no need to go further to make the point of non-proportional growth.

The extraordinary thing which emerges, even from a quick perusal of these data, is that there is no need of any particular elaboration. The pure and simple observation of any series of empirical data regarding the dynamics of various sectors in industrial economic systems, suggests, without any shadow of doubt, that in *all* countries a continuous process is in motion, leading to an irreversible tendency, concerning the relative change of the three broad sectors, as per-capita incomes increase. In the less developed countries, the agricultural sector (though increasing in absolute values) decreases relative to the other two sectors, as the economic system develops. In the more advanced countries, even the industrial sector is now

---

[4] Yearly data referring to the beginning of each decade are generally more reliable than those referring to intervening years, as they are normally based on censuses, which are held at ten-yearly intervals. For this reason, I have chosen the years 1961 and 1981, which – though only two decades apart – permit us a very significant comparison. The data for 1991 were not yet available at the time of going to press, but here follow the latest data published by the World Bank for the countries listed in tables 1 and 2, with reference to the GDP structure in 1989. (Publication of the data referring to the employment structure has been discontinued – one hopes temporarily).

Countries	Percentages of (1989) GDP in		
	Agriculture	Industry	Services
Ethiopia	42	16	42
India	30	29	41
Egypt	19	30	51
Brazil	9	43	48
Greece	16	29	55
Japan	3	41	56
Italy	4	34	62
France	4	29	67
Germany (F. Rep)	2	37	61
UK	2	37	61
USA	2	29	69

Source: World Bank, *World Development Report* 1991.

Table 1. *Sectoral structure of gross domestic product in selected countries*

| Countries | Per-capita GDP (In current dollars) | | Index numbers of per-capita GDP at constant prices 1960=100 | Percentage of domestic product in | | | | | |
| | | | | Agriculture | | Industry* | | Services | |
	1960	1981	1981	1960	1981	1960	1981	1960	1981
Ethiopia	42.85	140	n.a.	65	50	12 (6)	16 (11)	23	34
India	66.91	260	137.4	50	37	20 (14)	26 (18)	30	37
Egypt	145.90	650	220.0	30	21	24 (20)	38 (32)	46	41
Brazil	329.40	2,220	217.4	16	13	35 (26)	34 (27)	49	53
Greece	370.14	4,800	277.8	23	17	26 (16)	31 (20)	51	52
Japan	467.83	10,080	358.9	13	4	45 (34)	43 (30)	42	53
Italy	751.99	6,960	235.4	12	6	41 (31)	42 (29)	47	52
France	1,306.78	12,190	212.5	11	4	39 (29)	35 (25)	50	61
Germany (F. Rep)	1,334.51	13,450	189.3	6	2	53 (40)	46 (35)	41	52
UK	1,349.83	9,110	144.4	3	2	43 (32)	33 (20)	54	65
USA	2,750.05	12,820	164.4	4	3	38 (29)	34 (23)	58	63

* The percentages within brackets refer to manufacturing as part of industry

Sources:

UNO: *Statistical Yearbook*, 1962, 1963 and 1981.
IMF: *International Financial Statistics Yearbook*, 1988.
World Bank: *World Development Report*, various years.

Table 2. *Sectoral structure of employment in selected countries*

| Countries | Total population (in millions) | | Percentage of labour force in | | | | | |
| | | | Agriculture | | Industry | | Services | |
	1961	1981	1960	1981	1960	1981	1960	1981
Ethiopia	21.0[a]	32.0	88	80	5	7	7	13
India	441.6	690.2	74	71	11	13	15	16
Egypt	26.6	43.3	58	50	12	30	30	20
Greece	8.4	9.7	56	37	20	28	24	35
Brazil	73.1	120.5	52	30	15	24	33	46
Japan	95.0	117.6	33	12	30	39	37	49
Italy	49.5	56.2	31	11	40	45	29	44
France	46.0	54.0	22	8	39	39	39	53
Germany (F. Rep)	54.0	61.7	14	4	48	46	38	50
USA	183.7	229.8	7	2	36	32	57	66
UK	52.9	56.0	4	2	48	42	48	56

Note: [a] 1962.
Source: World Bank, *World Development Report*, various years.
UNO Statistical Yearbook, 1962 and 1963.

entering a phase of a decreasing quota, both with reference to the national product and with reference to total employment. It has by now even become fashionable to talk of 'de-industrialization'. It is of course significant to compare the situation of the less developed countries with that of the more industrially advanced countries. The former are now roughly – in terms of proportions – in a situation similar to the one in which the latter were a few decades ago. In any case, as can be seen, the tendencies of structural change are unmistakable, even when simply confining ourselves to the three main broad sectors (agriculture, industry, services).

If there is one assertion that we can make with absolute certainty on the long-term development of an industrialized economy or an economy which is becoming industrialized, this assertion is that the production structure does not remain constant, but undergoes *systematic* and *irreversible* changes. This can be seen over a period of time of only a couple of decades. It can be seen with even stronger evidence and clarity by examining longer periods of time (let us say fifty years or more).

The contrast between the picture immediately conveyed by these data and any idea of 'proportional dynamics' is truly striking; and yet, von Neumann's model and proportional dynamics models in general have exerted a sort of contagious fascination. For half a century, since the publication of von Neumann's article, the prevailing economic literature on theories of economic growth has not been able to deal with anything else but proportional growth models, either in the form of economic systems which are supposed to expand uniformly in all sectors, or in the further simplified form of models reduced to represent economies that produce one good only.

It is enough to take a quick look at the economic literature to become aware of the grossly unsatisfactory state of the theory of economic growth. Take just a single, yet significant and authoritative, example – the survey of the theories of economic growth that was commissioned by the editors of the *Economic Journal* to Professors Hahn and Matthews in the early 1960s (Hahn and Matthews, 1964). Such survey contains absolutely no reference to structural change. The most advanced analytic position reported is that associated with the 'turnpike theorem' – a temporary detour (for the sake of optimization) from the proportional dynamics pathway. The authors conclude the article with a section on 'future prospects', in which they express the 'feel[ing] that in these areas the point of diminishing returns may have been reached' (p. 890). Essentially, they invite the reader to abandon growth theory as it has become a sterile area for research. And indeed, from the literature they review – either completely aggregate or multi-sectoral proportional growth – one could hardly draw any different

conclusion. What is truly amazing is the authors' inability (or unwilling-
ness) to find, or catch a glimpse of, in the works of their colleagues, any
alternative line of research.[5]

Robert Solow (1988) seemed to have perceived the sad state of growth
theory research, when in the very title of his Nobel Memorial Lecture
('Growth Theory and After') he appeared to imply that growth theory had
by then come to an end.[6]

The present writer has had elsewhere the opportunity[7] to criticize the
models of proportional growth, and will not insist any further here. Two
important aspects of the limited interpretative capacity of the proportional
dynamics multi-sector models may however be usefully recalled: (i) the
structure of the economic system is supposed to remain absolutely
constant; thus these models can hardly tell us, *with regard to the structure*,
anything more than what we can discover already by looking at the static or
stationary models of inter-industry analysis; (ii) at the same time, a
structure that remains absolutely unchanged through time makes a
multi-sectoral model equivalent to a single-sector model (to be interpreted
as producing a single composite physical commodity). Thus these models
can hardly tell us, *with regard to the dynamics* of an economic system,
anything more than what we can already discover by looking at aggregate
growth models. The enormous interest that they have nevertheless
attracted is therefore rather puzzling. We shall come back to this point,
with a suggested explanation in chapter III.

[5] In a survey drawn ten years later for the *Journal of Economic Literature*, Ronald Britto
(1973) continues to report on macro-economic and proportionally dynamic models only;
but at the end allows a glimpse of hope: 'It is possible indeed that later, better theories of
economic growth might be built on quite different foundation from that currently
employed' (p. 1360).

[6] It is on the other hand very interesting to notice the recent reappearance in the economic
literature (see as a meaningful example Romer, 1990) of economic growth models that, even
if moving within the area of aggregate neo-classical models, take the crucial step of
introducing learning and technical change. They may well make a turning point, as their
inspiration seems to go back to the earlier works of Haavelmo (1954) on the rôle of
education, of Kaldor (1961) on the technical progress function and of Arrow (1962) on
learning by doing – all works that tried to 'endogenize' technical change in the earlier
economic growth literature. A non-linear 'endogenous' growth is now made to emerge by
various features – increasing returns to scale, externalities, diffusion of non-rival goods and
so on. Unfortunately, the explicit references – sometimes brilliant – to concrete facts of
industrial reality are most of the time translated into analytic expressions – generally based
on neo-classical production functions – which are aggregate and risk acting as a sort of
straitjacket. Besides hiding noted, well-known – but unsaid and unresolved – analytical
problems, they do not leave any space for structural dynamics, which is proposed here as
one of the most characteristic features of industrial reality.
   It is also reassuring that a new journal has recently started publication with the explicit
purpose of encouraging economic research of all kinds on structural change (*Structural
Change and Economic Dynamics*, Oxford University Press, vol. I, 1990).

[7] Pasinetti (1981).

4. Empirical studies on structural change

It is worthwhile pointing out, in spite of the general theoretical neglect, that hints at, and hindsights into, the problems of structural change have never ceased to emerge, even in the period between the two wars, mainly on the part of those authors who have paid attention to empirical or institutional aspects of economic systems. Even if it has sometimes only been a question of little more than intuition, those hints are worth noting. The same subjects have of course continued to crop up, and with much more insistence, in the post-war period.

Schumpeter has already been referred to earlier. Structural change was mentioned in the non-mathematical, or, in any case, in the non-formalized literature on the business cycles of the 1920s and 1930s, when there emerged a distinction between 'merely temporary influences and changes that produce permanent alterations in the fundamental relationships of economic systems or "structural changes" (*Strukturwandlungen*)' (Harms, 1926). A certain interest in the concept of 'economic structure' led to theoretical and applied work during the 1930s by economists such as Leontief (1936, 1951), Nurkse (1935), Perroux (1939), and later, Tinbergen (1952). Perroux explicitly used the term 'structural change' by defining the economic structure as made up of 'proportions and relationships that characterize ... an economic set in space and time' (Perroux, 1939, I, p. 194). This was the definition taken up and afterwards used by many other non-mathematical writers, and it became particularly widespread in the economic literature of Latin America, where a certain number of economists called themselves 'structuralists' and directed their research towards an institutional–historical–descriptive approach (see, for example, Furtado (1967)).

The literature on 'development economics' has all inevitably been concerned in some way or another with problems of structural change. Concepts such as 'big push' (Rosenstein-Rodan, 1943), 'unbalanced growth' (for example, Streeten, 1959), 'dual economies' (Lewis, 1954, Nurkse, 1953), and so on, are all inevitably connected with some changes in the system's structure. One may add that they have all indeed proved to be very hard to formalize,[8] which may also help to explain the poor reputational standing that development economics has at present among theoretical economists. Not very different has been the fate of attempts at grand historical generalizations, such as the one on the 'stages of economic growth' by W. W. Rostow (1960).

[8] Baumol (1967) is perhaps an exception. It was sufficient for him to use a simple two-sector differentiated-productivity growth model to reach immediately, in a few pages, some typical structural dynamics results.

But perhaps from no other set of works in the economic literature does the striking contrast between observed facts and strict theory emerge more sharply than from the empirical work on inter-country economic comparisons, that has been promoted, in the post-war period, by international organizations – in particular, by various United Nations agencies and especially by the World Bank. The original inspiration for this empirical work may be taken back to Colin Clark's book (1940), and to his insistence on the changes in employment in the primary, secondary and tertiary sectors, as 'economic progress' goes on. The scholars who then really did play the major rôle in the massive empirical work that has been carried out are undoubtedly Simon Kuznets and Hollis Chenery and his pupils.

Kuznets has devoted the whole of his life to the praiseworthy job of gathering, ordering and comparing data on relevant observable economic magnitudes in the different countries of the world. He has carefully pointed out a number of empirical generalizations on the variation of the economic structure. At the same time, he has been very careful to confine his elaborations to facts, sometimes stylized, but still facts, without pretending either to use or to develop any theory (see especially Kuznets, 1966, 1973). Chenery on his part started originally from input–output analysis. Later – first by himself and then with his pupils – he has gone into innumerable econometric exercises, trying to test simple hypotheses on the evolution of the economic structure, using 'reduced form' econometric relations rather than pretending to rely on, or to propose, any particular theory.

It seems to me very significant that these scholars, on any synthetic presentation of their works, have always very sharply distinguished two separate fields of analysis and research, which they call 'complementary', but which rather uneasily, they keep separate, namely: the field of research concerning changes in the economic structure – which they connect with long-term development, and which they do not integrate into any theory – and the field of research concerning prices and markets, which they do explicitly connect with a specific theory – the Walrasian general equilibrium theory – but which they openly acknowledge as being unhelpful to the investigation of structural change.[9] The curious thing is that they nowhere express any doubt on the adequacy of traditional general equilibrium theory; actually they say at various places that one will have to find a way to use it. Yet they do not use it, as it is avowedly unhelpful for their purposes.

One can indeed see very clearly the embarrassment and endless difficulties which have arisen when one has tried to relate received theoretic lines of thought – analytically so elegant, but inimical to the investigation of

---

[9] See, for example, Chenery's introduction to the second part (on 'structural transformations') of his voluminous *Handbook of Development Economics* (Chenery and Srinivasan, 1988, p. 197); see also Syrquin, 1988, p. 205.

structural dynamics – with the more practical facts of structural change, that do not lend themselves to be set easily in elegant terms, and yet are so much closer to the observable events of the real world.

5. Innovative methodological lines of research

What has been said in the foregoing sections naturally brings to mind the rather troubling suspicion that there may exist some sort of incompatibility – at least at the present state of our investigations – between empirical research on structural change and the requirements of a formally rigorous analysis of economic development. These doubts must be taken seriously.

The present work originally started from puzzles raised by such doubts. And I have finally come to a double kind of conviction. First, I have become convinced that there are analyses carried out in the past, especially by classical economists, that have fallen into oblivion, which are extremely helpful. They should be resumed. In line with this conviction is the contention, already mentioned in the Preface, about the singling out of pre-institutional fundamental features of an economic system – which may be connected with what the classics called 'natural'. Analytically, these should be investigated *before* the institutional relations are introduced. At least some implications of such contention will emerge in chapter VIII.

Secondly, I have become convinced that it may well be necessary to reconsider the entire approach to economic dynamics, by developing new tools of economic analysis, if we wish to avoid continually knocking our heads against the same seeming incompatibilities. In this connection, I shall mention here three innovative methodological lines of research (even if strictly speaking they go beyond the confines of the present work).

The first innovative methodological line of research consists in separating sharply the distinction between variables and constants from the distinction between unknowns and data. In traditional economic analysis these two distinctions tend to coincide because of the essentially static approach which is adopted: those magnitudes which are considered as unknowns are also considered as variables, and those magnitudes that are considered as data are also considered as constants. But in a dynamic context, to insist upon this coincidence makes no sense. Or rather, to insist on this coincidence is equivalent to frustrating the purpose of any investigation into dynamics.

It should be noted that there are magnitudes, such as technology or the attitudes and preferences of consumers, that an economic analysis may consider as exogenously given; and yet they are extremely, if not crucially, variable over time. At the same time, there are other typically economic magnitudes, that is, magnitudes that are within the area of economic analysis and which must therefore be 'explained' – e.g. the profit rate, the capital–output ratio, etc. – which can, in the long run, show no tendency at all to vary in any direction. To separate out the two distinctions mentioned above becomes, therefore, absolutely essential.

A second innovative line of research follows as a consequence of the preceding one, but goes methodologically deeper. It has become a general characteristic of economic investigations to formulate theories in the form of systems of equations. Now, in a system of equations, there are unknowns and there are data (or parameters). As long as the unknowns coincide with the variables and the parameters coincide with the constants no difficulties arise. But what happens if the parameters change in an essential way (as they actually do) over time? It would seem that we head towards a contradiction. The very methodological framework seems doomed to break down, and, in effect, I am convinced that it has been precisely the reluctance to face this apparent falling apart of the methodological framework that has been the underlying force behind the widespread tendency to keep the suppositions of constancy of the technical coefficients in all models of proportional dynamics.

In these models the unknowns are generally prices and quantities, while the data (or parameters) are the technical coefficients. It follows that one cannot admit that the technical coefficients can change; since, if they were to change, one should start over from the beginning on the basis of new technical coefficients, which, in turn, should be considered as data and therefore as constants. And if a new change were to happen, one should go back to the starting point and begin the construction of the model all over again. Every time that one begins, one finds oneself building an economic model that has nothing to do with the previously built one. The new economy is different from the preceding one; it is characterized by new solutions that share nothing with the previous economy. The paradoxical aspect is that each of these economies, which is built on the basis of different technical coefficients, is supposed to represent an economic system (with unvaried coefficients and therefore with unvaried structure) that expands for ever. In other words, the theorist constructs a model of an economy that grows indefinitely over time, even knowing in advance that the change of even a single technical coefficient (an event which is to be considered as quite normal in reality) would cause the whole model to break down. The logical implication seems to be that there must be something inherently wrong with the analytic tools themselves, which should obviously be either modified or changed.[10]

---

[10] Attempts have not been lacking. For example, John Hicks (1965 and 1973) has proposed to investigate what he called the 'traverse', or the passage from a certain steady growth equilibrium path to another steady growth equilibrium path that differs, with respect to the first one, by a once-for-all technical change. It is clear that, even if Hicks brings attention to

It is here that a third innovative line of research can be inserted. My proposal in this respect is a going over from a formulation in terms of the analysis of inter-industry relations to a formulation in terms of vertically integrated sectors. It is proposed that we go on using the analytic tools of inter-industry analysis, *à la* Leontief (1951) or *à la* Sraffa (1960), as long as we consider the economic system at a particular moment of time. But that we shift over, and conduct our analysis from another point of view, based on vertical integration with regard to the final goods, as soon as our inquiry begins to consider movements through time. In other words, it is argued that we need an appropriate set of rules in order to switch from inter-industry analysis, as it has been developed with regard to a given period in time, to vertically integrated analysis, to be used for investigations in time (that is, in a dynamic analysis), with the possibility of returning to inter-industry analysis at any moment when that is necessary or useful. Comparative statics and dynamics would thereby find an appropriate integration, and be used in a complementary manner.

In a theoretical framework of this kind, structural change should no longer present analytic problems. On the contrary, a dynamic analysis, in this context, far from creating problems, leads spontaneously to an analysis of structural change, that is, to *structural dynamics*.

In the present work, it will not be necessary to go into the technical aspects of shifting from inter-industry analysis to vertically integrated sector analysis, and vice versa, simply because the minimal theoretical model which is presented is so simple that, in it, a formulation in terms of inter-industry analysis automatically coincides with a formulation in terms of vertically integrated sectors. It will be recalled that the purpose of framing an economic system in terms of vertically integrated sectors is precisely that of preventing the system of equations from breaking down, owing to a change in the technical coefficients. In other words, the goal of framing an analysis in vertically integrated terms is that of rendering permanent, i.e., independent of technical change, the coefficients of the systems of equations considered. While the coefficients of inter-industry systems of equations change as soon as there is any change in technology, thereby causing the system of equations to break down, the coefficients that

the transition, the logic of proportional growth always is in the background and basically remains the term of reference. Adolph Lowe (1955, but see also Hagemann, 1990) has carried out similar traverse analyses, with a more flexible, but rather aggregate (basically a three-sector) model.

Very significant, therefore, appears the pragmatic approach adopted by the research workers of Richard Stone's 'growth project', which has been going on for years at the Cambridge University Department of Applied Economics. They have given up any grand theoretical scheme and have pursued all available methods – even *ad hoc* methods, such as interviewing engineers – in order to make direct corrections, and update, the coefficients of input–output matrices.

represent the vertically integrated sectors continue to hold, independent of technical change.[11]

It is this characteristic that gives meaningfulness and importance to the analysis to be carried out here. In the minimal, very simple, model which is here elaborated, it makes no difference whether we look at technology in vertically integrated terms or in inter-industry terms. The two types of coefficients come to coincide; but it is their vertically integrated characteristics that are responsible for their extraordinarily fruitful dynamic properties.

6. A note of warning

Before beginning, a warning may be helpful for those readers who are already familiar with my *Structural Change and Economic Growth* – the work from which the present one has originated. In the immediately following chapters, they may get the impression of being taken over already-familiar ground. To a certain extent, this is inevitable. The basic features of the theoretical scheme, on which the following arguments will be erected, have to be presented in their essentiality, and it is not possible to do this simply by referring to previous formalizations and saying that some coefficients are missing. The basic theoretical scheme has to be stated on its own, independently of how it has been arrived at or of how it is related to previous versions. Even where the results are the same, it is obviously important to realize which of them emerge independently of the introduction of capital goods. It would be no use staying with a complicated model where the same outcomes follow from a simpler one.

But the real question is much deeper and fundamental. A minimal model – precisely because of its essentiality – acquires a flexibility and a potential for generalization that the earlier, more complex, version could not have. This characteristic is by itself a source of novel results.

While all this will become quite apparent from chapter V onwards, when new ground will be broken, the attentive reader will find many instances emerging immediately, in the following pages, even where the connections with the previous work are more evident.

I should like therefore to make a plea, especially to the informed reader, for some patience (and generosity) at the outset.

[11] Such coefficients are, in truth, only two: a coefficient of vertically integrated labour and a unit of vertically integrated productive capacity. Now, a unit of vertically integrated productive capacity is essentially unvarying with regard to technical change, by definition. A coefficient of vertically integrated labour does change, but – since it aggregates all the changes that take place in the corresponding vertically integrated sector and reduces them to a single physical quantity of labour – it is susceptible of being represented according to a function portraying a specific hypothesis of change over time; for example, just to take the simplest of all hypotheses regarding temporal change, it can be represented by an exponential function of time, as will be done throughout the pages that follow. (For detail on vertical integration, see Pasinetti (1973 and 1988).)

II   A pure labour production economy

1. Introduction

It is possible to begin investigating the basic features and indeed the structural dynamics of an economic system characterized by production of goods and services, without the need to formulate from the start a complex analytic framework. There exists a minimal theoretical scheme that allows the representation of almost all the basic characteristics of the structural dynamics of a production economic system.

We must however be prepared to make an abstraction from the inter-industrial complexities of actual economic systems, and consider what may be called a *pure labour economy*. The aim is to go with ease and spontaneity right down to the roots of the phenomena that cause the structural dynamics of production systems, without letting ourselves get tied up by the straitjacket of an analysis of inter-industry relations in which the technical coefficients cannot but be considered as constants.

At the same time, the analytic expedient of a pure labour economy permits us to frame the entire analysis, right from the start, in vertically integrated terms, so as to prepare the way to a generalization to the normal situation in which the various commodities are produced by means of labour and capital goods.

In this chapter a theoretical scheme will be formulated of a pure labour economy, by considering the flows that occur within a given period of time (i.e. within the unit of time that is taken as the basis). From the following chapter onward we shall go on to consider the movements that occur over time.

2. A pure labour economy within a given period of time

The formulation of a theoretical scheme of production of a pure labour economy is presented here by following procedures already tested in earlier works (Pasinetti, 1962, 1965 and 1981). The present one is the simplest of all such formulations. In fact, as the reader will see, it turns out to be an extraordinarily flexible formulation, even if based on very few initial hypotheses and concerning some truly simple fundamental relations.

The theoretical elements of a pure labour economy can be traced back, in the history of economic analysis, to the original insights of Adam Smith (1904) [1776], who considered a pure labour production system by thinking of it as related to a primitive society, defined as a society in which the appropriation of land and the accumulation of capital had not yet occurred.[1]

There is, however, no reason, in our case, to relate a pure labour economy to a primitive society, as Adam Smith did. The elaborations of modern economists have made us familiar with much more radical theoretical abstractions. In the present theoretical attempt, the entire scheme will be related to a technologically advanced and perfectly developed society, which, however, is supposed to have the peculiar characteristic of employing labour *alone*. This is – as should be clear – an abstraction.

Let us suppose, therefore, an economic system in which a community of individuals carries out both an activity of production and an activity of consumption. The various goods and services, that in general we shall call 'commodities', are produced by means of labour alone. Following Sraffa, we may suppose 'labour to be uniform in quality or, what amounts to the same thing, any difference in quality to have been previously reduced to equivalent differences in quantity, so that each unit receives the same wage' (Sraffa, 1960, p. 10). But, according to our hypotheses, there is no need of any capital good or any intermediate commodity. It could be said, in a certain sense, that we are considering an economic system in which commodities are produced, exactly in the way Sraffa did, but that we reverse the starting point. Sraffa started by characterizing his economic system as 'production of commodities by means of commodities'; we start by characterizing it as 'production of commodities by means of labour alone'.

In the present theoretical scheme, all the commodities produced are obviously consumption goods, given that, *ex-hypothesi*, no capital goods exist. Labour is, therefore, the only factor of production. It is supposed, however, that production is carried out by means of an extensive division of labour and marked specialization. Each individual produces, or contributes to produce, only one kind of commodity. In this way, one can achieve very high levels of labour productivity. It follows that each individual will

[1] It is at the beginning of chapter 6 of book I of *The Wealth of Nations* that Smith writes: 'In that early and rude state of society which precedes both the accumulation of stock and the appropriation of land, the proportion between the quantities of labour necessary for acquiring different objects seems to be the only circumstance which can afford any rule for exchanging them for one another' (Smith, 1904 [1776], p. 49).

then have to obtain the consumption goods which he or she needs through exchange.

With reference to a given unit of time, within which production occurs, we shall represent the production process described above by means of a set of m labour coefficients: $l_1, l_2, \ldots, l_m$, for the production of m consumption goods (and/or services). The per-capita demand for goods and services (whatever be the process through which it is determined) is represented by means of a set of m coefficients of per-capita consumption: $c_1, c_2, \ldots, c_m$.

Of course, we suppose that:[2]

$$l_i > 0, \tag{2.1}$$

$$c_i > 0, \qquad\qquad i = 1, 2, \ldots, m. \tag{2.2}$$

Moreover we denote: the m physical quantities of goods produced with Q_1, $Q_2, \ldots, Q_m$, and the respective m prices with $p_1, p_2, \ldots, p_m$. We denote the price of labour, or wage rate, with w; and the total quantity of labour with Q_n, without for the moment making any distinction between total population and working population, the two being supposed to coincide. This simplification will be abandoned later on (in chapter IV), as soon as a distinction becomes important.

These magnitudes can be grouped in a production scheme according to Leontief's closed model. In our simple case, this model consists of two systems of $m+1$ (that we shall also call n) linear and homogeneous equations:[3]

$$\begin{bmatrix} 1 & 0 & \cdots & 0 & -c_1 \\ 0 & 1 & \cdots & 0 & -c_2 \\ \cdot & \cdot & \cdot & & \cdot \\ \cdot & \cdot & \cdot & \cdot & \cdot \\ \cdot & \cdot & \cdot & \cdot & \cdot \\ 0 & 0 & \cdots & 1 & -c_m \\ -l_1 & -l_2 & \cdots & -l_m & 1 \end{bmatrix} \begin{bmatrix} Q_1 \\ Q_2 \\ \cdot \\ \cdot \\ \cdot \\ Q_m \\ Q_n \end{bmatrix} = \begin{bmatrix} 0 \\ 0 \\ \cdot \\ \cdot \\ \cdot \\ 0 \\ 0 \end{bmatrix}, \tag{2.3}$$

[2] In the present work the various algebraic expressions will be marked by two numbers: the first one denotes the section in which it appears for the first time in the current chapter and the second one denotes the progressive order in which the expression appears for the first time in the current section. When, subsequently, in the text, it is necessary to refer to expressions that appear in earlier chapters, a (third) Roman numeral will be added – before the two Arabic numerals – indicating the chapter. Each notation without the Roman numeral, i.e. with only two Arabic numerals, must, therefore, be understood as referring to the chapter in which it appears. An analogous convention will also be followed for references to the sections of a chapter. A single Arabic numeral will be used for reference to a section in the current chapter, while a further Roman numeral will appear before the Arabic numeral for references to sections of other chapters.

[3] It may seem excessive or superfluous at first sight to use explicit matrix notation to frame such a simple scheme. Yet this notation serves the twofold purpose of showing immediately the connections with Leontief's closed model and its formal properties, and of rendering quite spontaneous (later on) the extensions to the introduction of intermediate commodities.

$$\begin{bmatrix} 1 & 0 & . & . & . & 0 & -l_1 \\ 0 & 1 & . & . & . & 0 & -l_2 \\ . & . & . & & . & . & . \\ . & . & . & . & . & . & . \\ . & . & . & . & . & . & . \\ 0 & 0 & . & . & . & 1 & -l_m \\ -c_1 & -c_2 & . & . & . & -c_m & 1 \end{bmatrix} \begin{bmatrix} p_1 \\ p_2 \\ . \\ . \\ . \\ p_m \\ w \end{bmatrix} = \begin{bmatrix} 0 \\ 0 \\ . \\ . \\ . \\ 0 \\ 0 \end{bmatrix} \qquad (2.4)$$

In any system of linear and homogeneous equations, there is, as is well known, a necessary condition that must be satisfied in order that there are non-trivial solutions. This condition is that the determinant of the coefficient matrix is zero. In our case, this necessary condition (as may be easily checked) is exactly the same for both systems and turns out to be:

$$\sum_{i=1}^{m} c_i l_i = 1. \qquad (2.5)$$

When this condition is fulfilled, it introduces a degree of freedom in each of the two systems of equations. This means that the solution of system (2.3) only determines relative quantities and the solution of system (2.4) only determines relative prices. These solutions turn out to be:

$$Q_i = c_i Q_n, \qquad (2.6)$$

and

$$p_i = l_i w, \qquad\qquad i = 1, 2, \ldots, m. \qquad (2.7)$$

If we now consider the working population as given:

$$Q_n = \bar{Q}_n, \qquad (2.8)$$

and, moreover, if we consider the wage rate as given:

$$w = \bar{w}, \qquad (2.9)$$

then the two systems of equations become determined.

As far as the price system is concerned, equation (2.9) is of course a convention, which is equivalent to considering the wage rate $\bar{w}$ as a unit for measuring prices. We might, even more simply, fix it directly:

$$w = 1, \qquad (2.10)$$

that is, express all prices in terms of classical 'labour commanded'; or else we might adopt as numéraire any commodity whatsoever, by closing the price system with the equation:

$$p_h = 1, \qquad (2.11)$$

where h is the particular commodity which is chosen as numéraire.

Whatever convention is chosen to close the two systems of equations, formulations (2.5), (2.6), (2.7) deserve a closer examination.

3. A Smithian pure labour theory of value and the Keynesian principle of effective demand

An interesting aspect of solutions (2.6) and (2.7) is that, in their amazing simplicity, they immediately call to mind the fundamentals of Smith's pure labour theory of value and of Keynes' principle of effective demand.

We may notice that there is a complete separation of the physical quantity system and the price system. These two systems of equations can be solved independently of each other – a characteristic that should be further investigated.

Looking at solution (2.7), concerning the price system, one sees that prices turn out to be proportional to labour coefficients: quantities of labour are multiplied by the wage rate. One can immediately feel here an unmistakable classical flavour; a result after all quite obvious. In a system in which the only factor of production is labour, prices cannot but be proportional to quantities of labour. There is not even any reason to distinguish between 'embodied labour' and 'commanded labour' (a distinction that caused so many complications to the classical economists). In a pure labour economy, the two notions necessarily coincide: the quantity of labour that each commodity can command is always exactly equal to the quantity of labour embodied in it. Precisely in this very connection the meaning of prices emerges as typically classical: they do not express *market* prices (that would inevitably depend on the temporary whims of market supply and demand). They express those prices which the classical economists called 'natural prices' – a more fundamental notion of price, which reflects permanent and fundamental determinants. And, in our case, the permanent determinants are the production costs, expressed as quantities of necessary labour.[4]

Going on to consider solution (2.6) for the system of physical quantities, we see that the quantities turn out to be proportional to the consumption coefficients. Per-capita quantities of demand for consumption goods are

---

[4] The distinction between 'natural' and 'market' prices goes back to Adam Smith (1904 [1776], book I, chapter 7). More accurate definitions can be found in chapter 4 of Ricardo's *Principles*, where the market prices are said to be 'disturbed by any temporary and accidental cause', due to the inevitable non-correspondence, at every instant, between the possibilities of production and the temporary whims of market demand. The 'natural' prices, on the other hand, are said to reflect the 'primary and natural' elements, that, being fundamental, are independent of demand (Ricardo 1951 [1817], pp. 88–92). It is to the 'natural prices' that all classical economists, and more specifically Ricardo, always referred their basic formulations.

multiplied by total population. And here we can unmistakably feel a Keynesian flavour. The solutions (2.6) bring to the surface a production theory dominated by effective demand. Independently of the way decisions are made, solutions (2.6) tell us that the physical quantities produced are determined by the effective demand that is actually being exerted for the various commodities. It could be said that the principle of effective demand emerges from the solutions of this system of physical quantities in a pure way, and in fact in a way which is clearer than in the elaborations of Keynes himself. As a direct result of the hypothetical absence of capital goods, the overall productive capacity in this model is represented by the multiform productive capacities of labour. And it is, therefore, a productive capacity, so to speak, widespread and undifferentiated, that makes itself available right there where demand so requires. The production is, in this sense activated, or, as is also said, generated by effective demand. And it is in this way that the Keynesian principle of effective demand here emerges, we might say, in its pure form.

There is only one constraint, not sectoral, but global or macro-economic. This is the constraint which is set by the overall existing productive capacity, i.e. in the present scheme, by the overall availability of total labour; namely by its full employment. Here we come up precisely against the problems raised by Keynes (1936), concerning the importance of a particular macro-economic condition, which in the present scheme is expressed by necessary condition (2.5).

4. A macro-economic condition for the achievement of full employment

An examination of the *economic* meaning of necessary condition (2.5) now becomes of particular interest.

Condition (2.5), as it concerns the determinant of the coefficient matrix, is exactly the same for both systems of equations. It is, therefore, a single condition. It should moreover be noted that it is independent of the number of production sectors. Whether the sectors are two, or whether they are thousands, this condition is just one – it emerges as the sum of all terms $c_i l_i$ $(i = 1, 2, \ldots, m)$ concerning the entire economic system. It represents, so to speak, a characteristic of the economic system as a whole, not of its sectoral features. We can, therefore, indeed say that condition (2.5) is a genuinely macro-economic condition.[5] Its economic meaning may be explored in two

---

[5] There are relations in economic analysis that take up a macro-economic form only when the entire analysis is carried out at a macro-economic level. These relations are 'macro-economic' only artificially: they cease to be such as soon as the analysis is carried out at a more disaggregate level. But there are other relations that maintain their macro-economic form independently of the degree of disaggregation at which the analysis is carried out. Only the latter relations can be defined as being genuinely macro-economic. Expression (2.5) is one of them.

ways: within the context of equation system (2.3) and within the context of equation system (2.4).

Within the context of physical quantity system (2.3), each term $c_i l_i$ represents the *proportion* of the overall employment that is required by the productive process of the ith commodity, as can easily be verified by examining the effects on the last equation of system (2.3). This equation says that the sum of all the requirements of labour from the various sectors must add up to the overall quantity of available labour. Evidently, equality (2.5), namely the condition that the sum of the mentioned proportions is equal to unity, therefore means that there must be full employment of the overall quantity of labour available. If we were to have an inequality, for example if we were to have:

$$\sum_{i=1}^{m} c_i l_i < 1, \tag{4.1}$$

and thus condition (2.5) were not satisfied, that would also mean that the last equation of system (2.3) is not satisfied. It would mean an incomplete utilization of the available quantity of labour. In other words, inequality (4.1) would mean that there is unemployment in the economic system.

But expression (2.5) also has an economic meaning in the context of price system (2.4). In this context, each term $c_i l_i$ represents the *proportion* of the potential national income generated in each ith sector by the expenditure channelled to that sector by the effective demand of the consumers, as can easily be verified by examining the effects on the last equation of system (2.4). This equation says that the sum of all the items of per-capita expenditure (which, in our case, refer entirely to consumption) must add up to the total average per-capita income, which in our case coincides with the wage rate. Clearly, equality (2.5), namely the condition that the sum of the mentioned proportions is equal to unity, precisely means that the expenditure of the overall national income must be complete. In the economic system that we are considering, all expenditure is on consumption goods. There is therefore no place for any savings, if by savings we mean – in Keynesian terminology – the difference betwen national income and overall consumption. Of course, there can be physical hoarding (an accumulation of physical durable consumption goods) or there can be savings on the part of certain individuals who accumulate credits, in terms of purchasing power (financial activities), towards other individuals, who, in their turn, accumulate debts (financial liabilities) – these aspects of the matter will be examined in chapter VI. But as far as the economic system as a whole is concerned, there can be no savings. Overall effective demand must exert itself at that level which generates an overall production equal to the entire potential national income of the economic system. If there were to emerge an inequality (4.1), i.e., if condition (2.5) were not to be satisfied, that would mean that in the economic system as a whole there is deficiency of effective demand.

The typically Keynesian economic meaning of necessary condition (2.5), required by the solution of the two systems of linear and homogeneous equations (2.3) and (2.4), now emerges fully, if we take advantage of both contexts considered above. Essentially, necessary condition (2.5) means that a complete expenditure of individual incomes must take place so that overall effective demand may reach that level which is capable of generating that amount of total production which assures the full employment of the available quantity of labour. This is precisely the message, in its pure form, of Keynesian theory.

But there are always two sides to every coin. Even if inequality (4.1), namely a situation of unemployment due to deficiency of effective demand, was considered by Keynes as the normal situation (and looking back to the 1930s, when he was writing, one could not blame him), also the opposite situation, namely that expressed by the opposite inequality:

$$\sum_{i=1}^{m} c_i l_i > 1, \tag{4.2}$$

always remains a possibility. Keynes (1936) did not consider it, but the theoretical model formulated here forces us to go (beyond Keynes) in that direction as well.

An effective demand that tends to overcome the possibilities of physical production cannot, in the physical quantity system, but come up against another physical constraint (represented by the physical impossibility of producing more than what the current technology permits, given the size of the available quantity of labour). But in the system of prices it can exert a pressure on their general level (an inflationary thrust). This is precisely the situation that Keynes (1936) did not consider. Yet it is a situation which is exactly symmetrical and opposite to the one he examined, and it is equally worthy of being investigated.

5. The two opposite situations of macro-economic disequilibrium – unemployment and inflation

The situations (which are each other's opposites) defined by the two inequalities (4.1) and (4.2) correspond to two opposite situations of macro-economic disequilibrium, due to a deficiency and an excess of effective demand, respectively, relatively to existing productive capacity. The first has immediately relevant effects on the physical quantity system (unemployment of labour); the second has immediately relevant effects on the price system (inflation of the general price level).

A particularly favourable formal property of the model may be noticed, on this respect. Non-fulfilment of necessary condition (2.5) does indeed mean non-existence of *equilibrium* solutions, but it does not exclude existence of non-equilibrium solutions. In fact, when necessary condition (2.5) is not fulfilled, in each of the two equation systems, the first *m* equations continue to hold. What breaks down is the last equation; and this, as pointed out above, respectively means less (or pressure for more) than full employment in the physical quantity system and less (or tendentially more) than full expenditure of national income in the price equation system. We might say that *sectoral* equilibrium may continue to hold, and that this is compatible with a macro-economic situation of disequilibrium (what has also been termed an equilibrium of Keynesian underemployment, or – we may now add – of inflationary expenditure).

At this point of our analysis, however, in order to proceed further, it would be necessary to introduce specific hypotheses regarding the behavioural response of the economic agents to the emergence of situations of macro-economic disequilibrium, within a certain well defined institutional set-up. But it is not our intention, at least for the time being, to go in this direction. We shall return to this matter in chapter VIII. Here we are content with having formulated the necessary condition that must be satisfied in order to obtain economically meaningful equilibrium solutions, and to have investigated the economic meaning of such condition when it is fulfilled, besides having pointed out its economic meaning when it is not fulfilled, in both directions.

6. The 'natural' level of employment and the 'natural' wage rate

We are, on the other hand, in a position to return to, and expand further on, the significance of solutions (2.6) and (2.7). These expressions, as has been pointed out above, hold in any case, whether condition (2.5) is fulfilled – a situation of macro-economic equilibrium – or whether it is not fulfilled – a situation of macro-economic disequilibrium.

But when macro-equilibrium holds, this gives particular macro-economic significance to the $(m+1)^{\text{th}}$ variable in each of the two equation systems, namely to Q_n in equation system (2.3) and to w in equation system (2.4).

The physical quantities $Q_1, Q_2, \ldots, Q_m$, are sectoral magnitudes. Each of them is determined by the effective demand which flows into the corresponding sector. The physical quantity Q_n on the other hand is a magnitude of national relevance. It represents a sort of pool of the physical quantity of labour that is available in the whole economic system. And it is clearly a matter of general concern that it should entirely be employed – i.e., that there should be full employment. This is what happens when the macro-economic equilibrium condition holds. If we were therefore to talk at all of a 'natural' level of employment, this could not but be the level of full employment. In the present context, a natural rate of unemployment would make no sense; or, if we like, it couldn't but be equal to zero.

In the price equation system, the same counter-position may be seen even more clearly. The m commodity prices, $p_1, p_2, \ldots, p_m$, taken together on the one side, and the wage rate, w, taken by itself on the other side, emerge as each other's counterparts. The 'natural' prices, by being proportional to physical quantities of labour (both embodied and commanded), channel back to each unit of physical labour an equal amount of purchasing power, that each recepient can then exert over all the consumption goods that are produced in the whole economic system. This is basically the meaning of the 'natural' wage rate. Essentially, the natural wage rate – emerging from the price equation system, when natural prices prevail and macro-economic condition (2.5) is fulfilled – represents each labourer's equal share into the net national product.

The macro-economic character of the natural wage rate thus emerges very clearly. This characteristic is, conceptually speaking, extremely important. As opposed to the 'natural' commodity prices, which express sectoral (or micro-economic) magnitudes, the natural wage rate represents an extraordinarily synthetic notion. Its *real* content is given by the basket of physical commodities that on average it can purchase. The natural wage rate thus expresses a synthesis of the characteristics of technology and of the characteristics of consumption choices of the economic system considered as a whole.

7. Importance of effective demand for the configuration of an economic system

We are in a position to go back to (2.5) and bring into relief yet another important aspect of this truly fundamental macro-economic condition, characterizing any production system.[6]

It is useful to note that, in the present theoretical scheme, all technical inter-industry relations have been left aside *ex-hypothesi*. No inter-industry relation is considered, no intermediate commodity is supposed to exist, no

---

[6] Incidentally, it will be noted that this macro-economic condition does not emerge from any of the neo-classical models used to represent an economic system. (The budget constraint equation of the Walrasian model of a pure exchange economy is of an entirely different nature. Actually, it can never be unsatisfied. It should not, therefore, be confused with equality (2.5).) This may also help to explain why it has also been so difficult, and in any case artificial, to insert Keynes' contributions on effective demand into the Walrasian model. Actually, the importance of Keynes' theory of effective demand can be truly understood and properly evaluated only if it is explicitly considered within a production model.

capital goods are necessary. And yet, despite this absence of technological inter-relations among the various sectors, the entire economic system is actually held together by necessary condition (2.5); that is, the entire economic system is inter-related, and truly forms a 'system', because of the effects of overall effective demand.

The ultimate explanation is given by the peculiarity of the organization of production, which is basically relying on division of labour and on specialization, at the same time as producing on a large scale. Each individual is so specialized that he or she contributes to produce only one type of good or even only a fraction of a good. But his or her demand concerns all, or most of, the goods produced. In other words, the individual's technical contribution achieves high productivity, but it is very concentrated and thus restricted. And it is concentrated (and thus restricted) precisely in order to achieve high productivity. At the same time, however, an individual's demand affects a multitude of goods and services, and, therefore, contributes to generating employment in the entire economic system.

This is one of the most basic and specific characteristics of any highly specialized production system; a typical characteristic of any industrially advanced economy. This is the source of its high productivity (on whose consequences we shall concentrate our attention in the following chapters) and, at the same time, of its intrinsic fragility, to which we shall return in chapter VIII.

8. Towards a dynamic analysis

Equation systems (2.3) and (2.4) – and corresponding solutions (2.6) and (2.7), subject to necessary condition (2.5) – represent flows of labour services and flows of production of consumption goods, respectively, that occur within a single unit of time. They are flows per year, if for the sake of simplicity we call 'year' the unit of time. But the year which has been considered will be followed by another, different, 'year', that will in turn be characterized by another, different, pair of systems of equations of type (2.3) and (2.4); and therefore by another, different, pair of solutions of type (2.6) and (2.7), with a corresponding macro-economic condition of type (2.5). This second time unit will then be followed by a third time unit with a third pair of systems of equations, and solutions, with their corresponding macro-economic condition, and so on, in ever-flowing temporal sequence.

In this way, in the most natural manner, there also emerges, besides the flows of the economic system under consideration, their *sequential* succession in time.

Now, in a sequence of 'years', there is no reason why the labour coefficients, the labour force, the consumption patterns should remain constant; and there is no reason why the various flows should always go on taking place in the same way. On the contrary, the most natural thing that may occur is that they undergo variations and changes. And there is no reason why these changes should be confined to either one or the other of the magnitudes taken into consideration. *All* magnitudes will, in general, vary (quite independently of the fact that there is no capital good in the system).

Therefore, as we prepare ourselves to carry our analysis beyond the single time unit considered up till now, we must add a time suffix, t, to each magnitude considered so far. Each magnitude thus becomes dated. We are taken from an analysis of the flows that occur within a given unit of time to the analysis of the flows that follow one upon the other over time – from a short-run analysis in the sense of Keynes (1936) to a dynamic analysis in the sense of Harrod (1948).

III Proportional dynamics

1. Analytic procedures

We are now ready for an investigation of the movements of the flows through time.

The analytic procedure which will be followed is first to formulate some specific basic hypotheses regarding the course over time of those magnitudes that are exogenously accepted from outside our analysis (population, technical knowledge, patterns of consumption); then to proceed to a search for those conditions that must be kept satisfied in order that there exist meaningful solutions for the magnitudes which are the object of our economic investigation; and finally to go on to examine the equilibrium paths of such solutions as time goes by.

We must first establish a preliminary analytic convention regarding the notion of time. There are two alternative procedures which may be followed here. Time may be considered as a succession of finite periods, thereby making the supposition that the changes occur between one period and another; or time may be considered as giving way to continuous variations, which means that the single periods become so short as to be infinitesimal. For most of our analysis, it is not important which one of these two conventions is adopted. But since the second one makes formulations analytically simpler, this is the one which will normally be followed, except that, from time to time, the arguments may be recast in terms of the first convention, whenever that appears useful or appropriate.[1]

However, we shall not venture immediately into the complex realm of structural change. For reasons of comparison and contrast, as well as for the purpose of preparing our way to the analysis that will follow, it will

---

[1] In any case, in the formulations concerning periods with finite length of time, it will be useful to continue to refer to the single time unit with the intuitive term of 'year'. Moreover, in the exponential formulations (with continuous time), the rates of change of explicit reference will always be yearly rates of change.

prove enlightening, as an intermediate analytical stage, to analyse first the hypothetical cases that bring about that proportional dynamics which has so far dominated most of growth theory, and which has been so severely criticized in chapter I. In this way, the artificial nature of such hypothetical cases will be shown even more clearly. At the same time, because of their simplicity and elegance, these hypothetical cases will serve the purpose of introducing formulations that are useful for the structural dynamics analysis which will be developed afterwards.

The present chapter, therefore, has a purely hypothetical nature and a purely analytical justification. It must be considered as an intermediate stage of analysis to prepare the treatment of structural dynamics, which will then be faced in the following chapters.

2. Population growth

The simplest of all cases of economic growth is that in which all technical coefficients and all consumption coefficients remain constant over time and the only exogenous magnitude that changes is population. In short, the only hypothesis of exogenous change over time is:

$$N(t) = N(0)e^{gt}, \tag{2.1}$$

where $N(t)$ is total population at time t, g is the percentage rate of growth per year and e is the well-known number ($e = 2,71828 \ldots$) which is the basis of the exponential functions (and of the natural logarithms).

Moreover, for simplicity's sake, we shall continue to suppose – a supposition which will be kept for the whole of the present chapter – that total population N and working population Q_n coincide, i.e.,

$$Q_n(t) \equiv N(t). \tag{2.2}$$

With hypothesis (2.1), the price system (II.2.4), the corresponding necessary condition for economically significant equilibrium solutions (II.2.5) and the solutions (II.2.7) all remain absolutely unchanged over time. Similarly, in the physical quantity system (II.2.3), all coefficients remain constant. Also constant remains the necessary condition for economically significant equilibrium solutions, which again is (II.2.5). But, in the physical quantity vector, the working population $Q_n(t)$ grows over time at the yearly percentage rate g, so that we can see from solutions (II.2.6) that all the physical quantities grow over time exactly at the same percentage rate of growth g.

A formal asymmetry therefore emerges between the physical quantity system and the price system. This asymmetry may be eliminated by redefining the physical quantities in per-capita terms, namely by denoting with $q_i(t)$:

$$q_i(t) = \frac{Q_i(t)}{N(t)}, \qquad\qquad i = 1, 2, \ldots, m, n. \qquad (2.3)$$

Now, $Q_i(t)$ and $N(t)$ grow, in equilibrium, at exactly the same percentage rate, g, so that $q_i(t)$ remains absolutely constant over time.

By therefore rewriting the physical quantity system, on the basis of (2.3) and (2.2), i.e.,

$$
\begin{bmatrix}
1 & 0 & . & . & . & 0 & -c_1 \\
0 & 1 & . & . & . & 0 & -c_2 \\
. & . & & . & & . & . \\
. & . & & . & & . & . \\
. & . & & . & & . & . \\
0 & 0 & . & . & . & 1 & -c_m \\
-l_1 & -l_2 & . & . & . & -l_m & 1
\end{bmatrix}
\begin{bmatrix}
q_1(t) \\
q_2(t) \\
. \\
. \\
. \\
q_m(t) \\
1
\end{bmatrix}
=
\begin{bmatrix}
0 \\
0 \\
. \\
. \\
. \\
0 \\
0
\end{bmatrix},
\qquad (2.4)
$$

we obtain the necessary condition:

$$\sum_{i=1}^{m} c_i l_i = 1, \qquad\qquad (2.5)$$

and the solutions for the physical quantities:

$$q_i(t) = c_i, \qquad\qquad i = 1, 2, \ldots, m. \qquad (2.6)$$

We still do not have a perfect formal symmetry. But if we now set $w = 1$ in the other system of equations (that of prices), namely if we express all prices in terms of the wage rate, we may also rewrite the price system:

$$
\begin{bmatrix}
1 & 0 & . & . & . & 0 & -l_1 \\
0 & 1 & . & . & . & 0 & -l_2 \\
. & . & & . & & . & . \\
. & . & & . & & . & . \\
. & . & & . & & . & . \\
0 & 0 & . & . & . & 1 & -l_m \\
-c_1 & -c_2 & . & . & . & -c_m & 1
\end{bmatrix}
\begin{bmatrix}
p_1(t) \\
p_2(t) \\
. \\
. \\
. \\
p_m(t) \\
1
\end{bmatrix}
=
\begin{bmatrix}
0 \\
0 \\
. \\
. \\
. \\
0 \\
0
\end{bmatrix},
\qquad (2.7)
$$

The solutions of this homogeneous system of equations, when necessary condition (2.5) is satisfied, turn out to be:

$$p_i(t) = l_i, \qquad\qquad i = 1, 2, \ldots, m. \qquad (2.8)$$

The two systems of equations (of physical quantities and of prices), rewritten in this way, are dually symmetrical with respect to each other; and they are absolutely invariant over time. The $q_i(t)$ and $p_i(t)$, $(i = 1, 2, \ldots, m)$ have been written with the suffix t, because we started by considering movements over time, but such a time suffix actually becomes redundant, because all solutions do not vary.

We may also say that equation systems (2.4) and (2.7), as written here, and their solutions, represent the *structure* of the economic system being considered. This structure remains absolutely constant over time. This means that such an (hypothetical) economic system, once it has reached the position of equilibrium at time zero, will stay in equilibrium for good, by simply making no change in its proportions. The physical quantities $Q_i(t)$ all increase at the same yearly percentage rate g. The entire economic system, so to speak, swells up in absolute terms, without varying its proportions in any way whatsoever. Here we are obviously dealing with a very simple kind of economic growth, at constant technical coefficients (and thus constant returns to scale) – a growth which is due to population growth only. There is a complete absence of any structural change.

In the following analysis, the various formulations presented here will be alternatively adopted according to appropriate circumstances. Definition (2.3) and the ensuing formulations (2.4)–(2.8) have the property of formal symmetry. Given their invariance over time, they are useful whenever the constancy of the structure over time needs to be brought into relief. Definition (2.2) and the preceding formulations, even with their formal asymmetry, are on the other hand useful whenever the physical growth of the economic system needs to be brought into evidence.

3. Uniform technical progress and homothetic growth

We shall now consider a second hypothetical case. Suppose that, as time goes on, there is technical progress in the sense that labour productivity increases. However, we shall suppose that it increases, for all production processes, at exactly the same yearly percentage rate ρ. This means that all technical coefficients decrease uniformly over time at exactly the same yearly percentage rate ρ:

$$l_i(t) = l_i(0) \, e^{-\rho t}, \qquad\qquad i = 1, 2, \ldots, m. \qquad (3.1)$$

Moreover, we shall suppose that all the consumption coefficients (namely per-capita consumption) also increase uniformly at exactly the same yearly percentage rate r:

$$c_i(t) = c_i(0) \, e^{rt}, \qquad\qquad i = 1, 2, \ldots, m. \qquad (3.2)$$

This is equivalent to supposing that the elasticity of demand with respect to income is, for all commodities, equal to unity; an assumption which is indeed very common in growth theory.

Now, expressions (3.1) and (3.2) represent the basic specific hypotheses of this second case. We may also add for the time being, in order to isolate its analytic properties, the hypothesis of a stationary population over time, namely $g = 0$.

By substituting (3.1) and (3.2) into the two systems of physical quantities and of prices, the necessary condition for economically significant equilibrium solutions emerges as:

$$e^{(r-\rho)t} \sum c_i(0) \, l_i(0) = 1. \tag{3.3}$$

We can immediately see that, once satisfied at time zero, this expression remains satisfied for ever, the only condition being that:

$$r = \rho, \tag{3.4}$$

i.e. the only condition is that the yearly (uniform) rate of growth of per-capita consumption is equal to the yearly (uniform) rate of growth of productivity.[2] When this is the case, the exponent of the term outside the summation in (3.3) – which is zero at the initial point $t = 0$ – also remains zero for all $t > 0$, and the term itself always remains equal to unity. It follows that the entire expression remains absolutely constant over time.

With (3.3) permanently satisfied, the solutions of the two equation systems turn out to be:

$$Q_i(t) = c_i(0) \, e^{rt} \, \bar{Q}_n, \tag{3.5}$$

$$p_i(t) = l_i(0) \, e^{-\rho t} \, \bar{w}, \qquad\qquad i = 1, 2, \ldots, m, \tag{3.6}$$

where $\bar{Q}_n$ is constant *ex-hypothesi*, and $\bar{w}$ is constant because of our convention of assuming it as numéraire of the price system (see (II.2.9)). From (3.5) we see that all physical quantities produced increase over time at the same uniform rate r, so that their proportions remain unchanged. The physical structure of the economic system remains absolutely constant over time. Symmetrically, from (3.6) we see that all prices (in terms of the wage rate) decrease over time exactly at the same uniform rate ρ (which is equal to r); so that the whole set of relative prices, i.e. the price structure, remains

---

[2] From this point onward, some elliptical expressions will be adopted for brevity's sake. We shall speak of 'rates of increase' (of population, of productivity, etc.) omitting the adjective 'percentage' and the reference 'yearly'. Moreover, we shall speak of 'productivity' always meaning productivity of labour. Finally, we shall write the summation sign Σ without any explicit index, meaning that such index always goes from 1 to m. The words and indices omitted will however be added any time there might be risk of misunderstanding, or any time it becomes important to call attention to them.

absolutely constant. At the same time, the wage rate – even while remaining unvaried in nominal terms – increases in real terms (i.e. in terms of any physical commodity) at the percentage rate ρ. Of course, we could also use the alternative convention of adopting as numéraire any arbitrarily chosen commodity (see (II.2.11)), in which case all the absolute prices (expressed in terms of the numéraire commodity), and not only the relative prices, would remain absolutely constant over time, while the wage rate, expressed in terms of the numéraire commodity, would grow at the percentage rate ρ, i.e. at the rate of growth of productivity.

This kind of growth is homothetic in the sense that the entire system grows while maintaining its proportions unchanged. This case is homologous to the case of the preceding section. In that case, production in all sectors grows at a uniform rate g, because of population growth, while labour productivity is constant; here, production in all sectors grows at the uniform rate ρ ($=r$), because of the uniform growth of labour productivity, while the working population is constant. It is as if all workers, with the passing of time, uniformly increased their work potential. For this reason in this regard, in the economic literature, the term 'augmented' labour has been used, i.e., each worker, at every given moment of time, may be considered as equivalent to a worker of the preceding period of time augmented by the percentage rate ρ. In any case, in both kinds of growth, the expansion of the economic system over time is exactly proportional, both in each single sector and in the economic system as a whole.

It is easy enough at this point to combine these two kinds of growth by supposing both $g > 0$ and $\rho > 0$, i.e. by supposing that the economic system grows over time both because of growth of population and because of a uniform technical progress (and demand). The results are obvious and I shall spare the reader the trouble of a detailed reformulation. All the physical quantities grow over time at the rate of growth $(g + \rho)$, but relative quantities remain absolutely constant. All prices decrease at the same rate ρ (if we adopt the wage rate as numéraire), or they remain constant, while the wage rate grows at rate of growth of productivity ρ (if we adopt any arbitrarily chosen commodity as numéraire). In any case, relative prices remain absolutely constant, i.e., the price structure remains unchanged. The necessary condition for economically meaningful equilibrium solution (II.2.5) also remains constant over time, provided only that $r = \rho$. The physical structure of the entire economic system, in terms of both net product and unemployment, remains perfectly constant as time goes on.

As may clearly be seen, we are moving here in the realm of pure proportional dynamics, with absolute absence of any structural change (and dynamics).

4. Quasi-proportional growth

There is a third kind of economic growth that maintains the proportions among the various production sectors unchanged over time. This is a kind of growth which is even more artificial than the two cases of proportional growth examined above, but at the same time turns out to be more interesting from an analytic point of view.

In this hypothetical case, the following basic specific hypotheses are made:

$$l_i(t) = l_i(0) \, e^{-\rho_i t}, \qquad\qquad 1 = 1, 2, \ldots, m, \qquad (4.1)$$

where:

$$\rho_i \neq \rho_j, \qquad\qquad i, j = 1, 2, \ldots, m, \, (i \neq j), \qquad (4.2)$$

and:

$$c_i(t) = c_i(0) \, e^{r_i t}, \qquad\qquad i = 1, 2, \ldots, m, \qquad (4.3)$$

where:

$$r_i \neq r_k, \qquad\qquad i, k = 1, 2, \ldots, m, \, (i \neq k), \qquad (4.4)$$

but, and this is the crucial hypothesis,

$$\rho_i = r_i, \qquad\qquad i = 1, 2, \ldots, m. \qquad (4.5)$$

In other words, *in each single sector*, the rate of growth of productivity exactly coincides with the rate of growth of per-capita demand for the corresponding product, even if both rates of growth may be different from sector to sector.

As may easily be seen, after introducing hypotheses (4.1) and (4.3) in the price equation system and in the physical quantity equation system, respectively, it follows that both relative prices and relative quantities vary as time goes by.

There *is*, therefore, a structural dynamics! And, what is more, there is a structural dynamics with reference to both prices and physical quantities. However, the one movement exactly compensates the other *within* each single production sector.

With respect to the entire economic system, each sector keeps its relative weight constant over time. The physical quantities grow exactly at that pace which compensates the variation in the opposite direction of the corresponding prices, so that the growth of the various sectors turns out to be uniformly proportional, as in the previous two cases of proportional growth (in spite of there being variations both in the structure of physical quantities and in the structure of prices).

I have called this case of growth 'quasi-proportional', because the two structures (of prices and of physical quantities) both vary; and yet an exact compensation occurs within each sector. The result is that the proportion of each sector in the whole economic system – whether such proportion is evaluated in terms of production at current prices or in terms of employment – remains perfectly unchanged as time goes on.

All this may be seen quite clearly by substituting hypotheses (4.1)–(4.5) into macro-economic condition (II.2.5). Each addendum in the summation becomes:

$$c_i(t) = c_i(0)\, l_i(0)\, e^{(r_i - \rho_i)t}, \qquad i = 1, 2, \ldots, m, \qquad (4.6)$$

where, thanks to crucial hypothesis (4.5), the exponent becomes zero for all $i = 1, 2, \ldots, m$, and therefore completely cancels out the effects of the time variable. Each addendum, which precisely expresses, in terms of both net product and employment, the proportion of each sector (see section II.4), remains absolutely unchanged for all $t > 0$. Macro-economic condition (II.2.5), once fulfilled at time zero, remains fulfilled for ever.

We continue to remain, therefore – considering each sector at a time – in the artificial realm of proportional economic dynamics, even if there is a (perfectly compensated) structural dynamics *inside* each sector. The degree of artificiality of the analysis appears in this case very high. If nothing else, however, it is formally interesting.

5. Beyond proportional dynamics

The three cases of economic growth presented above share the common feature of being constructed by formulating their basic hypotheses in such a way as to avoid analytical complications (rather than in a way to get as close as possible to reality). This has imposed the avoidance of any structural variation. By supposing the structure of the economic system to be unchanging, in the sense that each sector always makes up the same proportion of the total, no new problem arises with the passing of time. Everything which characterizes the economic system at time zero continues to characterize it for all time.

But these three hypothetical cases, with increasing evidence from the first to the third, bring to the fore the artificiality of the particular dynamics which has been presented up to now. This makes one wonder, as has been hinted at already in chapter I, about the reasons why all traditional analysis of economic growth has precisely concentrated on proportional dynamics.

Perhaps, the static nature of traditional economic theory may have contributed significantly to the formulation of proportional dynamics. Perhaps, the macro-economic nature of most of the recent literature on economic growth may have contributed further, as macro-economic variables maintain their meaning in dynamic analysis only if the supposition is made that their composition remains unchanged as time goes on.

But the foregoing elaborations now suggest a further and more convincing explanation. The elaborations of proportional dynamics entail the setting up, in the simplest conditions, of an analytic apparatus that appears, if not absolutely essential, certainly very useful for then proceeding to an analysis of economic growth in more complex terms. They represent, so to speak, an intermediate analytic step. If this interpretation is correct, then the fault of proportional growth theory would appear to be that of not having gone further; i.e., of having stopped at an intermediate stage, by taking it for the final one.

In any case, whatever the reason behind past developments, proportional dynamics has been taken in the present discussion to serve a twofold purpose – the purpose of evincing explicitly the artificiality of the suppositions that one is forced to make when refusing to consider structural change, and the purpose of setting up analytical formulations which will be useful in the following elaborations.

We are now ready to go beyond proportional dynamics. To stop at it would mean to remain with a model, which is in sharp contrast with the long-run evolution of any actual industrial system that has ever existed or will ever exist.

IV   Structural dynamics

1. Introducing technical progress

As soon as we abandon the artificial hypotheses of proportional dynamics and try to move nearer the phenomena that characterize the reality of industrial economic systems, we have no choice but to find a way to introduce into economic analysis, explicitly and without artificial restrictions, that widespread phenomenon of individual and social learning which constitutes the *primum movens* of industrial societies. Without making too many distinctions, which would carry prejudicial concepts with them, we shall simply label it with the all-embracing term of 'technical progress'.

Obviously we do not intend to go into an investigation of the deep sources of technical progress; a complex social phenomenon, which cannot but be accepted here as a given external datum. However, to assume technical progress as a datum does not mean assuming technology as constant. What is here taken as a datum is its *dynamics*. That is to say, we are going to introduce explicitly into our analysis a few very general but essential dynamic features of technical progress. As will be seen in the following pages, this very simple but crucial analytical step – with respect to the traditional procedure of assuming technical coefficients as constant – has truly upsetting effects.

2. Technical change and the evolution of consumption patterns

Technical progress reveals immediately, in the economic sphere, two separate and distinct, though obviously connected, aspects.

The first and most apparent aspect is strictly technological. There are at least three characteristics of this technological aspect that may be openly brought out, because of their important impact on the dynamics of economic systems:

(i) the widespread division of labour tasks, and therefore the marked specialization of each labourer, with regard to the tasks he or she carries out. (This characteristic, as will be recalled, was immediately pointed out by Adam Smith.);

(ii) the non-homogeneity and differentiation – from sector to sector, from time to time – of the effects of technical change on the variations of the labour coefficients, i.e. on labour productivity;

(iii) the tendency not only, and at times not so much, to improve existing technical operations, but also, and sometimes above all, to introduce new techniques and new goods and services, through the discovery and/or development of new technical production processes, new materials, new sources of energy.

But technical progress does not merely have a 'technical' aspect. Increased productivity endows single individuals with the possibility of obtaining larger amounts, or a larger number, of goods and services, or entirely new goods and services altogether. This is a second aspect of technical progress, which is quite distinct from the first one. It means concretely increased possibilities of consumption (an increased real per-capita income), which give way to further, autonomous, decisions, which are not implicit in the first aspect. In fact, in order that technological improvements may bring forth effective changes of production, it is necessary that there occur decisions regarding the demand for specific goods and services. It thus becomes necessary to discuss the relation that exists between increases in real income and expansion of demand for consumption goods.

Unfortunately, in this area, one must make some disappointing remarks. The theory of consumer demand which is offered to us by today's dominant economic analysis is a theory on the one hand extremely elegant (because of the rigour and sophistication of the analytical tools that are used) and on the other hand incredibly limited, at least with regard to the aim, which is of our concern here, of a dynamic analysis. With regard to the problem of the evolution of the composition of consumption as incomes grow, such a theory is, as it has also been said, 'agnostic' – an elegant euphemism meaning that it does not say anything. It is a theory which, on the dynamics of demand, is amazingly poor of information.

Fortunately, at least with regard to the present analysis, we do not need to develop a complete theory of demand. It will be enough to remain on the objective ground, previously trod by classical economists, of the variations of the physical quantities of the various goods and services demanded as income changes. At the same time, however, it will not be possible to continue to remain agnostic with regard to the evolution of the demand for consumption goods when labour productivity – and therefore per-capita income – increases continuously. In this regard, a dynamic analysis requires a decisive enrichment of the reference framework. And here the information we do have is already plentiful and overwhelming.

As is well known, all empirical research carried out on this subject has revealed that the structure of consumption always varies as income changes. This has been called 'Engel's Law'. Such a law has remained, even in our own days, at the state of an 'empirical uniformity', i.e. a statement of facts that come directly from empirical observation. Yet it is of the utmost practical importance. As is well known, it has been associated with the statement, originally made by a Saxon statistician of the nineteenth century (Ernst Engel (1857), after whom it is named), that, as real wages increase through time, the proportion of them spent on food decreases.[1]

But even for goods that are not of primary necessity, empirical studies have shown, everywhere and with a wide generality, that the proportion of any individual's expenditure devoted to any consumption good is never constant as personal income increases. Not only this, but: all empirical research has shown that consumers' demands follow well defined paths, before slowing down and eventually reaching saturation (see Houthakker's survey (1957), written as a centennial commemoration of Engel's Law). In effect, the most widespread of all time paths of demand (d) for each consumption good, following an increase in personal per-capita income (y), has turned out to be the one shown in figure 1.

This is exactly the kind of curve that has generally been taken as the typical expression of Engel's Law (Aitchison and Brown, 1957), and that, when applied to the demand for a succession of consumer goods, traces out for their overall demand a typical hierarchical structure.

The generality of these patterns is truly surprising. The path described above by the Engel curves has come out everywhere, and applies to the demand of single individuals as well as to the (aggregate) demand of groups of individuals. What is even more interesting is that the variations of the price structure (while obviously influencing the demand for the single goods

---

[1] This is certainly not a very surprising statement. It is not necessary to carry out complicated theoretical elaborations to realize that, at low levels of income, the demand for consumption goods is, by necessity, confined to those goods that are essential to survival, such as food, above all. Equally, there is no need for any complicated and detailed elaboration to realize that, with an increase of personal incomes, the primary necessity needs quickly reach saturation, and the demand for consumption goods moves towards less necessary goods, while many of the very primary necessity goods (the so-called 'inferior' goods) are replaced by consumption goods of higher quality. The typical path of demand for essential goods as there is growth of personal income is therefore shown by a movement tending towards a saturation level, and – in the typical case of the so-called inferior goods – even tending to a decreasing path after a certain point.

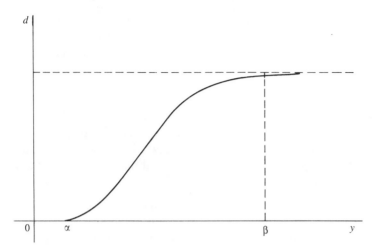

Figure IV.1 Typical shape of an 'Engel curve'

at each specific moment in time) are not affecting, eventually,[2] the basic kind of path that has been presented above![3]

For our purposes, therefore, that is for the purpose of an inquiry into the evolution of industrial systems over time, it will be enough to take advantage of a few essential characteristics, thereby enriching our theoretical framework with some entirely general and non-controversial pieces of information, which may be summed up in the following three points:

(i) as per-capita real income increases (whatever the price structure), a marked tendency emerges, for each consumer, not to increase proportionally the demand for the various goods, but rather to follow, in satisfying the various needs, a certain hierarchical order, by first

---

[2] For example, Houthakker and Taylor (1970), at the end of their econometric inquiry on consumer demand in the United States over four decades since 1929, could state that one of their 'major empirical findings' was that 'prices (relatively to income) play a fairly modest role in explaining United States consumption' (p. 305).

[3] Actually, with reference to any particular Engel curve, for example that of figure 1, if we subdivide the axis of abscissae into the three zones indicated, namely: $0-\alpha$, $\alpha-\beta$, $\beta-\infty$, we can safely state that price variations are practically irrelevant, for the consumer good considered, both in the first zone (because income is too low) and in the third zone (because income is already so high as to have brought saturation of demand for that commodity). It is only in the intermediate zone ($\alpha-\beta$) that variations in the price structure will exert an influence on demand. And yet, even in this intermediate zone, variations of the relevant prices can only steepen up or flatten out, without changing, the basic shape of the curve. They can only postpone or bring forward in time a dynamic path that, eventually, is bound to end up in the area of saturation, where demand becomes insensitive to both price and income changes.

satisfying essential needs and then gradually moving on to the satisfaction of those needs that are less and less essential;

(ii) the variation in the composition of consumption may well occur independently of the increase in income and of the changes in prices, as a consquence of the appearance on the market of newly invented goods and services;[4]

(iii) there is no good for which the consumption of an individual can increase indefinitely. A saturation level exists for the consumption of any good and service, even if this saturation level may be reached at different speeds for different goods or at different levels of per-capita income.

This minimal set of information on the evolution of consumption patterns, together with the minimal set of information earlier stated on the evolution of technology, will now be inserted, by appropriate procedures, into our formulations. Two successive stages of approximation will be followed. In section 3, the various time paths will be stated in terms of simple exponential functions of time (and for many of the consequences that will be investigated afterwards this first-approximation formulation will turn out to be by itself quite sufficient). In the subsequent section 4, the analytical formulations will be further refined, by means of appropriate modifications of the exponential functions, so as to make them, in practice, suitable for representing *any* kind of time movement.

3. The basic hypotheses

First of all, it is supposed that population grows over time at yearly percentage rate g:

$$N(t) = N(0) \, e^{gt}. \tag{3.1}$$

As we know, this is the exogenous movement which is easiest to consider, from an analytic point of view.

Secondly, it is supposed, as in section III.4,[5] that in all the production sectors labour productivity changes, through time, in a differentiated way from sector to sector, so that labour coefficients decrease according to exponential functions:

$$l_i(t) = l_i(0) \, e^{-\rho_i t}, \qquad\qquad i = 1, 2, \ldots, m, \tag{3.2}$$

---

[4] It may be noted that the phenomena under points (i) and (ii) entail a continuous process of new individual decisions, directed towards expenditures on consumption of better goods (to replace 'inferior' goods) and/or of new goods (both in the sense of goods that did not exist at all before, and in the sense of goods that did exist but were too costly).

[5] It will be recalled that references to sections are made with the same convention established for references to algebraic expressions (see footnote 2 of chapter II).

where, as already defined, ρ_i is the yearly percentage rate of change of labour productivity in the ith sector. In many of our following discussions, it will become convenient to adopt the convention of classifying the various production sectors in such a way that the rates of change of productivity are in a decreasing order, i.e.,

$$\rho_1 > \rho_2 > \ldots \rho_h > \ldots > \rho_m. \tag{3.3}$$

We shall take these rates to be positive, in general, without however excluding the case in which some of them – the last ones in the ranking order (3.3) – might be negative.

Thirdly, it is supposed, again as in section III.4, that the consumption coefficients change through time in a differentiated way, from one commodity to another, but – unlike what was supposed in section III.4 – it is here supposed that they change in a way which is *different* from that of the production coefficients. As will soon be noted, this hypothesis has consequences which are of crucial importance for all the analysis which follows. As a first approximation, we shall also use here exponential functions of time (but see, in this regard, the more detailed discussion of the following section), so that:

$$c_i(t) = c_i(0) \, e^{r_i t}, \qquad\qquad i = 1, 2, \ldots, m, \tag{3.4}$$

where r_i is the yearly percentage rate of change of the per-capita demand for the ith commodity. On the basis of the foregoing hypotheses, it follows that:

$$r_i \neq r_j, \qquad\qquad i, j = 1, 2, \ldots, m, (i \neq j), \tag{3.5}$$

and, above all:

$$r_i \neq \rho_i, \qquad\qquad \text{for all } i = 1, 2, \ldots, m. \tag{3.6}$$

Therefore, if we accept convention (3.3), then the $r_1, r_2, \ldots, r_m$, will *not* in general be in a decreasing order. (We could of course follow the alternative convention of classifying the $r_i, i = 1, 2, \ldots, m$, in a decreasing order, but then it would be the $\rho_i, i = 1, 2, \ldots, m$, to be no longer in a decreasing order.) Here too, the analysis will be carried out with the supposition that r_i is generally positive, without, however, excluding the possibility (and in fact considering this possibility as extremely probable) that some of them may be negative.

The basic hypotheses are all here, except for the refinements which will be made shortly. These hypotheses simply incorporate the statements of the preceding section and express them in terms of movements through time of the coefficients of the two equation systems which we are going to consider.

4. Further specifications of the basic hypotheses

The formalization carried out in the previous section, even if by itself it carries crucial implications, must nevertheless be considered as a first approximation. The statements made in section 2, even if very simple, require further refinements of the analytic specification of the time paths.

It will be useful to begin with the coefficients of per-capita consumption. These coefficients vary as a function of price changes and as a function of income changes. In the long run, it is the second type of change that is bound to play a dominant rôle, as has already been made clear. The information in this regard that was introduced in section 2 implies an evolution of demand for consumption goods over time of the inverted S-shape, as appears in figure 1 (a logistic curve, as it has been named) and, in any case, of a shape such as to entail accelerations and decelerations through time.

All this goes poorly with the time paths represented in the previous section by means of exponential time functions. From an analytical point of view, the exponential functions have the advantage of being extraordinarily simple, elegant and convenient for many purposes; and we shall use them on any occasion in which, for the purposes at hand, the particular shape of time evolution is not relevant. But for other purposes, the shape of the temporal evolution may become of crucial importance. The arguments carried out in section 2 lead us, in fact, with regard to the demand for consumption goods, to consider paths for which the rates of change are *not* constant over time.

In order to reconcile the requirements of simplicity and formal elegance with the needs of the actual non-constancy in time of the rates of change, we shall introduce an analytic expedient, which permits us appropriately to refine the basic hypotheses.

We shall suppose that time can be divided into finite stretches of length z, which we shall call 'phases'. A time phase is an elapsing of time, of a fixed length, longer than the unit of time considered, i.e. made up of a plurality of time units. It is supposed that, within each time phase, for each commodity i, the yearly percentage rate of change of demand, r_i, remains constant. Passing on from a given time phase to the following time phase (i.e. from one stretch of time of length z to the following time stretch), r_i changes, remaining however once again constant for another phase (i.e. another stretch of finite time z), and so on. Therefore, by now defining a new variable θ in the following manner:

$$\theta = t - \eta z, \tag{4.1}$$

where η is the largest integer that, multiplied by z and subtracted from t, leaves a positive remainder (θ), the time paths of the coefficients of per-capita demand, rather than by means of (3.4), can now be represented more generally in the following manner:

$$c_i(t) = c_i(t - \theta) \, e^{r_i \theta}, \qquad\qquad i = 1, 2, \ldots, m, \qquad (4.2)$$

where r_i is of course a function also of $(t - \theta)$. This functional dependence – in order not to complicate the formulations excessively – will not be explicitly written, except in those contexts where it may become particularly relevant. It shall, however, always have to be kept in mind.

Going on now to the technical coefficients, we can immediately say that there is no reason to suppose that the rates of change of productivity are constant over time; so that, similarly to what has been done for the coefficients of per-capita consumption, we may well substitute (3.2) with:

$$l_i(t) = l_i(t - \theta) \, e^{-\rho_i \theta}, \qquad\qquad i = 1, 2, \ldots, m, \qquad (4.3)$$

where the ρ_is now become functions of $(t - \theta)$, even if this will again not be written explicitly, except in those contexts in which this functional dependence becomes relevant.

For the sake of uniformity, we can finally also rewrite (3.1) in an entirely analogous manner, namely:

$$N(t) = N(t - \theta) \, e^{g \theta}, \qquad\qquad (4.4)$$

thereby making all the formulations of the basic hypotheses fully homogeneous.

5. Resuming earlier analytic formulations

We are now in a position to resume the analytic formulations that represent the production economic system which we are considering. We shall resume them in the most general possible way, and then, in the following sections, proceed to specify the time paths expressing the basic hypotheses that are made.

At any given moment of time, t, the theoretical framework that we have developed is expressed by two systems of equations, (II.2.3) and (II.2.4), in the physical quantities and in the prices, respectively. It should also be kept in mind that equation system (II.2.3) may be rewritten in the alternative form (III.2.4), whenever we wish to consider per-capita physical quantities, rather than physical quantities in absolute terms.

As time goes on, all the magnitudes that appear in the two equation systems are subject to variations. We may, therefore, imagine those two equation systems as rewritten here just as they are, with the addition only of a time suffix, t, for all the magnitudes that appear in them. Note that suffix t is to be appended to *all* magnitudes, i.e. to both the unknowns and the coefficients, as all of them vary over time.

The formulations that express the solutions of the two equation systems may also be considered as rewritten here, with the addition only of suffix t. However, in order to facilitate reference and display, it will be useful to rewrite them explicitly, and then go on to substitute therein the time paths corresponding to the basic hypotheses that are made. This will spare us from having to refer continually to formulations of previous chapters.

First of all, in each unit of time t, in order to have economically significant equilibrium solutions, the following necessary condition (which, as we know, has wide macro-economic implications) must be fulfilled:

$$\sum_{i=1}^{m} c_i(t) \, l_i(t) = 1. \tag{5.1}$$

Then we have the following solutions for the physical quantities and commodity prices:

$$Q_i(t) = c_i(t) \, N(t), \tag{5.2}$$

$$p_i(t) = l_i(t) \, w(t), \qquad\qquad i = 1, 2, \ldots, m, \tag{5.3}$$

which, however, only give us relative quantities and relative prices, respectively.

Solutions (5.2), for physical quantities, become determined if the time path of population $N(t)$ is accepted as exogenously given.

Solutions (5.3), for prices, become determined if a numéraire for the price system is exogenously fixed. This may be done in many alternative ways. It may be done by fixing:

$$w(t) = \bar{w}, \tag{5.4}$$

(where $\bar{w} \neq 1$), or even more specifically by fixing:

$$w(t) = 1, \tag{5.5}$$

i.e. by expressing all prices in terms of 'labour commanded'. Alternatively, determined solutions may be obtained by fixing to unity the price of any arbitrarily chosen commodity h (chosen as numéraire):

$$p_h(t) = 1, \tag{5.6}$$

or else by fixing to unity a weighted average of prices:

$$\sum \alpha_i p_i(t) = 1, \tag{5.7}$$

where the α_i ($\sum \alpha_i = 1$, and at least two $\alpha_i \neq 0$) represent arbitrarily chosen weight-coefficients, which obviously define a particular composite commodity. The expressions (5.4), (5.5), (5.6) or (5.7) represent of course alternative ways of choosing the numéraire of the price system – the choice of any one of them excludes the others.

6. Structural dynamics of prices

In the previous section, all formulations have been made 'dynamic' in the most general way possible, namely by the simple addition of a suffix t. But this generality would only permit us to make rather vague assertions. In order to be able to arrive at more relevant propositions, it is necessary to insert more specific hypotheses on the time paths of the basic magnitudes. It is with this aim in mind that the arguments of section 2 above have been developed, and then made analytically concrete through the formulations of sections 3 and 4.

We have spoken of a *primum movens* of the dynamics of modern industrial systems with reference to technical progress. It is therefore quite natural to begin by introducing some basic hypotheses concerning technical progress. According to the previous formulations, technical changes are expressed by exponential functions (4.3). Now we can see that the immediate effects are on the structure of prices. By substituting exponential functions (4.3) into (5.3), we obtain:

$$p_i(t) = l_i(t-\theta)\, e^{-\rho_i\theta} w(t), \qquad\qquad i = 1, 2, \ldots, m. \qquad (6.1)$$

As may be seen, if all $\rho_i > 0$, each price *decreases* over time, relative to the wage rate, at the particular rate ρ_i. (If some $\rho_i < 0$, then the corresponding price would of course increase.) In any case, all relative prices are moving; i.e. the entire price structure changes continuously. (6.1) expresses a widespread *structural dynamics of prices*.

In order to follow the movement of the absolute level of prices, it is necessary to focus attention on the choice of the numéraire. If we choose the wage rate as numéraire – namely if the price system is closed by (5.4) or by (5.5) – each price $p_i(t)$ decreases over time at rate ρ_i, while the wage rate remains constant *ex-hypothesi*, as is in fact explicitly shown by (6.1). If, instead, we choose as numéraire any commodity h – i.e. if the price system is closed by (5.6) – then it can be seen, after appropriate substitution, that:

$$p_i(t) = [l_i(t-\theta)/l_h(t-\theta)]\, e^{-(\rho_i - \rho_h)\theta}, \qquad\qquad i = 1, 2, \ldots, m. \qquad (6.2)$$

That is: each price changes in time at a rate of change that is the difference between the rate of change of productivity in the corresponding sector and the rate of change of productivity in the sector that produces the numéraire commodity. At the same time, the movement of the wage rate emerges as:

$$w(t) = w(t-\theta)\, e^{\rho_h\theta}. \qquad (6.3)$$

That is: the wage rate (expressed in terms of the numéraire commodity) grows over time at a rate that is equal to the rate of growth of productivity in the sector producing the numéraire commodity.

Within the present theoretical scheme, we are thus in a position to follow both the structural dynamics of prices and the movement of their general level. We shall return to this subject at more length in the following chapter.

7. Structural dynamics of production

It is important to realize that, unlike what happens in a regime of proportional dynamics, the variations of technical coefficients and thus of relative prices cannot here remain isolated. They produce a long chain of further effects. This can be seen immediately by looking at macro-economic condition (5.1). As coefficients $l_i(t)$ decrease, the macro-economic condition itself ceases to be satisfied, unless there is an increase of the demand coefficients $c_i(t), i = 1, 2, \ldots, m$. When there is technical progress, therefore, an increase of consumption is not only a possibility, it becomes a necessity.

In this way we are led to investigate the time paths of physical quantities. And here it will be useful to insert into (5.2) both (4.2) and (4.4). We obtain:

$$Q_i(t) = c_i(t - \theta) \, N(t - \theta) \, e^{(g + r_i)\theta}, \qquad\qquad i = 1, 2, \ldots, m, \qquad (7.1)$$

from which it emerges that an evolution through time of the production of each commodity is the result of two components: a scale component, due to the growth of population, and a structural component, due to the growth of per-capita consumption demand. The first component exerts its effect uniformly on *all* production sectors; the second component, on the other hand, exerts its effect on each branch of production, in a way that is specific to it.

Thus, also on the side of physical quantities, the present theoretical scheme brings to the fore a widespread *structural dynamics of production*.

8. Technology and effective demand, as determinants of 'natural' prices and sectoral production

It is worth stressing that a confirmation is obtained of the basic characteristics of the two systems of solutions, which emerged in chapter II from the discussion of an economic system in a given period of time. Expressions (6.1) and (7.1) maintain, in their evolution over time, the meaning pointed out in section II.3, with reference to the price system and the physical quantity system respectively.

First of all, there remains over time a clear separation between the two systems, which helps to bring out vividly the basic determinants. The price system is determined by the structural evolution of technology. The physical quantity system is determined by the structural evolution of consumption demand. Both technology and demand have therefore relevant (and symmetrical) rôles to play, but separately from each other – technology in the price system and demand in the system of physical quantities.[6]

Prices maintain over time their classical meaning, according to the most rigorous version of the pure labour theory of value. Each price evolves in time in proportion to the physical quantity of labour embodied, or commanded, by the corresponding commodity (and the two notions coincide). We are obviously dealing with 'natural' prices; i.e., prices that reflect the 'permanent and primary'[7] determinants, indepenently of any deviation, temporary or contingent, due to fluctuations of demand. In effect, these prices may also be regarded as 'efficient' prices, in the sense that they accomplish a correct allotment of equal purchasing power (labour commanded) for equal quantities of labour embodied.

Similarly, the expressions for physical quantities maintain over time their Keynesian meaning, in the sense specified at length in section II.3. In each sector, the evolving production is generated by the evolution of the corresponding effective demand.

9. The dynamic rôle of the 'natural' wage rate

There is something else – something really novel – that the entering of structural dynamics on to the scene of our analysis now enables us to see clearly and investigate further. This is the dynamic rôle played by the 'natural' wage rate.

We have seen in chapter II that, within the price equation system, the natural wage rate emerges as a logical counterpart to the 'natural' commodity prices. These prices, by being proportional to physical quantities of labour (both embodied and commanded), channel to each unit of labour an equal amount of purchasing power, that represents its share of national income.

In a *structural dynamic* context, this concept of natural wage rate actively generates far-reaching effects; and in two directions: an efficiency inducing direction and an income distribution direction.

---

[6] In Pasinetti (1981), pp. 138–142, it has been shown how this symmetry between the effects exerted by technology and the effects exerted by demand also solve the problem, raised by Marshall (1920), of the antithesis between the classical and marginalist theories of value. In a long run perspective, the classical theory of value turns out to be correct. 'Natural' prices are determined by the costs of production, i.e., by technology, just as the classical economists stated, and just as is clearly revealed by the present theoretical scheme. But there is another system of equations, besides that of prices. It is not true, therefore – contrary to what Marshall's arguments implied – that classical economic theory induces us to neglect demand. Demand is as relevant as production cost; but in a different (symmetric) context – that of the determination of physical quantities.

[7] See footnote 4, chapter II.

The natural wage rate exerts first of all a propulsive thrust on the whole production structure by propagating from its origin the shock of technical change. By growing over time at the same rate in all sectors (this being precisely a characteristic of its being 'natural'),[8] it immediately clashes against the differentiated variations, from sector to sector, of the technical coefficients. In those sectors where, for any reason whatsoever, productivity grows at a rate higher than average, the uniform growth of the wage rate tends to produce windfall gains. If efficiency is to be preserved, our theoretical scheme tells us that, in those sectors, the prices of the goods produced *must* decrease with respect to the average. Conversely, in the other sectors – even where, to take a limit case, nothing were to happen on the technological front – an increase of the natural wage, imposed by the rèst of the economic system, tends to cause losses, unless productivity can be pushed up. Each sector cannot therefore isolate itself from the rest of the economic system. Precisely the growth of the natural wage prevents it from doing so. And it is this growth of the wage rate that eventually ties together all the production sectors, with an inevitable spilling over into each sector of the consequences of what occurs in all the others. To the extent that it is not possible for a particular sector to increase its productivity, prices *must* increase with respect to average. This means that no sector can remain inert in the face of technological innovations in the rest of the economic system. In each sector, either productivity is increased, or prices must increase (relative to the prices of the other sectors).

There is another side to the same coin – another aspect of the same process. Jointly with the propulsive effect on the entire production structure, the uniform growth of the natural wage rate plays another (very important) function concerning income distribution. The flowing of the purchasing power that represents the natural wage increases at the same rate over all sectors (independently of the differentiated changes of the sectoral technical coefficients). This puts into operation a process of distribution of the benefits of technical progress over the entire economic system. In other words, all the participants in the production processes, in whatever sector they contribute their labour (whether in sectors enjoying strong increases in productivity or in sectors characterized by weak productivity increases, or even in sectors with no productivity growth at all), come to enjoy the fruits of technical progress that is under way in the economic system as a whole. The uniform growth of the natural wage rate is precisely the channel through which this distribution of benefits takes place.

---

[8] It is important to realize that the implications that are explored here refer to a uniform *growth* of the wage rate. The results obtained would therefore stand even if we were explicitly to consider different wage rates in different sectors, provided that the differentiated wage rates all grow at the same rate.

The macro-economic character of the natural wage rate, which had been pointed out in section II.6 with reference to an economic system at a given point in time, emerges here, in a dynamic context, in an extraordinary vivid way.

10. Available labour and full employment

After considering the dynamics of the 'natural' wage rate (in the price equation system), we may go on symmetrically to consider the dynamics of its dual magnitude, namely the total quantity of available labour, in the equation system of physical quantities. But what is it that may be considered as the quantity of available labour?

Up till now, for simplicity's sake, we have supposed that total population $N(t)$ coincides with total working population $Q_n(t)$, the latter representing the amount of labour available in a given unit of time. At this point, however, it is worth dropping this simplification and writing:

$$Q_n(t) = \mu(t) \, v(t) \, N(t), \tag{10.1}$$

where the two parameters $\mu(t)$ and $v(t)$, which are obviously themselves functions of time,[9] represent the proportion of active population relative to total population, and the proportion of time actually devoted to work relative to total time available, respectively. Of course:

$$0 < \mu < 1, \tag{10.2}$$

and

$$0 < v < 1. \tag{10.3}$$

The complement of μ to unity, i.e. $(1 - \mu)$, represents the proportion of total population that does not contribute to production activity, even though it does contribute to demand for consumption goods (non-active population), and the complement of v to unity, i.e. $(1 - v)$, represents the proportion of the unit of time that is devoted to leisure.

At this point of our analysis, even if magnitude $N(t)$, and its path through time, may still be considered as exogenously given, magnitude $Q_n(t)$, and its path through time, will depend on coefficients $\mu(t)$ and $v(t)$, which in turn depend upon a complex set of circumstances of a social, besides individual and technological, nature.

In any case, at the appropriate parameters $\mu(t)$ and $v(t)$, particular to any period of time, the quantity of labour available, $Q_n(t)$, resulting from (10.1),

---

[9] For these parameters too the convention will be adopted of omitting to write out explicitly their time functions, except in those circumstances where it may be necessary to draw attention to the relevance of their dependence on t.

has two important characteristics. On the one hand, it represents the size of potential production of the economic system (given prevalent technology). On the other hand, precisely in order that potential production becomes effective, it represents the quantity of labour that must be absorbed by the productive processes; in other words, it expresses the size of *full employment*.

In the present theoretical framework, as we know, full employment requires the fulfilment of necessary condition (5.1). This condition must now be re-examined, with reference to the new formulations that have been introduced.

Note, first of all, that the introduction of the new parameters μ and v does not cause changes in the form of solutions (5.2) and (5.3). However, the definition of the two kinds of coefficients which they contain must be modified in an appropriate manner. Labour coefficients $l_i(t), i = 1, 2, \ldots, m$, must be understood as referring to the fraction of time actually devoted to labour (i.e., so to speak, to the actual 'hours' of work) and to the fraction of total population that actually works (active population); while per-capita consumption–demand coefficients $c_i(t), i = 1, 2, \ldots, m$, continue to refer to the entire time unit and to total population. Precisely for this reason, in order to make the two kinds of coefficients compatible with each other, a modification must be introduced into macro-economic condition (5.1), which becomes:

$$\{1/[\mu(t)\, v(t)]\} \sum c_i(t)\, l_i(t) = 1. \tag{10.4}$$

We can actually go on and explicitly substitute in it the time paths resulting from (3.2) and (3.4). By using the more complete notation for the time variables (see section 4), we obtain expression:

$$\{1/[\mu(t-\theta)\, v(t-\theta)]\} \sum_{i=1}^{m} c_i(t-\theta)\, l_i(t-\theta)\, e^{(r_i - \rho_i)\theta} = 1. \tag{10.5}$$

This is the version that is taken, at this stage of our analysis, by the necessary condition to be kept satisfied over time in order that the economic system may grow with equilibrium full employment.

Expression (10.5) – by representing at this stage of our analysis the macro-economic condition for equilibrium growth – warns us that maintaining full employment over time is a truly complex problem. It presents two distinct aspects – a macro-economic aspect and a structural aspect. We shall examine them separately, starting with the structural aspect.

11. Structural dynamics of employment

We can see clearly that there is a further and important process of structural dynamics that is in operation in addition to, though following as a

consequence of, the two processes of structural dynamics already considered in sections 6 and 7 above. This is the process of structural dynamics of
employment.

To bring this process into relief, we may well start from expression (10.5),
in which each term $c_i(t)\, l_i(t), i = 1, 2, \ldots, m$, represents, as we know, the
proportion of total employment engaged in the ith sector. And, to set the
macro-economic aspect aside for the time being, we may suppose, for the
moment, that expression (10.5) is kept satisfied in some way as time goes on
(in other words, we suppose that full employment is in some way
maintained in the economic system as a whole).

A striking contrast emerges immediately with the previous cases of
proportional dynamics. Here, *each single addendum* in the summation
varies continually, even if their sum were to be kept constant. This means
that employment in the various sectors changes continually. In other
words, in some sectors employment turns out to be expanding and in other
sectors it turns out to be contracting. More precisely, each ith sector
expands, maintains constant, or contracts its share of total employment
over time according to whether:

$$r_i \gtreqless \rho_i, \qquad\qquad i = 1, 2, \ldots, m, \qquad (11.1)$$

i.e. according to whether the corresponding rate of growth of per-capita
demand is greater than, equal to, or smaller than, the corresponding rate of
growth of productivity.

Thus, even if we start from the hypothesis that total full employment is in
some way maintained over time, expression (10.5) reveals that the
maintenance of full employment at a global level requires a continuous
process of re-proportioning of employment at the sectoral level. It requires
a continuous process of *structural dynamics of employment*.

12. Sectors with declining employment in a process of economic development, and the challenge of labour mobility

The conclusion of the preceding section brings forth a quite novel outcome,
with respect to the corresponding cases of proportional dynamics, and a
quite disturbing one, if one thinks of its inevitable social implications. The
structural dynamics of technology and of demand engender a structural
dynamics of employment, which, even if we impose the constraint of full
employment, makes it necessary to have inter-sectoral mobility of labour.

It is possible to make at once some evaluation of the quantitative
relevance of this phenomenon, if we go into detail a little further.

The first impression which one gets from (10.5) would seem to be
disastrous. If all sectors are moving, then half of them on average will enjoy

an expanding sectoral share of employment into total employment, but the other half will suffer a contracting share of employment. This might make one think at first of the necessity of an exasperated mobility of labour. But this picture regards *shares* of employment. The actual mobility of labour concerns individual persons, not proportions of total employment. In order to evaluate the phenomenon quantitatively it is therefore necessary to evaluate it in terms of absolute quantities (rather than in terms of shares). Now, the employment in each sector i ($i=1, 2, \ldots, m$) – that we may represent here with the symbol E_i – turns out to be, by using the preceding formulations and making the appropriate substitutions, from the following expression,

$$E_i(t)=l_i(t) \ Q_i(t)=l_i(t-\theta) \ c_i(t-\theta) \ N(t-\theta) \ e^{(g+r_i-\rho_i)\theta},$$
$$i=1, 2, \ldots, m. \qquad (12.1)$$

From these we can see that there is another component influencing sectoral employment, besides the variations of the technical coefficients and of the consumption coefficients. This is the increase of population that, when it is positive, brings with it a factor of expansion of demand, and therefore of employment, in *all* sectors.

This is not all. It can be noticed that, even in the limiting case of a perfectly stationary population, the working population has, in itself, another component of variation, which is made up of the natural turnover of the generations (every year a certain cohort of workers retire and is replaced by a younger cohort of workers). It is, therefore, possible to carry out a certain redistribution of labour among the various sectors by simply not replacing those workers of contracting sectors that retire, while directing the younger generations to those sectors which are expanding. If we call δ_i the yearly percentage rate of retirement in each sector i ($i=1, 2, \ldots, m$), the inequality that indicates the watershed point, as it were, between the sectors that absorb new workers and the sectors that are compelled to lay off workers (or, in any case, to carry out alternative measures, that have the same effects) may be written as follows:

$$g+\delta_i+r_i \gtrless \rho_i, \qquad\qquad i=1, 2, \ldots, m. \qquad (12.2)$$

The term on the left hand side of this inequality is made up of three components, all of which have a positive effect on sectoral employment; while the term on the right hand side is made up of only one component (the rate of growth of productivity), which exerts a negative effect. On the average, and fortunately, therefore, the number of sectors that need to hire new workers turns out to be greater than the number of sectors that actually have to lay off workers.

In spite of all this, and with all the mitigating circumstances of the situation considered above, it is nonetheless necessary to admit that there always will be sectors that actually face the necessity of laying off workers. These are those sectors in which the sum of the three magnitudes $r_i + g + \delta_i$ (rate of growth of per-capita demand, rate of growth of overall demand due to population growth, and rate of retirement) is not sufficient to counterbalance the laying-off effects exerted on sectoral employment by the rate of growth of productivity ρ_i, i.e., by technical progress (think, in this regard, of the agricultural sector and, nowadays, even of some manufacturing sectors).

We are here stumbling upon a phenomenon that on the surface appears paradoxical, but that is, in effect, an inherent aspect of the processes generated by technical progress. The present structural dynamics scheme brings to the fore one of the most alarming phenomena of modern industrial systems: the inevitable decline of employment in certain production sectors, as a result of the process of economic development.

13. Ways to counter the tendency towards technological unemployment

We may now go back to the macro-economic aspect of necessary condition (10.5).

The arguments developed in the previous section (regarding the necessity of a certain inter-sectoral labour mobility, as an unavoidable result of the existence of sectors with declining employment, owing to technical progress) were carried out on the assumption that condition (10.5) is kept satisfied, namely on the assumption that full employment is in some way maintained over time. But this cannot at all be taken for granted. In a structural dynamics context, unlike what occurs in the case of proportional dynamics, each single addendum in the sum that appears in (10.5) does not remain unchanged over time. And if each single addendum changes, it becomes quite natural to ask ourselves, and begin to investigate, what can happen to their sum.

First of all, if technical progress – according to our initial hypothesis – is the *primum movens* of a production economic system, an immediate effect is a continual decrease of technical coefficients. This means that, in order to keep macro-economic condition (10.5) satisfied, the coefficients of per-capita demand not only can, but must increase, as has been already hinted at. And yet we know, from the discussion of section 2, that the demand coefficients, as a result of the phenomenon of consumption saturation, cannot increase indefinitely. It follows that, because of technical progress, macro-economic condition (10.5) is bound to show a tendency to become less than satisfied, that is, to generate unemployment, as time goes on. This is that kind of unemployment which has acquired the name of 'technological unemployment'.

The question therefore arises: is technological unemployment unavoidable? An answer to this question requires some further elaboration.

What emerges as unavoidable, as a result of technical progress, is the tendency to generate technological unemployment. However, from the present theoretical scheme, we can also single out various ways by which such a tendency can be held up. We can see that, with technological progress, the economic system inevitably generates unemployment, if in the meantime nothing else occurs, or only occurs with insufficient speed. But there are many things which can occur. There is, in effect, not just singularity, but multiplicity of possible movements which can hold up, if not completely check, the above-mentioned tendency.

A first way to counter the process which creates technological unemployment has already been touched upon: it is an increase of per-capita demand. We have also noticed, however, that demand for every commodity is sooner or later bound to reach thresholds of saturation. Therefore the increases in demand for available consumption goods (which, among other things, could also occur in sectors different from the ones in which increases in productivity are most relevant) can never be enough by themselves. (It may be added, incidentally, even if the argument cannot be developed here as we are moving, at least for the moment, within the bounds of a closed model, that as soon as international relations are introduced into the analysis, it also becomes necessary to consider, for each sector and for each country, the possibility of exports, with the addition however of also considering the opposite effects generated by imports.)

A second way of holding up the tendency towards technological unemployment is the introduction of new processes for the production of new (or better) goods and services. In effect, this is another important and normal aspect of technical change in industrial systems, as has already been noted in section 2. Technical progress is never restricted just to quantitative reductions of inputs for given outputs, but it also – and sometimes mainly – goes on in the direction of the invention, experimentation, and diffusion of new goods and services. In the present theoretical scheme, the introduction of new goods and services generates no analytic difficulty. It only implies that the list of production processes and produced goods lengthens (the size of the production matrix becomes larger) over time. We may simply consider the number m (of sectors and goods) as itself a function of time, by writing it $m(t)$. In this regard too, for simplicity's sake, we shall not insist upon writing this symbol as an explicit function of time, except in those circumstances in which it may become important to call attention to such aspect; yet the reader should always consider it as varying in time. In the summation that appears in (10.5), therefore, the long-run tendency of each addendum to decrease over time (due to the saturation of per-capita consumption demand) can be counteracted by the increase over time of the number of addenda themselves (i.e. by the increase of the number of sectors and of goods produced).

And yet the list of possibilities is not exhausted. Precisely the distinction, made in section 10, between total population $N(t)$ and working population $Q_n(t)$, along with the introduction of parameters μ and v, brings to us a further way to counteract the effects of the tendency towards technological unemployment. This consists in the progressive diminution over time of parameters $\mu(t)$ and $v(t)$, which means a diminution of the activity rate of total population (spreading of part-time employment and/or early retirement) and/or a diminution of the fraction of time actually devoted to work (i.e. increasing leisure time). We are clearly touching here upon well-known phenomena, that are becoming more and more apparent in all industrialized economic systems.[10]

It is, in any case, important to stress that all these ways of holding up the tendency toward technological unemployment are not alternative to one another and are not, therefore, mutually incompatible. They are indeed mutually complementary. In other words, they can all be brought in together, albeit in different proportions. The total effect of the unemployment 'compensation' (as it has also been called in the economic literature) will therefore arise as a result of the combination of all the above-mentioned processes.

14. Problems of employment connected with technical progress: non-uniqueness and time specificity of the full employment solution

An examination of the requirements for the fulfilment of macro-economic condition (10.5) brings us close to the complexity of the employment problems raised by technical progress.

We have started by finding that, even when macro-economic condition (10.5) is successfully kept satisfied and thus full employment is maintained, this can only occur with an appropriate and complex structural dynamics of production and employment. We have then gone on to realize that there is no reason one should take for granted that expression (10.5) remains satisfied as time goes on.

It is right here that we come across the crucial difference with respect to the case of proportional dynamics. As seen in chapter III, with proportional

---

[10] In the work from which the present one has originated a further important channel is examined that permits avoiding the actual sackings of workers (Pasinetti, 1981, p. 228). This is associated with the development of multi-product firms, which – by producing new goods, with expanding demand, side-by-side with old goods that have entered the phase of saturated demand – are able, so to speak, to internalize sectoral labour mobility.

dynamics, no new problem arises with the passing of time, because each single component of macro-economic condition (III.2.5) remains unchanged. Once this condition is satisfied at the beginning, it remains satisfied for ever. On the contrary, with structural dynamics, the corresponding expression on the left-hand side of macro-economic condition (10.5) *does not* remain unchanged; in fact, it undergoes variations in *all* its components.[11] The problem of bringing macro-economic condition (10.5) into fulfilment is therefore specific to each single period of time, precisely because it has to be obtained in a different way from one period of time to the next. In other words, even though the fulfilment of (10.5) can occur in many ways, the particular way in which it can occur in every given period of time is necessarily different from the way in which it occurred in the preceding period and is necessarily different from the way in which it will occur in the period that follows. Condition (10.5) assigns to each period of time its own specific problem. There can be no solution of (10.5) which is permanent over time.

Therefore, the solution of the problems posed by (10.5) is paradoxically various in the sense that it offers a variety of choices, but at the same time it is punctually specific in the sense that it concerns each single specific period of time. Structural dynamics never allows us, so to speak, to rest on our laurels; it requires alert and specific decisions at every single moment in time.

In terms which are closer to common sense, we might put the questions which have emerged in the following way. Technical progress brings with it a continuous flow of new productive potential, permitting us vast and varied choices: a greater quantity of consumption goods with the same effort, or new and better goods, or a diminution of efforts with the same level of production, i.e. an increase of the amount of leisure time for all people or for some people, or all these things together, in the particular proportions which are thought to be appropriate. But all this does not come about without constraints. The whole process is subject to a

[11] It is possible to give a very elegant proof of the impossibility – with a given number of coefficients and corresponding rates of change through time – of fulfilling macro-economic condition (10.5), as time goes on. By taking the derivatives, with respect to time (t) of both sides of the equality, it is seen immediately that the derivatives of the right-hand side are all zero, while the derivatives of the left-hand side are all non-zero. More precisely, all the derivatives of even order are necessarily positive, except in the very particular case in which $\rho_i = r_i$, for all $i = 1, 2, \ldots, m$. This evidently means that the case of quasi-proportional dynamics examined in section III.4 (which, for this purpose, includes as particular cases also the cases of proportional dynamics examined in sections III.3 and III.2) is indeed the only case in which condition (10.5), once satisfied at a given moment of time, remains satisfied for ever. But in general, when $\rho_i \neq r_i$ ($i = 1, 2, \ldots, m$), condition (10.5), even if it turns out to be satisfied for any $t = \bar{t}$, will no longer be satisfied as soon as $t > \bar{t}$. The implication of this is that, if condition (10.5) is to be kept satisfied, the necessity arises of acting from outside on some of its components.

macro-economic constraint imposed by condition (10.5). It is precisely this macro-economic constraint which characterizes the most troubling aspects of the effects of technical progress. It imposes, at every moment in time, not just the possibility, but the *necessity* of making choices. There does not exist the alternative of not choosing! Technical progress does not present itself in the form of a free gift, which, as it might always be refused, could only increase (or, at least, not decrease) existing wellbeing. Rather it presents itself in the form of an impetuous flow which cannot be stopped, but which must always be channelled into new directions, which must themselves, bit by bit, be discovered and invented, as the old ones continuously become saturated. And if the new directions do not emerge, or are not found, or are not found soon enough, that impetuous flow, precisely because it cannot be stopped, may well upset or overthrow acquired positions or cause considerable damage (in the form of unemployment) to existing positions, or at least to some of them. Technical progress can therefore – through unemployment – also cause net losses of wealth or of social wellbeing in general, if the problems that it poses to the economic system in its whole are not resolved.

In the present theoretical scheme, the synthesis of all these problems is expressed by necessary condition (10.5), which precisely represents a macro-economic constraint permanently imposed on the economic system as a whole.

15. A few remarks on familiar problems relating to Keynes' principle of effective demand

The structural dynamics problems connected with the fulfilment (or non-fulfilment) of macro-economic condition (10.5) have been considered, in the previous sections, from the standpoint of full employment (and unemployment). But each of the arguments proposed can also be looked at from the symmetric standpoint of overall effective demand (or rather of tendencies to insufficiency of overall effective demand); since, as we have seen earlier, the fulfilment of macro-economic condition (10.5) has a twofold meaning – on the one side it means full employment of available labour and on the other side it means equality between actual and potential overall demand. This is the point generally associated with Keynes' principle of effective demand.

Without tiring the reader by repeating the same concepts from another point of view (that of effective demand), it will nevertheless be useful to put into relief those aspects of the discussions on effective demand that go beyond Keynes' short term analysis.

We are able to see immediately here the conditions, indeed very restrictive, under which no problem concerning total effective demand would arise, as time goes on. In the case of an economic system which were to expand in a perfectly proportional manner – and *a fortiori* in the case of a stationary economic system – the preceding analysis shows that macro-economic condition (10.5), which also represents the condition for a correct overall level of effective demand, once satisfied at a certain time, would remain satisfied for ever.

But in the case of economic systems that develop with structural change, to any increase in personal incomes, there will not automatically correspond an increase of effective demand, because new consumption decisions will have to be taken. This is the key point. Problems concerning the consumption decisions, and therefore, as a reflection, overall effective demand, emerge anew in every single period of time. They are original and specific to that particular period of time, corresponding to the particular stage at which, in the economic system, the structures of technology, and consumption have arrived. They are of course susceptible to multiple, not unique, solutions, but they are there, and require specifically (never automatically) to be solved in that particular period of time.

Basically, this is the same point which has been made in the previous section with regard to unemployment, here looked at however from the (symmetric) point of view of overall effective demand. Unlike what might have appeared from Keynes' analysis, the problem of effective demand is indeed an ever present, permanent, problem that has to be solved, one period after another, as times goes on.

16. The challenging task of pursuing the goal of full employment – problems of macro-economic coordination

What makes the problems, specific to each period of time and synthesized by macro-economic condition (10.5), so complex is that all coefficients vary as a consequence of discoveries or of decisions made by different persons and organizational bodies, that are not necessarily coordinated among themselves. Some of the decisions require individual choices; others require choices of particular groups, still others cannot in the end but require collective choices. Even if we have not given ourselves the task of going into the complex field of decision theory and adaptation mechanisms, or of individual and collective choice, it may be useful to point out how macro-economic condition (10.5) shows us, with great clarity, the existence of a problem of macro-economic coordination, which concerns the entire economic system. This is not a problem which is impossible to solve; on the contrary, it must be stressed that the problem has (not just one, but) multiple possible solutions. However, in order to solve this problem, the choices cannot help but vary from any one period of time to the next.

Above all, it is useful to call attention to the fact that the coordination problem concerns the economic system as a whole. Precisely because the fulfilment of macro-economic condition (10.5) requires decisions made by different persons and/or different groups of people, there is no *a priori* basis for expecting that it will occur automatically. On the contrary, the coordination problem raises a series of questions – institutional questions (which institutions are to be promoted to ensure or, at least to pursue, a certain coordination of the various decisions?), questions of economic policy (what is there to be done in the cases where the spontaneous interaction of individuals and groups does not prove to be sufficient?), etc.

The theoretical scheme here proposed, which has already, as has been noticed in chapter II, brought us to the problems once raised by Keynes, is at this point taking us well beyond Keynes' terms of reference. It shows that the problems connected with full employment are not confined to any single period of time (i.e. to the short run), but are constantly present in a *sequence* of periods of time, when the complex structural dynamics of a production economic system unfolds itself. In fact, it shows, in extremely clear terms, the existence of a permanent problem of coordination at the level of the economic system considered as a whole. It shows the existence of a permanent, and challenging, task of pursuing the macro-economic goal of an adequate global effective demand and full employment.

We shall return to these problems later on, after completing the general theoretical framework.

V The evolving structure and level of prices

1. Asymmetries between the price system and the system of physical quantities

In the two equation systems considered in the previous chapter, the solutions for physical quantities and the solutions for prices have emerged in a formally symmetrical manner. They determine the time paths of *relative* quantities and the time paths of *relative* prices, respectively. This means that, in each equation system, the time path of one of the unknowns must be determined exogenously.

However, in point of substance (as against the formal appearance), the two equation systems evince more than an asymmetry. In the physical quantity system (IV.5.2), the exogenously determined unknown is, quite obviously, $N(t)$, i.e., population. The (exogenous) time path of $N(t)$ determines, through (IV.10.1), the total quantity of available labour $Q_n(t)$, which in turn determines the evolution of the scale of operation of the entire economic system. On the other hand, it is not so evident which of the unknowns is exogenously determined in the price system (IV.5.3). Actually, in this equation system, there is no unknown that may obviously be said to be determined from the outside. The choice of the unknown to be exogenously determined, which means in this case the choice of the numéraire of the price system in its evolution over time, is arbitrary.

In a dynamic context with structural change, this gives way to a whole series of intricate relations, to which we shall devote the present chapter.

2. Two degrees of freedom in the exponential dynamics of prices

It is important to realize that the solutions for the price system, obtained in the preceding chapter, concern entire dynamic movements. Therefore the arbitrary choice of the numéraire of the price system concerns the entire dynamic path of one of the unknowns. Now, a dynamic path may take very complicated forms. But here the elegance and analytic properties of the exponential functions come to help. These functions are very convenient because each one of them defines a dynamic path with the minimum number of parameters; in fact two parameters only – an initial value and a rate of change over time.

This means that, in an analysis like the present one in which we use exponential functions, the choice of the numéraire of the price system comes down to a choice, to be made exogenously, of two magnitudes: the absolute value of the numéraire at the initial point of time and its rate of change over time.

Resuming now the analysis of section IV.5, we can say that, when the arbitrary choice of the numéraire falls on the labour unit – classical 'labour commanded' – and therefore the price system is closed by (IV.5.5), then the use of exponential functions is an analytic device that is equivalent to specifying the wage rate $w(t)$ as a function of time:[1]

$$w(t) = w(0)e^{\sigma_w t}, \tag{2.1}$$

where $w(0)$ is the wage rate at time zero and σ_w is the yearly percentage rate of change of the wage rate over time; and, at the same time, inserting into equation (2.1) the two particular values:

$$w(0) = 1, \tag{2.2}$$

$$\sigma_w = 0. \tag{2.2 bis}$$

Similarly, when any particular physical commodity (or composite commodity) h is chosen as numéraire of the price system and the same system is closed with equation (IV.5.6), using exponential functions is equivalent, in general, to specifying p_h as a function of time:

$$p_h(t) = p_h(0) \, e^{\sigma_h t}, \tag{2.3}$$

where $p_h(0)$ is the price of commodity h at time zero and σ_h is the percentage rate of change of such price over time; and at the same time inserting into (2.3) the two particular values:

$$p_h(0) = 1, \tag{2.4}$$

$$\sigma_h = 0. \tag{2.4 bis}$$

Expressions (2.1) and (2.2)–(2.2 bis) may at first sight seem a more complicated way of writing (IV.5.5); and, similarly, expressions (2.3) and

---

[1] For simplicity's sake, we shall maintain here and afterwards the notation t, to indicate time, whenever constancy or variability of the rates of change is not relevant for the arguments that are carried out. But we shall go on (see, for example, section 6 further on) to the more complex notation defined in section IV.4, involving z and θ, any time the variability of the rates of change becomes relevant.

(2.4)–(2.4 bis) may seem a more complicated way of writing (IV.5.6). But these new expressions have considerable analytic properties, which allow us to go much deeper into the intricacies of the structural dynamics of prices.

To begin with, they permit us to express clearly the two degrees of freedom contained in the time paths of the price system. In its most general expression, the price system:

$$p_i(t) = l_i(t) \, w(t), \qquad\qquad i = 1, 2, \ldots, m. \qquad (2.5)$$

appears to be made up of m relations in $(m+1)$ unknowns, but, as has already been stressed above, the relations, and the unknowns, are time paths.

By introducing the more specific exponential functions of time, defined above, (2.5) becomes:

$$p_i(0) \, e^{\sigma_i t} = l_i(0) e^{-\rho_i t} w(0) \, e^{\sigma_w t}, \qquad\qquad i = 1, 2, \ldots, m. \qquad (2.6)$$

or also:

$$p_i(0) \, e^{\sigma_i t} = l_i(0) \, w(0) \, e^{(\sigma_w - \rho_i)t}, \qquad\qquad i = 1, 2, \ldots, m. \qquad (2.7)$$

where, in general, σ_i is the percentage rate of change of price p_i over time. Now we can see from the outset that, in order to be satisfied, (2.7) requires two distinct conditions. First, it requires that, for $t = 0$,

$$p_i(0) = l_i(0) \, w(0), \qquad\qquad i = 1, 2, \ldots, m. \qquad (2.8)$$

namely it requires, in the initial time unit, the satisfaction of the usual system of m equations in $(m+1)$ unknowns, represented by m commodity-prices $p_i(0)$, $i = 1, 2, \ldots, m$, and by the wage rate $w(0)$. This is a system of equation with one degree of freedom.

But (2.7) requires yet another condition! Besides (2.8), it also requires, for $t > 0$, that:

$$\sigma_i = \sigma_w - \rho_i, \qquad\qquad i = 1, 2, \ldots, m. \qquad (2.9)$$

which in turn makes up *another* system of m equations in $(m+1)$ unknowns, represented by the m rates of change of prices, σ_i, $(i = 1, 2, \ldots, m)$ plus the rate of change of the wage rate, σ_w. This system of equations is additional, and quite distinct from the previous one, and has an additional degree of freedom.

As may now be seen explicitly, in a dynamic context, the choice of the numéraire for the price system entails the choice of two exogenous magnitudes: one in equation system (2.8) (where the data are represented by the technical coefficients), and another one in equation system (2.9) (where the data are represented by the rates of change of productivity). In other words, the choice of the numéraire of the price system entails in effect two choices: the choice of the unit of account of the price system at the initial point in time and the choice of the rate of change of the unit of account over time.

3. Physical numéraires and nominal numéraires – an important asymmetry

It is important to call attention to the existence, in general, of two distinct degrees of freedom in the price system.

In the traditional way of dealing with the price system, there is a tendency to think in terms of only one degree of freedom. This occurs in an obvious way when one is moving within a static context, in which one finds oneself confined to the degree of freedom of the initial system of equations (2.8). But it may happen also when, while going over to a dynamic context, the two available degrees of freedom are not utilized independently of each other. This happens whenever the choice of the numéraire occurs in physical terms.

The choice of a unit of measure of the price system of the kind 'so many ounces of gold' or 'one day of work' has the property of closing both degrees of freedom at once. As has already been pointed out in the preceding section, the decision to express prices in terms of a particular commodity h simultaneously implies both $p_h(0) = 1$ and $\sigma_h = 0$. Similarly, the decision to express prices in terms of 'commanded labour' simultaneously implies both $w(0) = 1$ and $\sigma_w = 0$. In other words, the decision to use a *physical* numéraire has the noteworthy property of blocking the separate and independent utilization of the two degrees of freedom with which the price system is intrinsically endowed.

But, from a logical point of view, there is no inherent need in the price system for rigid pairings like those due to the choice of a numéraire in physical terms. The degrees of freedom are truly two and can be used independently of each other. This became obvious quite early on in the evolution of monetary systems. The ancient phenomenon of 'debasing' metallic money is the first example of an attempt to avoid the above-mentioned pairing, by means of a change in time of the physical content of the unit of account of the price system. The complete decoupling of the degree of freedom regarding the *choice* at a certain moment in time of the unit of account from the degree of freedom regarding the *variation* in time of the unit of account occurred more recently, with the adoption of monetary regimes based on paper money, and more generally on purely nominal units of account. In paper-money regimes, the banks of issue have no longer any obligation to convert paper money into any fixed amount of physical commodities.

There exists, therefore, an important asymmetry between monetary regimes in which the numéraire of the price system is physical, and monetary regimes in which the numéraire of the price system is a purely nominal unit of account, not linked to any quantitative specification of any particular physical commodity.

In the following pages, we shall examine the first (and more traditional) type of monetary regime to begin with. It will be shown that, in a structural dynamics context, this opens up an intricate problem concerning the conditions of stability of the price level; and it will further be shown that a stable price level is by no means a characteristic of physical numéraires, except in a very peculiar, and very interesting, case. The way will then become open to going on to examine the monetary regimes based on purely nominal units of account.

4. Physical numéraire and 'non-stability' of prices

Let us begin with an examination of the dynamics of prices in the case in which the two degrees of freedom in the price system are closed simultaneously, by means of the choice of a numéraire in *physical* terms.

Suppose that commodity h is chosen as numéraire. As we know, this means that, at time zero, prices are determined by equation system:

$$p_i(0) = l_i(0) \, w(0), \qquad\qquad i = 1, 2, \ldots, m; \qquad (2.8)$$

$$p_h(0) = 1, \qquad\qquad (2.4)$$

and, over time, their rates of change are determined by equation system:

$$\sigma_i = \sigma_w - \rho_i, \qquad\qquad i = 1, 2, \ldots, m; \qquad (2.9)$$

$$\sigma_h = 0. \qquad\qquad (2.4 \text{ bis})$$

Note that this second system of equations may be rewritten in the following alternative manner:

$$\sigma_w = \rho_h, \qquad\qquad (4.1)$$

$$\sigma_i = \rho_h - \rho_i, \qquad\qquad i = 1, 2, \ldots, m, \qquad (4.2)$$

which is a formulation of notable interest. It allows us to make at least two important remarks.

The first remark is about (4.1). In a dynamic context, the rate of change of the wage rate, σ_w, provided of course that it is fixed in the appropriate relation (4.1) with the rate of growth of productivity in the sector of the numéraire commodity, comes forth in a *general* manner (and no longer only in the case of the wage used as numéraire) as the variable of reference in closing the price system. Once σ_w is fixed, according to (4.1), all the other rates of change (including that of the numéraire commodity, that will turn out to be equal to zero) will then be determined by (4.2).

Of course, it can be seen at this point that among the $(m+1)$ exponential functions (2.1) and (2.3), any one of them – and not necessarily the one that represents the path of the numéraire – can be used in order to close the price system, provided that its two parameters (its initial value and its rate of change) are fixed in the appropriate relation to those of the time path of the numéraire. But while the choice of any of the other exponential functions would make the formulations unnecessarily complicated, the choice of exponential function (2.1), concerning the time path of the wage rate, has the noteworthy property of making the formulations much simpler. Exponential function (2.1) is therefore suitable for being used always and in general for the closing of the price system.

In the case under consideration, in which commodity h is chosen as numéraire, this means that – as an alternative to the use of exponential function (2.3), with parameters (2.4), (2.4 bis) – we may close the price system with exponential function (2.1), by fixing its two parameters $w(0)$ and σ_w with the particular values:

$$w(0) = \bar{w}_h(0), \tag{4.3}$$

$$\sigma_w = \rho_h, \tag{4.3 bis}$$

where $\bar{w}_h(0)$ is the wage rate at time zero, expressed in terms of commodity h, and ρ_h is the rate of growth of productivity in the sector that produces the numéraire commodity.[2]

The second remark which (4.1) and (4.2) suggest concerns price variations. As may immediately be seen from (4.2), a monetary regime with a physical numéraire does not mean at all that prices remain constant over time. Prices would remain constant only in the limiting case in which all ρ_i $(i=1, 2, \ldots, m)$ were equal to zero, i.e. in the limiting case in which the technical coefficients were constant. This limiting case, which from the present analysis appears as trivial, is after all precisely the case traditionally considered. The present analysis, even though very simple, has already gone far beyond this case.

Indeed we can now see very clearly that a technical progress which is differentiated from sector to sector (i.e., $\rho_i \neq \rho_k$; $i,k = 1, 2, \ldots, m$; $i \neq k$) makes stability of prices over time *impossible*, if this stability is understood in the sense of a constancy over time of all prices. Structural dynamics, as a

---

[2] Among other things, it may be interesting to note that the general use of exponential function (2.1) in the closing of the price system unexpectedly comes to re-introduce a certain symmetry into our theoretical scheme, by attributing to (2.1) a central rôle in the price system, in symmetry with (IV.3.1), concerning the time path of population in the system of physical quantities.

necessary consequence of differentiated technical progress, means precisely that *all* prices vary, relative to one another, even when these prices are expressed in terms of a physical unit of any commodity *h*. (It should of course be remembered that all present analysis refers to 'natural' prices, or, in the sense pointed out in section IV.8, to 'efficient' prices.)

It follows that, within the context of the present discussion, the term 'price stability' cannot be referred to the individual prices. Nevertheless it is reasonable to continue to use such a term, provided that it is made clear that it is understood in the more general sense of a constancy of the average, or, with a more widely used term, of the general level, of prices. Such stability evidently entails an increase of certain prices and a decrease of other prices, with the restriction of constancy over time imposed on their average. From now on, therefore, the term 'stability of prices' will always be understood in this more general and common sense, i.e. in the sense of a constancy over time of the average (or general level) of prices.[3]

But an even more interesting outcome which now emerges is that the stability of prices, precisely in the more general and common sense just specified, is not at all a characteristic of a numéraire in physical terms. From a simple inspection of (4.1) and (4.2), it can immediately be seen that, once commodity *h* has been chosen as numéraire, the price paths are determined by the difference between the various rates of growth of productivity and the rate of growth of productivity in the sector that produces the numéraire commodity. This latter rate of change therefore takes up a central rôle. This means that the price paths, and the path of their average, are not independent of the choice of the numéraire of the price system. The σ_is in (4.2) turn out to be *different* – and therefore the paths over time of the various prices, and consequently of their average, turn out to be different – according to the particular commodity that is chosen as numéraire.

It is possible to develop these propositions a little further, at least briefly, at this stage. Suppose that the rates of growth of productivity are ranked in a decreasing order, from commodity 1 to commodity *m*, as indicated by (IV.3.3). If commodity *m* were chosen as the numéraire, then all prices, and therefore also their average, would decrease over time – a deflationary path. Conversely, if commodity 1 were chosen as the numéraire, then all prices, and therefore also their average, would increase over time – an inflationary path. These are two extreme cases. The choice of a numéraire commodity whose rate of change of productivity is to be found between those two extremes would entail a decrease of all the prices that refer to the commodities with rates of growth of productivity greater than that of the

---

[3] Let me stress explicitly that in adopting this commonsense meaning – i.e., constancy over time – of the term 'stability of price level', nothing is implied regarding whether there actually is in operation any mechanism that makes for a tendency towards it.

numéraire commodity, and an increase of all the prices that refer to commodities with a rate of growth of productivity lower than that of the numéraire commodity. It is not possible to tell *a priori* which will be the path of the price average; in any case, in general, its rate of change will not be zero, i.e., the general price level will not be stable. It will be farther away from stability – it will be the more inflationary or the more deflationary – the farther away is the rate of growth of productivity, ρ_h, of the numéraire commodity from the point which is intermediate between the two extremes.

The important result of this analysis is that the stability of not only the individual prices, which would be impossible, but also of the general level of prices is not at all a property of the regimes in which a physical commodity is used as a unit of account. On the contrary, the general level of prices will not in general be stable, but will be moving; and this will depend on the particular rate of change of productivity in the sector producing the commodity that is chosen as the numéraire.

In a structural dynamics context, as opposed to what occurs in a proportional dynamics context, the choice of a numéraire in physical terms entails, in general, non-stability over time of the general price level.[4] If we wanted specifically to introduce the objective of average price stability, that would impose a restriction on the choice of the numéraire. Such a choice would, thereby, cease to be arbitrary. More specifically, the objective of price stability – if we want to pursue it – requires the solution of a well-defined and by no means easy problem of choice of the numéraire of the price system.

5. The search for a particular physical numéraire that keeps the general price level stable over time

From the analysis of the foregoing section we come up with a specific problem – the problem of the search for a particular physical commodity that, when adopted as numéraire, keeps the general price level stable over time.

It should be noted that, within the context of traditional analysis (in which it is supposed that all technical coefficients remain constant, or that they all vary at precisely the same percentage rate – in our analysis, in the cases considered in sections 2 and 3 of chapter III), this problem does not

---

[4] It should be recalled that, historically, the adoption as numéraire of even a physical commodity with particularly favourable properties (like a precious metal such as gold or silver), has led to periods in which there have sometimes been considerable rises and sometimes also falls of the general price level – i.e. to inflation or deflation. This was obviously due to price falls or rises of the precious metals, relative to all other prices (for example, because of the discovery of new and richer mines or because of the impoverishment of older ones).

arise, or rather it becomes trivial, because *any* physical commodity satisfies the property specified above, which means that any commodity, if chosen as numéraire, maintains unchanged over time the overall average of prices. However, when there are differences among the rates of growth of productivity in the various sectors (which incidentally already occurs in the case of quasi-proportional growth considered in section III.4), then the problem is no longer trivial but, on the contrary, becomes rather complex.

In the general case, *no* physical commodity, if chosen as numéraire, will have the property of keeping the general price level perfectly stable over time (although the degree of instability associated with each commodity may be different from one commodity to another). But this statement needs further elaboration.

From the arguments expounded in the previous section it follows that the degree of maximum instability (within the physical numéraires) is associated with the choice of one or the other of the two commodities – commodity 1 or commodity m – that are found at the two opposite ends of the ordered scale (IV.3.3) of the rates of change of productivity. Clearly, the degree of instability decreases as we move towards the central area of such a scale; and ideally reduces to zero (reaching stability), if it were possible to choose that particular commodity which lies exactly half way between the two extremes. More precisely, instability would be eliminated if we were able to choose as numéraire that particular physical commodity to which there corresponds the average (appropriately weighted) of the rates of growth of productivity of the entire economic system.

Very rarely, however – or rather only by chance – will such an ideal physical commodity be tracked down among the various physical commodities actually produced. Above all, even if it were possible to track it down at a certain moment of time, such a commodity would not, in general, maintain its already peculiar property in the subsequent moment of time, when all the other rates of growth of productivity – as generally happens – will change, and when the proportions of the various commodities demanded will change, thus making the weighting coefficients and the weighted average change.

The conclusion to be drawn is that the ideal physical commodity, which, if adopted as numéraire, has the property of keeping the general price level perfectly stable over time, in practice does not exist. But at this point we have all the elements for constructing such a commodity analytically. We have to concoct a composite commodity characterized by a rate of growth of productivity that represents the weighted average (according to a formula yet to be found) of the rates of growth of productivity of the entire economic system.

6. The 'standard' rate of growth of productivity

One should notice the essentially dynamic character of the properties of the ideal physical commodity that, if adopted as numéraire, would solve the problem of stability of the general price level. It is singled out – not in terms of its physical composition, but in terms of the rates of change of its components.

The task comes down to the search for the appropriate method of weighing up the rates of change of labour productivity, which have been ordered in (IV.3.3). But a moment's thought reveals that the appropriate weighting coefficients are already implicit in the foregoing analysis.

While considering macro-economic condition (IV.5.1), or its earlier versions, which concern both the price system and the physical quantity system, we found (see especially sections II.4, IV.10–14) that the addenda which appear under the summation entering such expression have a precise economic meaning: each of them represents the share of total employment (as well as the share of total national product), which is accounted for by the sector to which each addendum refers. In other words, in (IV.5.1), the terms:

$$c_i(t) \; l_i(t), \qquad\qquad\qquad i = 1, 2, \ldots, m,$$

represent, without any ambiguity, the shares of total labour required by the various sectors. The weighting coefficients that are needed for the weighted average in question cannot but be precisely these terms.

We already know that, when there is technical progress, only in a very particular case will each of these terms remain unchanged through time. This case is the hypothetical one – considered in section III.4 – in which, within each single sector, the rate of growth of per-capita demand coincides with the rate of growth of productivity. In this particular case, the calculation of the weighted average of all ρ_i, $i = 1, 2, \ldots, m$, is immediate.

However, in general, there is no necessity whatsoever, as we know, that the terms remain unchanged or even that the rates of growth of productivity remain unchanged over time. To deal with the general case, we may take advantage of the more complete formulation (IV.10.5) of the macro-economic condition and of the analytic device presented in section IV.4, which allows us to approximate any type of time movement by breaking it up into discrete exponential phases of time of length z. By using this analytical device and by here denoting the weight coefficients by the symbol λ_i, we obtain:

$$\lambda_i(t-\theta) = \frac{1}{\mu(t-\theta) \; \cdot \; v(t-\theta)} c_i(t-\theta) \; l_i(t-\theta),$$

$$i = 1, 2, \ldots, m(t-\theta). \qquad (6.1)$$

To generalize these expressions even further, we may suppose that, when new goods are introduced, they are introduced only at the beginning of each time phase. Weight coefficients (6.1) thus remain unchanged within each of the phases in which time is divided (i.e. within each finite time of length z – see section IV.4), but of course they change from each such time phase to the next.

Hence, for each time phase, the summation:

$$\rho^*(t-\theta) = \sum_{i=1}^{m(t-\theta)} \lambda_i(t-\theta)\, \rho_i(t-\theta),\tag{6.2}$$

gives us the weighted average of the rates of growth of productivity of the entire economic system.[5]

We shall call magnitude $\rho^*(t-\theta)$ the 'standard' rate of growth of productivity of the economic system under examination. Standard rate $\rho^*(t-\theta)$ remains unchanged within each time phase, but in general it will be changing, in a discrete way (i.e. at the end of each time phase of length z), as time goes on.

7. The 'dynamic standard commodity'

We are now able to express the price system in terms of that particular composite commodity for which labour productivity grows through time at a rate equal to the 'standard' one. This particular composite commodity will be called the 'dynamic standard commodity'.

Note that, if we knew the dynamic standard commodity, i.e. if we knew a particular basket of goods, which we may denote by

$$\alpha^*_1(t-\theta),\ \alpha^*_2(t-\theta),\ \ldots,\ \alpha^*_m(t-\theta),\tag{7.1}$$

which, at time $(t-\theta)$, is characterized by a rate of growth of productivity that satisfies definition (6.2), then we could close the price system by applying formulations (2.4) and (2.4 bis). In other words, by denoting by h^* the dynamic standard commodity (7.1), when used as numéraire, we could write:

$$p_{h*}(t) = \sum \alpha^*_i(t-\theta)\, p_i(t) = 1,\tag{7.2}$$

and we would know, by construction, that

$$\sigma_{h*} = 0.\tag{7.2 bis}$$

---

[5] Expression (6.2), by being an average of rates of change, with weight coefficients referred to the beginning of the time phase, has the properties of a logarithmic average of the Laspeyres type. But the weight coefficients might well be referred to the end of the time phase (Paasche method) or to any average of the two points, without changing, for the purpose of the present analysis, the properties of magnitude ρ^*.

We would also know that (7.2), by becoming the standard of the price system, would keep the general price level constant over time.

It must be admitted, however, that, in order actually to construct composite commodity (7.1), the computation might be laborious. The reason is that composite commodity (7.1) is defined in terms of its dynamic requirements, and therefore in an indirect way; it is that particular commodity whose components are in such proportions to one another as to make the weighted average of the corresponding rates of growth of productivity yield the result defined by (6.2). Now, through time, i.e. from one time phase to the next, when in general all coefficients are changing, the composition of (7.1) that satisfies the definition of the standard dynamic commodity is bound to change. Therefore the computation of such physical composition will have to be done all over again at the beginning of each time phase.

But – we might ask – how can we adopt as numéraire of the price system a composite commodity the physical composition of which changes over time? The answer to this question is simply that we have all the elements that enable us to carry out, at the beginning of each time phase, the computation in question. Even if it were a laborious computation, it is a well defined one.[6]

But the interesting property of our formulations is that – for the purpose of fixing the numéraire of the price system – no laborious computation is necessary at all!

Here we are aided by that alternative method of closing the price system (which in this regard reveals all its analytic relevance) that has emerged from the analysis of section 4 – see formulations (4.3) and (4.3 bis). Its application to the case of the dynamic standard commodity is straightforward. Instead of using (2.4), (2.4 bis), which, when applied to the dynamic standard commodity, would give way to (7.2), (7.2 bis), we can close the price system with exponential function (2.1), and then, as particular values of the two parameters $w(0)$ and σ_w, insert:

$$w(0) = \bar{w}^*(0), \tag{7.3}$$

and

$$\sigma_w = \rho^*, \tag{7.3 bis}$$

where $\bar{w}^*(0)$ is the wage rate at time zero, measured in terms of the dynamic standard commodity, and ρ^* is the standard rate of growth of productivity defined by (6.2).

---

[6] We have in fact all the elements necessary to compute the chain-index implied in going over from each time phase to the next.

Expression (7.3) raises no problem. The level $\bar{w}^*(0)$, to which the nominal wage rate is fixed at the beginning, is indeed arbitrary. Since the dynamic standard commodity is a composite commodity, granted that, in order to begin with, we fix any arbitrary level, it is of no importance which fraction or which multiple of that level is chosen as numéraire. Along with the fixing of the level of the nominal wage $\bar{w}^*(0)$, we implicitly fix at the beginning a physical unit made up of that particular basket of commodities that the wage rate $\bar{w}^*(0)$ can purchase. Then, expressions (2.8) determine at the initial time all commodity prices in terms of such a basket of commodities.

It is then relation (7.3 bis) which plays the crucial role. From it, relations (4.2) become:

$$\sigma_i = \rho^* - \rho_i, \qquad\qquad i = 1, 2, \ldots, m, \qquad (7.4)$$

which define the time paths of all commodity prices relative to the time path of that commodity for which productivity grows through time at rate ρ^*, i.e., relative to the time path of the dynamic standard commodity.

Now examine (7.3 bis) and (7.4). The wage rate grows over time at the standard rate ρ^*. That means – precisely from (7.4) – that half of the prices on (weighted) average increase (those prices that refer to commodities with rates of change of productivity smaller than the average ρ^*) and the other half of the prices on (weighted) average decrease (those prices that refer to commodities with rates of growth of productivity greater than the average ρ^*). It follows that the general level of prices neither increases nor diminishes, i.e., it remains perfectly constant.

Expressions (7.3) and (7.3 bis) therefore close the price system in such a way that all commodity prices and the wage rate are expressed in terms of that particular commodity (the 'dynamic standard commodity') whose rate of growth of productivity through time is equal to (weighted) average ρ^*. This keeps the general price level stable over time.

The surprising outcome is that particular values (7.3) and (7.3 bis), when substituted into relation (2.1), implicitly define the dynamic standard commodity, and automatically insert it into the price system as a physical standard of measure, without it even being necessary for the commodity itself to be explicitly constructed. We end up by expressing all prices in terms of the dynamic standard commodity, without having to know what the commodity itself is actually made up of.[7] Such is the analytic relevance, in this context, of the use of function (2.1) for closing the price system!

---

[7] Note how parallel this property is to the analogous property of Sraffa's 'standard commodity'. As is well known, the latter is implicitly defined (without having to construct it explicitly, and without even knowing what it is in fact made up of) by a linear relation of the wage rate and the rate of profit, which is inserted in order to close Sraffa's price system (see Sraffa, 1960, pp. 31ff.; also Pasinetti, 1977, pp. 117ff).

8. Formal properties of the 'dynamic standard commodity'

It may be useful to pause for a moment and take a look at the formal properties of that particular composite commodity which is here called the 'dynamic standard commodity'.

It is not easy to visualize such a composite commodity, precisely because it is defined not so much in terms of its composition (which actually varies over time), as in terms of the (weighted) rates of change of labour requisites of its components.

Note, to begin with, that the dynamic standard commodity is not necessarily unique. The simpler the dynamics of the economic system, the more widespread we find the properties that characterize it. In effect, as has been mentioned already, in the two cases of growth considered in sections 2 and 3 of chapter III, *any* commodity satisfies the requisites of the dynamic standard commodity. In the hypothetical case of section III.4, an overall average becomes necessary, but the physical composition always remains unchanged. In the general case, the physical composition of the dynamic standard commodity will be changing as time goes on.

In general, therefore, the dynamic standard commodity is nowhere to be found in reality. And yet, at any moment of time, even if in a different way through time, it can always be constructed by putting together a basket of commodities which are in such proportions to one another as to yield result (6.2), where the various rates of productivity change have been weighted up appropriately.

We may well obtain a multiplicity of such physical commodity baskets. However this is no complication, because, as it should be noted, the property of uniqueness is in any case maintained in dynamic terms. More precisely, the uniqueness of the dynamic standard commodity is always maintained when referred to the rates of change. The rate of growth of productivity in the (composite) productive process that produces the dynamic standard commodity is defined by weighted average (6.2); and this is unique, no matter which or how many (single or composite) commodities there are whose rates of change of productivity satisfy the definition.

What the dynamic standard commodity accomplishes is that it singles out something very profound and fundamental, which remains constant through time, despite all the complex variations brought about by structural change. This something profound and fundamental is what in the economic literature has been called 'augmented' labour. As time goes on, technical progress makes labour more and more productive, but at a different speed from one sector to another. The dynamic standard commodity is that particular commodity for which the growth of labour productivity is exactly equal to the overall average. In a theoretical scheme, like the present one, in which technical progress typically augments the labour potential, such a physical commodity emerges as a sort of dynamic version of Ricardo's 'invariable measure of value'; as the physical standard *par excellence*, dreamed of by Ricardo, which keeps the price level perfectly stable through time. It is a commodity, which 'now and at all times requires precisely the same quantity of labour to produce it',[8] to be interpreted in a dynamic sense, i.e. in the sense of labour 'augmented' by technical progress. Indeed, in terms of (augmented) labour, the dynamic standard commodity always 'commands' through time as many physical commodities as correspond to the quantity of (augmented) labour embodied into them. It is a composite commodity physically reducible through time to a constant physical quantity of augmented labour.

For this reason, it has here been called the 'dynamic standard commodity'. It provides us with an analytic tool that gives rigorous physical content to the norm of stability of the general price level.[9]

9. Inflation from structural dynamics

The singling out of the dynamic standard commodity – a composite physical commodity that, if adopted as numéraire, keeps the general price

---

[8] As is well known, the 'invariable measure of value' was defined by Ricardo as a particular commodity, which satisfies two requisites: (i) a commodity which 'now and at all times requires precisely the same quantity of labour to produce it' (Ricardo, 1951 [1817], p. 17n); and (ii) a commodity the value of which is invariant to changes in income distribution. Piero Sraffa concentrated on the second requisite. He 'froze', so to speak, the economic system at a given technique and constructed a composite commodity (his 'standard commodity') whose value is invariant to changes in income distribution. In the present analysis a symmetrical approach is followed, by focussing on the first of Ricardo's requisites, interpreted in dynamic terms. Starting from a stage at which the problem of income distribution between profits and wages has not yet arisen, a composite commodity is constructed (the 'dynamic standard commodity') which through time always requires the same amount of 'augmented' labour to be produced.

[9] It may also be interesting to confront the concept of a dynamic standard commodity with an idea of Luigi Einaudi's, which was another version of Ricardo's 'dream'. This is the idea of an 'imaginary' or 'ideal' unit of account, that is meant to assure 'stability of the general price level'. In an unusually provocative way, Einaudi (1937) claimed that such an imaginary unit was actually aimed at in practice for a thousand years, since medieval times. He pointed out that it never existed in material shape, it was never coined, it couldn't be coined, as its rate of exchange with precious metals was subject to continuous changes. Yet, according to Einaudi,

> Books and pamphlets and statutes of the ninth to the eighteenth century are unintelligible if one does not bear in mind the distinction between money of account or imaginary money and effective or coined money. Usually the money of account was called *libra*, *livre*, *lira*. Men kept accounts, drew instruments of debts, sold and bought goods and securities and property rights in imaginary money, which they never saw ... the *libra*, the monetary unit of account, was something invariable, however changing was the price or quotation of the effective moneys (pp. 265–6).

level stable through time – now allows us to go back to, and conclude, the earlier analysis concerning the non-stability in general of the price level, when a physical numéraire is adopted.

We have seen in section 4 that, when any physical commodity h is chosen as numéraire of the price system – which means inserting particular values (4.3) and (4.3 bis) into exponential function (2.1) – the wage rate grows in time at rate ρ_h. This rate of growth of the wage rate will in general be different from the 'standard' rate of growth, ρ^*, which is by definition that rate of growth of the wage rate that would keep the general price level constant. The difference:

$$\rho_h - \rho^*, \tag{9.1}$$

precisely represents the rate of increase (or decrease, if negative) of the general price level.

Expression (9.1) expresses therefore the (average) rate of inflation (or deflation, if it is negative) of the general price level, due to the structural dynamics of prices. We shall call the general price movement (9.1), associated with any physical commodity h adopted as numéraire, *inflation from structural dynamics*.

There is only one way of avoiding this inflation, namely the adoption as numéraire of the dynamic standard commodity, which would mean inserting into exponential function (2.1) the particular values (7.3) and (7.3 bis), instead of the values (4.3) and (4.3 bis) of the general case. The dynamic standard commodity is the only physical commodity that, if adopted as numéraire, prevents any type of inflation (or deflation), including the inflation from structural dynamics.

It should be noted that expression (9.1) precisely quantifies the deviation of the general movement of prices – associated with any physical numéraire h, and thus with $\sigma_w = \rho_h$ – from the norm of price stability. It precisely represents the rate of inflation of the general price level, due to the structural dynamics of prices.

It follows that, in general, the difference between the rate of growth of the wage rate and the 'standard' rate of growth of productivity:

$$\sigma_w - \rho^*, \tag{9.2}$$

must be taken as a key magnitude of reference for any discussion concerning the stability of the price level.

It will be seen in the following pages that the difference $(\sigma_w - \rho^*)$ continues to remain a key magnitude of reference well beyond the adoption of any physical numéraire. It remains the key magnitude of reference for evaluating any deviation of the general price level from the norm of price stability, in an entirely general context.

10. A nominal or 'monetary' unit of account

It may seem paradoxical that rigorous stability of the general price level can be obtained, not by the adoption of a unit of account made up of a specific and unchanging quantity of a physical commodity, but rather by the adoption of a unit of account made up of a basket of various commodities whose composition, far from being 'stable', is variable through time.

And yet this analytic circumstance may help us, among other things, to understand some of the evolutionary characteristics, otherwise not easily explicable, of modern economic systems. It may contribute to explaining, for example, why industrial economies have through time all gone over from physical to purely nominal numéraires. In all industrial economies, prices are now expressed in terms of nominal units of account (the 'monetary units' – the pound sterling, the dollar, the mark, the lira, etc.) that are printed on paper money, issued by central bodies (the issuing banks, which everywhere have by now become central banks).

These nominal units of account make it possible to unhook the price system from any specific physical commodity. This means that they can also make it possible to adopt particular numéraires that satisfy certain conditions; for example, that of maintaining the stability of the general price level. At the same time it is necessary to be aware of the fact that the adoption of a unit of account which is purely nominal also makes the *deviations* of the general price level from the stability conditions much easier. This makes the singling out of the characteristics of the dynamic standard commodity even more relevant, as it provides us, in a completely general context, with a standard of reference for the evaluation of any deviation.

Returning therefore to the end of section 3 above, we may resume our examination of the characteristics of the price system, when – instead of considering as numéraire a physical commodity, which simultaneously blocks both degrees of freedom inherent in the price system – we introduce a nominal unit of account, which makes a separate utilization possible of the two degrees of freedom.

We may indeed use here too, for the closing of the price system, exponential function (2.1), thanks to its general properties, and insert into it the particular values:

$$w(0) = \bar{w}^{(M)}(0), \tag{10.1}$$

$$\sigma_w = \bar{\sigma}_w, \tag{10.1 bis}$$

where $\bar{w}^{(M)}(0)$ is the wage rate expressed at the initial time in terms of the monetary unit of account, whatever it may be (e.g. the pound sterling, the dollar, the mark, the lira, etc.) and $\bar{\sigma}_w$ is the rate of growth over time of the wage rate, expressed in terms of the adopted (monetary) unit of account.

The expressions (10.1) and (10.1 bis) are now independent from each other. Expression (10.1) does not imply (10.1 bis) and the latter does not imply the former. We may recall that, in the preceding cases in which we adopted a specific physical commodity h as numéraire, the initial condition could be arbitrarily fixed, but, once fixed initially, it automatically implied also the fixing of the rate of change of the wage rate through time. In the present case, this is no longer so. Both the initial condition and the rate of change over time can indeed be fixed arbitrarily, independently of each other. The unit of account is purely nominal and is no longer tied to any real standard. Hence the wage rate can be fixed in nominal terms. Then, this nominal wage can grow at *any* (nominal) rate of increase, which is independent of the initial level.

Of course, any arbitrary growth of the monetary wage rate has only 'nominal' consequences. The problem therefore arises of evaluating the 'real', as against the purely nominal, meaning of wage and price movements. In order to do this, we must look for their relations with the movement of the general level of prices. This means looking for their relations with the movement of the price of the dynamic standard commodity, which from previous analysis has emerged as the key standard of reference.

11. Unconstrained monetary inflation (made possible by decoupling the two degrees of freedom inherent in the price system)

The introduction of a nominal unit of account for the price system brings to light important opportunities and possibilities, at the same time as bringing to light great risks previously unknown.

A physical numéraire places a physical constraint on price inflation. When a physical quantity of commodity h is adopted as numéraire, it fixes *ipso facto* – as we have seen – both the unit of account at the initial time and the rate of increase of the wage rate over time, which turns out to be $\sigma_w = \rho_h$. That does not mean stability of the general price level. As we have seen (see (9.1)) the general price level will be moving at rate of change $(\rho_h - \rho^*)$, which precisely represents the rate of inflation (or deflation, if negative) due to structural dynamics. But $(\rho_h - \rho^*)$ is a rate of change that refers to physical magnitudes and is, therefore, finite, and in most cases not excessively high. At most, if we were to choose as numéraire that particular commodity – commodity 1, in our scheme – that is produced at the highest rate of growth of productivity, inflation from structural dynamics would reach the rate, $(\rho_1 - \rho^*)$; and this is truly the upper limit. In practice, the numéraire commodity (since it must satisfy certain requisites) will not usually be that one which is characterized by the highest rate of growth of productivity, and this means that the rate of inflation from structural dynamics (which in any case is finite) cannot be excessively high.

But when a nominal unit of account is adopted as numéraire of the price system, there is no longer any physical limit to the possible rate of inflation. When, after fixing the nominal unit of account in the initial period, through (10.1), we go on to (independently) fix its rate of change over time, through (10.1 bis), the difference, which we shall call σ_M, between the rate of growth of the wage rate, $\bar{\sigma}_w$, in terms of the nominal unit of account, and the standard rate of growth of productivity ρ^*, in physical terms, namely:

$$\sigma_M = \bar{\sigma}_w - \rho^*, \tag{11.1}$$

denotes, in a way in all respects similar to (9.1), the rate of change over time of the general price level. Now, however, in (11.1), only ρ^* refers to a physical magnitude. Rate of change $\bar{\sigma}_w$ refers to a magnitude expressed in terms of a purely *nominal* unit of account, so that the difference $(\bar{\sigma}_w - \rho^*)$ is no longer subject to any physical constraint. Rate σ_M is a (physically unconstrained) rate of change, which concerns a unit of account whose purchasing power, in terms of *any* (single or composite) commodity, varies continually over time. Rate of change σ_M represents a rate of *monetary inflation*.

It should be stressed that the dynamic situation of stability of the general price level remains in any case defined by:

$$\sigma_w = \rho^*, \tag{7.3 bis}$$

(namely by $\sigma_M = 0$, or zero rate of monetary inflation). If (7.3 bis) were to hold, the price system would implicitly be measured in terms of the dynamic standard commodity and therefore would turn out to be rigorously stable over time. When (7.3 bis) does not hold, it remains nevertheless the standard of reference and comparison for evaluating any distance of the actual price movement from the ideal situation of dynamic stability.

It might also be remarked that (7.3 bis), even though an essential term of reference, may hardly be accomplishable in reality. In general, magnitude (11.1), i.e. σ_M, by being completely free from any physical bond, is subject to no physical constraint. Therefore, price inflation, when prices and wages are expressed in nominal (monetary) units of account, have the possibility of reaching extraordinarily high levels, incomparably higher than any level conceivable for (9.1).

These propositions too have found historical confirmation in many cases of so-called 'hyperinflation'.

The actual going over from monetary regimes based on units of account linked to specific physical commodities to monetary regimes based on units of account that are purely nominal has brought with it the pathological possibility of hyperinflation, at the same time as it has brought the actual possibility of achieving a rigorous stability of the general price level.

12. Breaking down the general dynamics of prices into an inflationary component and a structural component

When the goal of price stability is not achieved, it becomes important to be able to distinguish, and separate out, the real effects and the purely nominal effects in any price change. For this purpose, we must turn to the movement over time of our term of reference – the price of the dynamic standard commodity (as it expresses the movement over time of the general price level).

When adopting a nominal monetary unit of account as the basis for the price system, constancy through time of the general price level would be assured by equality $\bar{\sigma}_w = \rho^*$, as we have seen above. But when:

$$\sigma_w \neq \rho^*, \tag{12.1}$$

the general price level is moving.

The equality of these two rates of change, as against the (positive or negative) difference between them – which we have called σ_M, see (11.1) – precisely marks the discriminating point between the real and the purely nominal effects. More specifically, when:

$$\sigma_M = \sigma_w - \rho^* = 0, \tag{12.2}$$

then, the general price level is absolutely stable, even if the single prices are moving, relative to one another. But when:

$$\sigma_M = \sigma_w - \rho^* > 0, \tag{12.3}$$

then the general price level is increasing (as the price of the dynamic standard commodity is increasing). Expression (12.3) precisely represents, as pointed out in the previous section, the rate of inflation of the general price level.

At the same time, the single commodity prices will be moving in time in a more complex manner. When $\sigma_w \neq \rho^*$, all prices undergo the same thrust that pushes the price of the standard commodity, i.e. (12.3). But each commodity price also undergoes a further (positive or negative) thrust, due to the specific change of productivity in the sector to which it refers, relative to the average variation of productivity in all other sectors.

Going back therefore to relations:

$$\sigma_i = \sigma_w - \rho_i, \qquad\qquad i = 1, 2, \ldots, m, \tag{2.9}$$

representing the system of equations by means of which all the rates of change of commodity prices are determined (once the rate of change of the wage rate, σ_w, has been fixed), we may rewrite such relations in the following manner:

$$\sigma_i = (\bar{\sigma}_w - \rho^*) + (\rho^* - \rho_i), \qquad\qquad i = 1, 2, \ldots, m. \qquad (12.4)$$

These expressions now appear as general formulations of considerable interest, as they relate the rates of change of all commodity prices to the rate of growth of the wage rate, the sectoral rates of growth of productivity, the 'standard' rate of growth of productivity and the rate of change of the general price level. From (12.4), we can see explicitly that the rate of change of each commodity price is made up of two components: a general component $(\bar{\sigma}_w - \rho^*)$, which is common to all prices, including that of the dynamic standard commodity; and a particular component $(\rho^* - \rho_i)$, which is specific to each price, and which is zero, by definition, for the dynamic standard commodity.

The general component $(\bar{\sigma}_w - \rho^*)$ is nothing but σ_M, already defined by (11.1): it is the 'rate of inflation of the general price level'; or, as we shall simply and shortly say, the 'rate of inflation'. It is a purely nominal, that is inflationary, component. Specific component $(\rho^* - \rho_i)$, on the other hand, concerns the price structure, which is in continual evolution; it expresses how each specific price $p_i(t)$ evolves because of the difference between the rate of growth of productivity in the specific sector to which it refers and the average rate of growth of productivity of the entire economic system. It is a *structural* component. Each commodity price $p_i(t)$ therefore varies through time at a rate of change, σ_i, which is the sum of these two components; one of which is inflationary, the other structural.

We could also consider these same paths in a reciprocal manner. Rate of change σ_i, if we place the negative sign before it, also represents the rate at which the purchasing power of the monetary unit diminishes, in terms of each specific commodity i ($i = 1, 2, \ldots, m$); while rate of change σ_M, with a negative sign (i.e. the opposite of the rate of increase of the monetary price of the dynamic standard commodity), also represents the rate at which (on a weighted average) the purchasing power of the monetary unit of account decreases through time; what could simply be defined as the rate of decrease through time (because of monetary inflation) of the purchasing power of (paper) money. It represents the degree of deviation of the general price level from the norm of price stability.

13. The goal of stability of the general price level – another macro-economic objective

The practical relevance of breaking down the general dynamics of the price system into its two components – the structural component and the inflationary component – should appear quite evident at this point. Both components have important and pervasive implications, but of a very different nature. The structural component is tied up with problems of attainment of efficiency in each single branch of production. The inflationary component concerns the economic system as a whole. The first component poses questions, at a sectoral and micro-economic level, that recall investigations rather familiar in economic analysis. The second component brings to light the involvement of the economic system as a whole – a field of investigation which has not been nearly so well explored.

Incidentally, the reader will not miss the implications that the change-over from monetary regimes with physical numéraires to monetary regimes with purely nominal numéraires must have had on the appearance, as has happened by now in every country, of a central banking institution.

Although we do not aim here, as has been repeatedly pointed out, at entering into any discussion of the institutional set-ups of the various economic systems (with the exception of what will be said in chapter VIII), yet it is important to underline how clearly, at the present stage of analysis, one can see emerging the necessity, with regard to the economic system considered as a whole, of stating an objective concerning the movement through time of the general price level.

The obvious objective would appear to be precisely that of achieving stability of the general price level, or at least, when the pursuit of rigorous stability generates too many difficulties, that of not going beyond a moderate increase of the general price level, provided that it is at a steady rate of variation.

What seems important to point out here is that such an objective concerns the *whole* economic system. Within the framework of nominal numéraires, one cannot see how it could be pursued by single individuals or by single groups. It seems indeed to require a central banking institution.

This is the second time that, from the present analytic scheme, there emerges the existence of a macro-economic task – i.e. a task which cannot be pursued by single individuals, but necessarily involves the economic system as a whole. At the end of chapter IV there emerged the macro-economic task of pursuing full employment. Now there emerges the task, again typically macro-economic, of pursuing the stability of the general price level.

VI Consumption, savings, rate of interest and inter-temporal distribution of income

1. Impossibility of transferring consumption over time for the economic system as a whole

In a pure labour economy there can be no savings for the economic system as a whole. If by savings we define, following Keynes, the difference between total national income and overall consumption, there clearly is no place for overall savings in a pure labour economy.[1] Since *ex-hypothesi* there are no capital goods, the entire productive capacity[2] is available for the production of consumption goods only.

But the macro-economic equilibrium condition for effective demand, since its first formulation (II.2.5), has been telling us something else, which is less evident but even more important. The productive capacity, within each production period, *must*, in its entirety, be devoted to the production of consumption goods. If overall demand (and consequently overall production) of consumption goods turned out to be less than total potential national income, the difference would represent, for the community as a whole, non-realized and therefore lost consumption; i.e. it would represent consumption goods that could be, but are not, produced, and are therefore lost, because of non-utilization of productive capacity. This is one of the most characteristic aspects of production economies. To have brought it into relief appears, from the present theoretical scheme, as one of the most important contributions of Keynes' *General Theory* (1936).

All this also means that, for an economic system as a whole, the consumption that, in any period of time, were not to be realized because of

---

[1] Overall savings, in Keynesian terms, would of course enter the scene the very moment the model were to be extended to production with capital goods (as in Pasinetti, 1981). The purpose of the present analysis is to investigate those characteristics that hold even if no overall savings are possible.

[2] It may be useful to recall the particular features of the notion of 'productive capacity' in a pure labour economy (see end of section II.3).

lack of effective demand, cannot be transferred to any other time period. It is lost for ever.

There remains of course the possibility of producing, and then hoarding, durable consumption goods, in physical terms; thereby transferring them physically through time. This hoarding in physical terms is always possible, but is subject to rigid physical constraints. In order to make the present relations emerge in a clear manner and without complications, we shall suppose, in this entire chapter, that all consumption goods are perishable, and therefore that there is no possibility to store them up in physical terms. (The possibility of physically storing up non-perishable consumption goods can always be introduced at a second stage of analysis.)

Having therefore supposed, for the sake of analytic simplicity, that there does not exist any durable consumption good, the impossibility of overall savings emerges even more clearly; and just as clearly there emerges the impossibility for the economic system as a whole to transfer consumption through time. In each time period, overall consumption can (and in full employment equilibrium must) be equal to overall productive capacity. Any upward deviation would be physically impossible. Any downward deviation is indeed physically possible, but it means a loss of the consumption goods that could have been produced (as well as corresponding unemployment for those people who could have been employed to produce them); it is not possible to make them up in other time periods. The loss of consumption goods that fail to be produced because of lack of effective demand is final and irretrievable.

2. Wide possibilities of personal savings and dissavings

Yet, although the possibilities of overall savings for a (pure labour) economy are zero, the possibilities of savings for single individuals are entirely open, and they are enormous. Overall impossibility does not imply any *personal* impossibility to save and transfer consumption through time, positively or negatively. The only condition is that the decisions to postpone or to bring forward consumption, and therefore to carry out (positive or negative) savings, exactly compensate each other in the aggregate.

More precisely, even by making the extreme assumption that all goods are perishable consumption goods, and therefore have to be consumed within each single time period, this does not entail any impossibility of personal savings, positive and negative. Any single individual may indeed abstain from consuming part of his or her current income, and postpone consumption in time, provided that he or she can find some other individual, or individuals, who are willing to do the opposite.

Operations of this sort may be carried out to a very large extent indeed. Individuals have natural lives that are longer than their active lives; moreover they normally have families whose components vary in age, requirements, and number, in each particular time period. This means that the time profile of each family's consumption needs will normally differ from the time profile of the same family's incoming income, even when their total sums coincide. Hence there may be periods in which a particular family needs to save (income exceeding consumption) and periods in which the same family needs to dissave (consumption exceeding income). Normally these needs for savings and dissavings will arise at different times for different families, so that – within each period of time – those people whose incomes are in excess of their consumption needs may lend their excess purchasing power to those people whose incomes fall short of their consumption needs, and then have it back when the personal situations have reversed, or else let this right be exerted by their heirs.

It is quite evident that, in an economic system with millions of individuals, inter-personal lending and borrowing may take place (directly or through intermediaries) to a large extent, with very few complications. In theory, in each single period of time, any individual may lend to others an amount of purchasing power up to the whole amount of his or her current income; and, at other times, may even borrow multiples of the amount of purchasing power corresponding to his or her current income.

There is no limit, in theory, to these possibilities of personal lendings and borrowings. The only constraint is of a different sort – it is the macro-economic constraint which is imposed by the overall effective demand equilibrium condition. Within the bounds of such macro-economic constraint, in any closed economic system, all personal lendings and borrowings must cancel each other out. There can be no net savings or dissavings for the economic system as a whole, however large personal savings and dissavings may be.

3. Public savings and dissavings

Similarly, and in addition, to the possibilities of transferring consumption among individuals, within a total consumption which is given, there are possibilities of transferring consumption between the single individuals on the one side and the whole community considered as a single entity, on the other side.

The community as a whole – which we may imagine as represented by a public authority, for brevity's sake let us say the 'government' – is taking charge of the provision of many public goods and services (as will be hinted at in a little more detail in the following chapter). And the normal way to do this is to impose taxes on private citizens, i.e. to impose the surrender to the government (for purposes of public expenditure) of a part of the private citizen's purchasing power, according to various criteria. But the flows of government taxes and of government expenditures, within each time period, may not coincide exactly. There may be times at which public expenditure exceeds taxation, thereby generating a public deficit – and thus debts – and there may be other times at which taxation exceeds public expenditure, thereby generating a surplus, and thus credits, or, more likely, abatement of previously cumulated debts.

It is evident that in this case too, as in the previous case of debt/credit relations among single individuals, there can be no transfer of overall consumption through time. Yet, there may be a redistribution of consumption within each time period. For those single individuals who undertake savings, this may be a way to transfer personal consumption through time, to the extent that the whole community (of which those citizens themselves are a part) does the opposite.

In the case of public savings and dissavings, a further, important, concern must of course be introduced. The community as a whole (unlike the single individuals) cannot in general take decisions on redistribution of public versus private consumption, without paying explicit attention also to the overall effective demand constraint. There may be times at which overall effective demand tends to be larger than overall productive capacity; and there may be other times at which overall effective demand tends to be less than overall productive capacity. Public concern about these problems is bound to interfere with the decisions on inter-sectoral transfers of consumption. In other words, government policy as to taxation and public indebtedness is bound to be inserted as part of the wider concern with the appropriate ways to achieve fulfilment of the macro-economic condition for overall effective demand. We shall come back to this point in the final section of this chapter.

The point to be stressed here, however, simply regards the many ways in which savings and dissavings (and the possibilities of inter-temporal transfers of consumption) become possible individually and sectorally, even if they cancel out in the aggregate. Dissavings (or savings) may indeed take place, even for the entire community taken as a single entity, if savings (or dissavings) in the opposite direction are undertaken by private citizens. And these possibilities are very wide indeed.

4. The coming into being of financial assets and liabilities

The debt/credit relations described above (among single individuals or between private citizens and a public authority) have a very important tangible consequence.

Lendings and borrowings entail the coming into being of *financial* assets and liabilities. This means that, even when no physical stocks of commodities are carried through time (as in the case we are supposing here), the economic system will normally carry financial stocks through time, representing claims to future consumption by some individuals against others.

Overall, as has been pointed out, positive and negative claims – i.e. financial assets and liabilities – necessarily cancel each other out. Yet the stocks of financial assets for some individuals (and for some organizational bodies) and of corresponding financial liabilities for other individuals (and for other organizational bodies) may grow to very large amounts indeed. Through financial assets, some individuals have the possibility of building up stocks of purchasing power for the command of future consumption goods; and, what is more, of postponing to the future any decision about such consumption goods. Through the corresponding financial liabilities, other individuals (and/or organizational bodies) have the possibility of making their present annual consumption go well beyond the (physically determined) amounts of present annual incomes, with the undertaking (which precisely represents their liability) of surrendering purchasing power back to their creditors in another, or in other, time periods.

It will be realized that all this is far from being a trivial matter. Even if financial assets and liabilities cancel out overall, they build up an intricate network of inter-personal, and private–public, relations, which go beyond those emerging from production activity, and which may profoundly affect through time the distribution of income among the members of the economic system.

5. The emerging of a rate of interest

The relations of debt and credit, among the various individuals and/or between private citizens and a public authority (and therefore the coming into being of financial assets and liabilities) have another immediate and important consequence.

They insert so to speak a wedge, they open up a gap, between the inflows of incomes and the actual outflows of expenditure (or vice versa), for each single individual. The connection remains committed to the choice of the numéraire of the price system. Existence of financial assets and liabilities necessarily requires the choice of a specific numéraire, in terms of which they are denominated. This means that they are bound to remain constant through time *only* in terms of such numéraire. But if all the 'natural prices' vary through time, as we are supposing here, it follows that the purchasing power of all financial assets and liabilities will vary through time in terms of *all* commodities (and, what is more, in a different manner from one commodity to another), with the exception only of the commodity chosen as numéraire. This is another reason for which, in the presence of structural dynamics, the choice of the numéraire of the price system, far from being an arbitrary, or irrelevant, decision, becomes a very important decision indeed.

If the percentage rates of growth of productivity in the m (vertically integrated) sectors are $\rho_1, \rho_2, \ldots, \rho_h, \ldots, \rho_m$, ranked in a decreasing order, and if commodity h is the one that is used as numéraire, which means that all debts and credits are stipulated in terms of commodity h, then all debts and credits will clearly remain constant through time only in terms of commodity h. In terms of any other commodity, the purchasing power of all debts and credits will change. More precisely, over time, all debts and credits will revalue at rate $(\rho_1 - \rho_h)$ in terms of commodity 1, at rate $(\rho_2 - \rho_h)$ in terms of commodity 2, ..., at rate $(\rho_{h-1} - \rho_h)$ in terms of commodity $(h-1)$. And they will devalue at rate $(\rho_h - \rho_{h+1})$ in terms of commodity $(h+1)$, ..., at rate $(\rho_h - \rho_m)$ in terms of commodity m.

In order to make the implications of this structural dynamics (of the purchasing power of financial assets and liabilities) emerge clearly, suppose that, at a certain moment, we wanted to change the numéraire of the price system. Clearly, if we did so, the evolution through time of all debt/credit relations would, in *real* terms, be altered. To express the problem more cogently, suppose that we wanted to change the numéraire, but at the same time we wanted to keep inter-personal relations unaltered through time in real terms. Then, we would have to introduce a correction – precisely in the form of a rate of interest,[3] even if no rate of interest had originally been stipulated on the debts and credits in terms of commodity h. For example, if a change of numéraire were to be made from commodity h to commodity 1, in order that all debt and credit relations remain unaltered in real terms through time, a rate of interest equal to $(\rho_1 - \rho_h)$ would have to be introduced on all debts reckoned in terms of the new numéraire (on top of whatever rate of interest had been stipulated already when debts were reckoned in terms of the old numéraire).

The conclusion is important. The coming into being of financial assets and liabilities, reflecting inter-personal or private–public debt/credit relations, implies *inevitably* (i.e., even if nothing had been stipulated on the matter), the emergence of a rate of interest.

6. A whole set of own-rates of interest, implied by the same (actual) rate of interest

We may notice that the existence of financial assets and liabilities, when coupled with a structural dynamics of natural prices, implies the existence

---

[3] For simplicity's sake, as before, we shall talk of a 'rate of interest' to mean a *percentage* rate of interest per period of time.

of not just one rate of interest, but of a whole set of rates of interest. More precisely, it implies the existence of a particular own-rate of interest for each commodity.

To illustrate the point, suppose that the wage rate is chosen as the numéraire through time, i.e. $w(t) = 1$, and suppose that loans, in terms of the wage rate, are stipulated at a rate of interest equal to zero. Thus, when a loan expires, the lender simply receives back from the borrower an amount of purchasing power (in terms of labour) equal to the amount that was lent at the beginning, without receiving any interest in the meantime. However, the natural price of each commodity j, in terms of labour, has been decreasing in the meantime at the percentage rate ρ_j, $(j = 1, 2, \ldots, m)$. Hence the amount of the loan repaid, at time t, although unchanged in terms of labour, could purchase a quantity of each commodity j equal to $q_j(0)e^{\rho_j t}$, where $q_j(0)$ is the quantity of commodity j which the amount that is repaid could have purchased at time zero. This means that the amount of the loan, though unchanged in terms of labour, has grown, in terms of each specific commodity j, at a compound rate of interest equal to ρ_j, $(j = 1, 2, \ldots, m)$. Percentage rate ρ_j therefore represents, in this case, what may be called the *own-rate of interest* for commodity j. There are m such own-rates of interest, namely:

$$\rho_1, \rho_2, \ldots, \rho_m, \tag{6.1}$$

for commodities 1, 2, ..., m, respectively; all implied by an actual rate of interest equal to zero in terms of the wage rate.

If the actual rate of interest, stipulated on loans in terms of the wage rate, were $i_w > 0$, instead of being zero, then the set of own-rates of interest implied by i_w would be:

$$(i_w + \rho_1), (i_w + \rho_2), \ldots, (i_w + \rho_m), \tag{6.2}$$

for commodities 1, 2, ..., m respectively.

The same concepts may alternatively be illustrated with reference to the case in which a particular commodity (instead of the wage rate) – let us say commodity h – is chosen as numéraire in terms of which loans are reckoned through time, i.e., the case in which $p_h(t) = 1$. In this case, if an actual rate of interest i_h is stipulated, to be paid on loans reckoned in terms of commodity h, then this actual rate of interest i_h clearly implies a set of own-rates of interest:

$$(i_h + \rho_1 - \rho_h), (i_h + \rho_2 - \rho_h), \ldots, (i_h + \rho_{h-1} - \rho_h), \tag{6.3}$$

$$i_h + \rho_h - \rho_h = i_h, (i_h + \rho_{h+1} - \rho_h), \ldots, (i_h + \rho_m - \rho_h),$$

for commodities $1, 2, \ldots, h-1, h, h+1, \ldots, m$, respectively; and also an own-rate of interest,

$$i_h + 0 - \rho_h = i_h - \rho_h, \tag{6.4}$$

for 'labour commanded'.

A particularly interesting case is that one in which the chosen numéraire is the 'dynamic standard commodity', which has been denoted by h^*. In this case, if i_{h*} is the actual rate of interest, stipulated on loans denominated in terms of the dynamic standard commodity, such rate of interest implies a set of own-rates of interest

$$i_{h*} - (\rho^* - \rho_j), \qquad j = 1, 2, \ldots, m, \tag{6.5}$$

for the m goods, and an own-rate of interest

$$i_{h*} - \rho^*, \tag{6.6}$$

for 'labour commanded'.

As may be seen, the own-rate of interest for labour commanded is simply, in this case, the difference between the actual rate of interest and the standard (i.e. average) rate of growth of productivity; while the own-rate of interest for each commodity j ($j = 1, 2, \ldots, m$), is given by the difference between the actual rate of interest and the (positive or negative) excess of the standard rate of growth of productivity over the rate of growth of productivity in the specific j^{th} sector.

7. Nominal or 'money' rate of interest

The rates of interest considered in the previous section (though one of them is explicit, and the other m own-rates are implicit) are all 'real' rates of interest, in the sense that each of them refers to purchasing power in terms of a specific physical commodity (simple or composite).

But in modern economic systems the chosen numéraire normally is a *nominal* unit of account (a paper-money unit). And when it is this nominal unit of account (which we shall simply call money unit) to be adopted in the stipulation of debt and credit relations, the rate of interest will be expressed in the same terms, i.e. it will be a nominal, or, as we shall call it, a 'money' rate of interest.

If we denote such a nominal or money rate of interest by i_M – a rate of interest stipulated on loans denominated in terms of a nominal (money) unit of account – it is evident that such a rate of interest, to acquire a meaning, must be put into relation with the movement over time of the general level of prices.

8. The relation between nominal rate and real rates of interest – the 'standard' (real) rate of interest

When the inter-personal debt/credit relations are denominated in terms of a nominal unit of account (a paper-money unit), and the rate of interest on the loans so denominated has been stipulated at level i_M (a money, or nominal, rate of interest), it becomes necessary to take our analysis behind the time movement of all prices, to find the corresponding real rates of interest.

Resuming notation σ_j, $(j = 1, 2, \ldots, m)$ and σ_w of the previous chapter for the rates of change of the commodity prices and of the wage rate, respectively (all expressed in terms of the nominal or 'money' unit), we may express, first of all, the (real) own-rate of interest for each commodity j by the difference:

$$i_M - \sigma_i, \qquad\qquad i = 1, 2, \ldots, m, \qquad\qquad (8.1)$$

and the (real) own-rate of interest for 'labour commanded' by the difference:

$$i_M - \sigma_w. \qquad\qquad (8.2)$$

But in order to compare these expressions with the previous ones, we must go much deeper. We can take advantage of (V.12.4) of the previous chapter and re-write (8.1) and (8.2) as:

$$i_M - (\sigma_w - \rho^*) - (\rho^* - \rho_j), \qquad\qquad (8.1 \text{ bis})$$

and

$$i_M - (\sigma_w - \rho^*) - \rho^*, \qquad\qquad (8.2 \text{ bis})$$

respectively.

As may be seen, these expressions, when compared with the corresponding (6.5) and (6.6), reveal the algebraic addition of a new addendum, namely $(\sigma_w - \rho^*)$, which – as we know – represents the rate of monetary inflation, and which we have called σ_M (see (V.11.1)). Therefore (8.1bis) and (8.2 bis) may also be rewritten:

$$i_M - \sigma_M - (\rho^* - \rho_j), \qquad\qquad j = 1, 2, \ldots, m, \qquad (8.1 \text{ ter})$$

and

$$i_M - \sigma_M - \rho^* \qquad\qquad (8.2 \text{ ter})$$

respectively.

This means that, when the unit of account is the nominal (money) unit, in order to obtain the (real) own-rates of interest, it is necessary to deduct the rate of monetary inflation σ_M from the nominal rate of interest i_M. Then we are back to the formulations of the previous sections – compare (8.1 ter) with (6.5), and (8.2 ter) with (6.6).

Notice that, for the dynamic standard commodity, (8.1 ter) reduces to:

$$i_M - \sigma_M, \tag{8.3}$$

that is to say: the own-rate of interest for the dynamic standard commodity is simply given by the difference between the nominal, or money, rate of interest, and the rate of increase of the general price level (i.e., the rate of monetary inflation).

Expression (8.3) represents a sort of average 'real' rate of interest for the economic system as a whole. We may call it the 'standard' (real) rate of interest.

9. Which rate of interest?

The foregoing analysis has already yielded a very important result indeed.

It would make no sense to posit the question of whether there should or should not be a rate of interest. A whole structure of rates of interest exists in any case, whatever the actual 'nominal' rate of interest (even if it were equal to zero), and whatever the numéraire chosen as the basis of the price system. In other words, a whole structure of own-rates of interest – all of them 'real' – is inevitably inherent in the structural dynamics of relative prices, as soon as this structural dynamics is accompanied by inter-personal debt/credit relations.

The problem to be posited is therefore another one, namely the problem of finding the appropriate level at which to peg the whole structure of the own-rates of interest. More specifically, the problem is that of singling out *which* money rate of interest is the appropriate one to apply to all debt/credit relations, stipulated in terms of the money unit. This is in fact the only variable that still has remained indeterminate in the present theoretical scheme, since the introduction of inter-personal debt/credit relations. It has been pointed out already (in section 5) that the coming into existence of debt/credit relations has opened up a gap between the inflow of personal incomes and the outflow of expenditures. Now we can say more precisely that it has opened up a new degree of freedom in the price system. The closure of this degree of freedom requires the determination of a rate of interest.[4]

The question is: which rate of interest? Here we must go back to

---

[4] In more detail, each wage earner has the possibility, through debt/credit undertakings, of decoupling his or her current personal consumption from personal current wage. He or she can carry through time a personal (positive or negative) stock of financial wealth, which, at

fundamentals. If a new variable has entered the price system, this variable must obviously be determined in a way which is logically consistent with the rest of the theory. Now, from among all possible price systems, the present theoretical scheme has adopted the 'natural' price system (i.e., prices proportional to physical quantities of labour, 'embodied' or 'commanded'). The determination of the rate of interest must be consistent with this theoretical scheme.

The question may therefore be restated in the following terms. From all possible levels of the actual rate of interest (and by implication of the whole structure of the own-rates of interest), is there a particular one, which may legitimately be claimed to be the 'natural' level of the rate of interest? (And, by implication, is there a natural structure of the own-rates of interest?)

10. The 'natural' rate of interest

The question just stated, in order to be answered, requires the adoption of a well-defined criterion; and the criterion that is adopted here is a direct one – namely that of logical consistency. We shall come back to justifying this choice in section 12 below, with more elaborate arguments, which will yield a different, but in fact equivalent, definition. For the time being, let us proceed straightaway.

Definition of 'natural rate of interest' (logical consistency version)
In an economic system in which all contributions to, and benefits from, the production process are regulated on the basis of physical quantities of labour ('natural' prices being proportional to labour, both 'embodied' and 'commanded'), the natural rate of interest is that rate of interest that maintains through time the equality between labour embodied and labour commanded, i.e. that maintains unaltered through time all purchasing power relations in terms of labour.

This means a zero rate of interest in terms of labour.

the end of each time unit, will be the algebraic sum of: wages minus consumption, initial financial assets minus initial financial liabilities, interest received minus interest paid on financial stocks. Although all these items cancel out in the aggregate, as the economic system we are considering can carry, as a whole, no net wealth through time (total wages being always equal to total consumption, i.e. to total production), yet a very articulated structural dynamics takes place in the amounts of *personal* purchasing power. We know that, given the numéraire in terms of which debt/credit relations have been denominated – let us say a conventional money unit – and given the rate of change of the money wage rate (or alternatively the rate of change of any one of the commodity prices), there exist well-defined relations between the evolution of the money prices and the evolution of the purchasing power of the money unit, in terms of each single physical commodity. This means that the evolution of the actual distribution of real purchasing power among all individuals is not determined until the current rate of interest is fixed.

We have seen already, in section 6, that a zero rate of interest in terms of labour implies a rate of interest equal to ρ_1 in terms of commodity 1, a rate of interest equal to ρ_2 in terms of commodity 2, ..., a rate of interest equal to ρ_m in terms of commodity m, and, we may now add, a rate of interest equal to ρ^* in terms of the dynamic standard commodity. We may therefore call this the 'natural' structure of the own-rates of interest.

Clearly, given this structure of own-rates of interest, what the *actual* rate of interest will have to be in order to bring such structure into being depends on the numéraire in terms of which debts and credits are denominated. Hence, the (actual) natural rate of interest does depend on the numéraire of the price system. If we denote the natural rate of interest by an asterisk, i.e. if we represent it by i^*, we shall normally have to add a subscript to this symbol in order to specify the numéraire in terms of which all debt/credit relations are reckoned.

When the numéraire chosen is the wage rate (i.e. when $w(t)=1$) and all debt/credit relations are reckoned in terms of labour, then the natural rate of interest, to be denoted by i^*_w, turns out to be:

$$i^*_w = 0. \tag{10.1}$$

When the numéraire chosen is any commodity h (i.e. when $p_h(t)=1$) and all debt/credit relations are stipulated in terms of commodity h, then the natural rate of interest i^*_h turns out to be:

$$i^*_h = \rho_h, \qquad\qquad h = 1, 2, \ldots, m. \tag{10.2}$$

And when, as a particular case, the numéraire chosen is that singularly interesting composite commodity which we have called the 'dynamic standard commodity', then the natural rate of interest (which we may denote in this case by i^*_{h*}) turns out to be equal to the 'standard' rate of productivity growth:

$$i^*_{h*} = \rho^*. \tag{10.3}$$

The usual case, however, will be one in which the numéraire chosen is a conventional money unit of account and all debt/credit relations are stipulated in terms of such a money unit. In this case, the natural rate of interest (in terms of money) may be expressed with reference to the average movement through time of all prices. We know that such movement coincides with the movement through time of the price of the dynamic standard commodity. Hence we only need to take (10.3) and add to it the rate of change, σ_M, of the price of the dynamic standard commodity. We obtain:

$$i^*_M = \rho^* + \sigma_M. \tag{10.4}$$

This is the natural, *money*, rate of interest. It is simply equal to the standard rate of growth of productivity plus the rate of inflation of the general level of prices.

We may note that all these expressions are equivalent, in real terms. They simply represent different ways, in relation to the particular choice of numéraire, of making the price system produce the same 'real' effects, i.e. of making it produce the same structure of (natural) own-rates of interest and thus of preserving intact through time the original purchasing power of all loans in terms of labour.

But there is a particularly interesting expression that emerges from all these elaborations. Since

$$\rho^* + \sigma_M = \rho^* + \sigma_w - \rho^* = \sigma_w$$

then (10.4) may be written:

$$i^*_M = \sigma_w. \tag{10.4a}$$

But the same may also be said of (10.3), of (10.2), of (10.1)! In other words, these three expressions may also be written, respectively, as:

$$i^*_{h^*} = \sigma_w, \tag{10.3a}$$

$$i^*_h = \sigma_w, \tag{10.2a}$$

$$i^*_w = \sigma_w, \tag{10.1a}$$

where the wage rate is measured, in each expression, in terms of the corresponding numéraire. Thus, in general, whatever be the numéraire, the natural rate of interest possesses the remarkable property of always being equal to the rate of growth of the wage rate.

We may therefore write, without the need of any subscript,

$$i^* = \sigma_w, \tag{10.5}$$

where σ_w is the percentage rate of change of the wage rate, expressed in whatever numéraire is chosen as the basis of the price system, and thus of the debt/credit relations. This is the simplest of all expressions of the 'natural rate of interest'.

The definition stated at the beginning of this section may therefore be simply re-expressed by stating expression (10.5). Whatever be the numéraire in terms of which debts and credits are stipulated, the 'natural' rate of interest is equal to the rate of growth of the wage rate. This is the rate of interest that preserves intact through time the purchasing power of all loans in terms of labour.

11. A 'labour principle of (inter-temporal) income distribution'

The definition of the natural rate of interest, which has just been given, has a practical implication of some relevance. Average labour productivity normally grows at a positive rate. This implies that the (actual) natural rate of interest will normally be positive, at least with reference to the numéraires so far considered (the only exception occurring when the numéraire chosen is the wage rate, which implies by definition $\sigma_w = 0$, and thus a natural rate of interest is equal to zero). This means that, when a natural rate of interest is adopted, interest will normally have to be paid on loans, at the end of each time period. And it may not be immediately evident what implications this may have for income distribution, in an economic system in which income is to be distributed in proportion to labour contributed to the production processes.

To investigate this question, we may begin by considering first the case in which the numéraire chosen is precisely the wage rate and all debt/credit relations are reckoned in terms of labour, at a rate of interest equal to zero (the natural rate of interest). One can see clearly, in this case, that in each time period the whole national income is distributed to people in proportion to labour contributed. Then, side by side with the income distribution process carried out by natural prices, a whole series of debt/credit relations may come into being, owing to the needs of single individuals to transfer personal consumption through time. Some people may save and other people (or groups of people, among whom we may include the community as a whole) may dissave, by exchanging positive and negative purchasing power among themselves, while all financial transactions cancel out for the economic system as a whole. Since all debts and credits are in terms of the wage rate, and the natural rate of interest is equal to zero, each creditor will receive, at maturity, an amount of purchasing power, in terms of labour, which is exactly equal to the amount originally lent. It appears absolutely clear, in this case, that – thanks to natural prices and to the natural rate of interest – an income distribution process is in operation, at any given point in time as well as through time, which distributes all national income to people in proportion to the labour they have contributed to the production process. We may well say that income is distributed (at any point in time as well as through time) according to a 'labour principle of income distribution'.

But we can also easily see that the situation remains exactly the same, in real terms, with any other numéraire, *provided that* a natural rate of interest is charged. Suppose for example that a particular (single or composite) commodity h is taken as the numéraire of the price system and that all debt/credit relations are reckoned in terms of commodity h. Then the natural rate of interest on loans is $i^*_h = \rho_h$. Suppose that this is the actual rate of interest that is stipulated. At the end of each time period, the national income, measured in terms of commodity h, is distributed, through the natural price system, in proportion to labour contributed to the production process. But now loans are stipulated in terms of commodity h at rate of interest $i^*_h = \rho_h$. Since, as time goes on, labour productivity in sector h is increasing at rate ρ_h, the wage rate, in terms of commodity h, will grow through time at rate ρ_h. This means that, in terms of the wage rate, all financial assets are devaluing through time at rate ρ_h. It is precisely in order to compensate for this devaluation that the (natural) rate of interest $i^*_h = \rho_h$ has to be paid on all loans. If interest was in fact not paid, but cumulated, at the end of each time period, with the amounts of the loans, all financial assets and liabilities would grow in time at rate ρ_h, in terms of commodity h, but would remain constant in terms of labour. In real terms, the situation would be exactly the same as in the previous case, in which $w(t) = 1$. If, on the other hand, as is more usually the case, interest is actually paid at the end of each time period, then the illusion might be created that some income is distributed to rentiers. But this is not the case. When interest is reckoned at the *natural* rate, the interest which is paid correctly compensates the creditors for the devaluation of loans in terms of labour.

The payment of natural interest is therefore revealed to be a partial reimbursement of debt.

Exactly the same arguments could be restated for the case in which a conventional money unit of account (paper money) is used as the numéraire, in terms of which all debt/credit relations are stipulated. We have seen that, in this case, the natural rate of interest is $i^*_M = \sigma_M + \rho^*$ (see (10.4)) which is also equal to σ_w, the rate of increase of the money wage rate. This is precisely the rate at which all financial assets and liabilities devalue through time in terms of labour. Therefore, the payment of the natural rate of interest – a rate of interest in this case equal to σ_w – again is revealed to have the character of a correct compensation of creditors for the devaluation of all loans in terms of labour.

To conclude and summarize: whatever the numéraire in terms of which loans are stipulated, the definition of a natural rate of interest given in the previous section, enables us to say that the actual payments of natural interest on financial assets have the character of partial repayments of debts, since the debts themselves – when they are stipulated in terms of a numéraire other than the wage rate – normally devalue through time, by undergoing a diminution, in terms of labour, precisely by the amount that is paid as natural interest. Only the payment of natural interest correctly compensates for the devaluation of financial assets through time, thereby ensuring that their purchasing power remains unchanged in terms of labour.[5] In a nutshell: only the payment of interest at the 'natural' rate prevents through time any distortion from the 'labour principle of (inter-temporal) income distribution'.

12. An alternative definition of 'natural' rate of interest

The arguments developed in the previous section now enable us to state an alternative definition of 'natural' rate of interest (with respect to the one given in section 10).

We may notice, to begin with, that any actual rate of interest, when it differs from the natural rate of interest, inevitably distorts the inter-temporal distribution of income from taking place in proportion to labour contributed to the production process. More precisely, a higher than natural rate of interest distorts the distribution of income in favour of creditors (by enabling them through time to command more labour than they have contributed); and conversely a lower than natural rate of interest distorts income distribution in favour of the debtors (by enabling them through time to repay an amount of purchasing power which can command less labour than they have been able to use). Only a natural rate of interest (provided of course that natural prices prevail) ensures no distortion in income distribution through time.

Here is therefore a very simple definition of natural rate of interest, alternative but equivalent to the one given in section 10 above.

Definition of 'natural rate of interest' (*income distribution version*)
The natural rate of interest is that rate of interest which realizes through time a distribution of income among the participants to the production process, which is proportional to the physical quantities of labour they have contributed (i.e., a rate of interest that realizes the 'labour principle of income distribution').

This is a rate of interest equal to zero in terms of labour, which in turn means a real rate of interest equal to the rate of growth of labour productivity in terms of every single physical commodity that is produced in the economic system.

Any rate of interest that is different from the natural rate of interest

---

[5] Note that the notion of 'natural' rate of interest, as a compensation for a loss of purchasing power, recovers the original etymological meaning of the term 'interest', as distinct from 'usury'. Let me give a couple of references. Noonan (1957) points out that in Roman law, the term 'interest' arose 'In discussing applications for damages because of the nonfulfilment of contractual obligations ... *Quod interest*, the difference, is what the delinquent party is held to pay the damaged party' (p. 106). Homer (1963) notices that 'The Latin verb *intereo* means "to be lost"; a substantive term "*interisse*" developed into the modern term "interest". Interest was not profit but loss' (p. 73).

causes distortions in the inter-temporal distribution of income (in favour of debtors or in favour of creditors), by preventing income distribution from taking place (at any given moment in time or through time) in proportion to physical quantities of labour.

13. The rentier in a pure labour economy

We are in a position to investigate further the meaning and implications of any particular way of closing the degree of freedom which inter-personal debt/credit relations have opened up in the overall price system.

In the very simple context of a pure labour economy governed by natural prices, all income is distributed to wages, i.e. to labour. There are no profits, *ex-hypothesi*, as there are no capital goods. And yet this is not enough to ensure that national income is actually enjoyed, in terms of consumption, in proportion to physical quantities of labour contributed to the production process. As we have just seen, in order to ensure proportionality between labour and actual consumption through time, a further condition must be satisfied, namely that the rate of interest on inter-personal debt/credit relations be fixed at its natural level. Invariance through time of the purchasing power of all financial assets (and therefore of postponed or advanced consumption), in terms of labour, is ensured only if the rate of interest is fixed at its 'natural' level.

This means that any time the rate of interest is not at its natural level, even in the hypothesis that income is originally distributed in proportion to labour (through the natural price system), income undergoes through time a redistribution among debtors and creditors, that makes it no longer proportional to physical quantities of labour. When, to cite a specific example, the actual rate of interest is higher than its natural level, some individuals (those who have credits and receive interest – the creditors) come into possession of an amount of purchasing power greater than that which is justified by the labour they originally contributed: in fact, they come to enjoy extra-incomes (with respect to labour-income), due to their position as rentier. Conversely, the debtors – as a result of their paying interest at a rate greater than the natural one – are deprived of a part of the purchasing power they had originally obtained by means of the labour they had contributed.

We therefore descry, in an economic system of pure labour, the economic figure of the rentier (who appropriates purchasing power going beyond that which is justified by the labour he or she has contributed); and similarly we descry the economic figure of the debtor, who is deprived of part of the purchasing power obtained through labour, owing to indebtedness at a too burdensome rate of interest. It is hard to avoid defining this income redistribution as 'exploitation'. This has actually been a too familiar phenomenon in the course of past centuries (and still is at present), which gives a justification to the censures of moral philosophers against loans at usury.[6]

But our analysis also brings to light the characteristics, theoretically equally possible, of situations which are symmetrically opposite. When the rate of interest is lower than its natural level, income is redistributed through time in exactly the opposite direction. In this case, it is the creditor who is deprived of a part of the purchasing power obtained from his or her labour services and who is exploited; and it is the debtor who is put in a position to buy something more than what he or she would be entitled to, on the basis of the labour he or she has originally contributed. Historically, situations of this kind have been rare, if not practically impossible, with monetary regimes that were in the past based on physical units of account; but, with the advent of monetary regimes based on nominal units of account (paper money), these situations have become perfectly possible, even in spite of very high nominal rates of interest, and they have in fact punctually come into being, in the cases of strong money devaluations (hyper-inflation).

An interesting feature to note is that the historical situations of exploitation of creditors (as opposed to the historical situations of exploitation of debtors) have not been so severely denounced by moral philosophers, even though there has been wide sympathy expressed for the low-income, 'poor' savers, who have ended up with financial assets nominally unchanged, but practically emptied of real content.

One may wonder: why is it that so little sensitivity is found for the exploitation of creditors? Perhaps one, not unimportant, reason may be found in the fact that creditors (except for the classic case of 'widows and orphans') generally belong to high income-bracket categories. Their exploitation may appear, from a strictly moral point of view, less preoccupying than the opposite kind, resulting from consumption loans, and usury.

But there is another reason, which undoubtedly is not irrelevant. During major money devaluations, the rôle of the advantaged debtor is by and large taken up by the State, as a major holder of debt – the public debt. One may therefore ask: what justification is there – if there is any – for the community as a whole, represented by the State, to exploit the single individual savers?

---

[6] One might say that any excess of the rate of interest over the natural level gives precise quantitative content to the medieval notion of 'usury' – no longer compensation for a loss but illicit gain. This result should not be surprising in the present context, in which all loans are consumption loans.

14. Income redistribution due to money inflation

It is obviously not reasonable – it is in fact iniquitous – that the State, which represents the community as a whole, should exploit private citizens through recourse to money inflation, after having asked them, in preceding periods of monetary stability, to underwrite long-term dated bonds at a fixed nominal rate of interest.

Yet, this has happened repeatedly throughout the history of many countries and it may well continue to happen. It remains to be asked whether the present theoretical scheme may be of some help in understanding the meaning and implications of these events.

First of all, it is clear that windfall benefits coming from income redistribution taking place during the processes of money inflation (when the nominal rates of interest remain fixed and the real rates become negative) accrue indistinctly to *all* debtors. To the extent that this redistribution is favouring private debtors, it is surely without any justification (i.e. it is iniquitous); just as unjustified (and iniquitous) is the income redistribution which occurs in the symmetrically opposite case, considered in the previous section.

To the extent that this income redistribution is favouring the State, i.e. the community as a whole, it raises more complex questions, which require further investigation.

One might say that this redistribution in favour of the State is equivalent to a supplementary tax. It has in truth been called 'inflation tax' – a tax which falls on those people who possess public-debt bonds, and in general on anybody who possesses any document representing a debt by the State, including paper money itself. But one must admit that such a tax puts into being a taxation criterion which is entirely arbitrary, and that in any case side-steps any of those decision-making processes that the community is explicitly and consciously setting up in order to distribute the total tax burden among its citizens.

One might however add that, if the public-debt bonds happened to be distributed among private citizens exactly in proportion to their incomes, it could be claimed that the inflation tax had after all turned into a supplementary and proportional income tax. Similarly (especially in a wider context, with many types of assets), if that public-debt bond distribution were exactly proportional to individuals' 'wealth', one could claim that the inflation tax had after all turned into a supplementary and proportional property tax. Yet one could hardly rely on the realization of these conditions, if nothing else because of the voluntary nature of the subscription of public bonds.

We may therefore conclude – with reference to inflation and public debt –

that precisely the non-realization, or the only partial realization, of the above mentioned conditions may be taken as an index of the degree of iniquity of the 'inflation tax', i.e. of the degree of non-justification and thus of iniquity of the divergence of the actual rates of interest on public debt from the natural rate of interest.

15. Public debt or taxation – remarks on the meaning of 'Ricardian neutrality'

The discussion of the preceding pages may also help to shed some light on the *vexata quaestio*, of Ricardian origin,[7] regarding the neutrality or non-neutrality of the two alternative options any government must face in covering its expenditures – taxation or public debt.

From the present logical scheme, it emerges clearly that transfers of consumption through time are not possible for the economic system as a whole. But they are perfectly possible between individuals (and therefore also between the public sector and the private sector of the economy), provided that – within the macro-economic constraint concerning full employment – they compensate each other in the aggregate, at any given moment of time.

In order to leave complications aside, we may begin by supposing that natural rates of interest are always applied, so as to avoid any distortion from the labour principle of inter-temporal income distribution. Furthermore, in considering the distribution or redistribution of consumption from the private to the public sector, or vice versa, we may consider each sector, as it were, as a whole.

Therefore, if at any time (let us say at time zero), the government decides to carry out an additional, let us say an 'extraordinary', expenditure (as against those expenditures that we may call 'ordinary' and that are already balanced by ordinary taxes), the two alternatives that are open – either imposing an extraordinary tax or issuing public debt certificates – have exactly the same effect on the present. They transfer consumption from the private sector to the public sector, leaving the total unchanged.

On future prospects a difference remains. The alternative of present taxation has the characteristic of, so to speak, closing the problem immediately. The alternative of public debt keeps it open until the debt is actually reimbursed. It is therefore necessary to state clearly the terms of the future reimbursement.

The real effects of the two methods of financing public expenditure would actually differ in the future if, at debt repayment, the government were to

---

[7] See Ricardo (1951) [1820].

reimburse it by drawing on the ordinary means of taxation (overall taxation being kept unvaried), thereby correspondingly reducing public consumption and public services, and effecting that inverse inter-personal transfer of consumption (this time from the public to the private sector) that is inherent in every loan among individuals.

But if, in the future – as Ricardo assumed, and as is generally assumed – the reimbursement of the loan is done by means of an imposition of a specific future tax, then the future reimbursement of the public debt to private citizens on the one hand, and the corresponding future taxation on the other, will balance each other out, thereby cancelling out any redistribution of consumption between public and private sectors.

Here we obtain, therefore, a typically Ricardian conclusion. The future taxation (because of the compensation brought about by the reimbursement of the loan) no longer causes any redistribution of consumption between private and public sectors. The only redistribution of consumption remains the present one (from the private sector to the public sector); and this redistribution is exactly the same, whether the government has recourse to taxation or to public debt.

This seems to be precisely the meaning – and the present context, of typically classical inspiration, brings it out very clearly – of the 'neutrality' inherent in Ricardo's arguments.

It is to be noted that this neutrality is *not* dependent on any hypothesis concerning the supposed rational behaviour of single individuals.[8] It is a much more general, and indeed a much more fundamental, result. It emerges from the inherent characteristics of a 'production' economic system, which are here defined and investigated, *independently* of any hypothesis on the behaviour (rational or other) of single individuals. The explanation of the neutrality of the two methods of public financing – taxation or public debt – is simply due to the fact that in a production economic system it is intrinsically impossible to transfer consumption through time for the economic system as a whole.

16. More on the importance of the effective demand macro-economic condition

It would of course be unjustified to accept the conclusions of the preceding section in a rigid way. Despite the background 'Ricardian neutrality' of the choice between taxation and public debt, these two alternative ways of financing public expenditure can never in practice produce exactly the same effects, either for the single individuals or even more for the economic

---

[8] As the more recent interpretations given by the so-called 'new classical macro-economics' is claiming. See, for example, in this regard Barro, 1974.

system considered as a whole, owing to many and various circumstances that may intervene.

For the single individuals, the inter-personal distribution of the burdens deriving from taxation may materialize in very different ways (even if the overall amount is exactly the same), according to whether it is done now or it is put off to a future date. Objective, personal and institutional conditions may substantially change in the intervening time.[9] When public debt is undertaken, we must also keep in mind that it entails the payment of interests, which – to the extent that they differ from their natural level – engender further inter-temporal redistribution of personal incomes (in either direction), as has been seen in the previous pages.

But the different consequences of the two alternative methods of financing public expenditure may be particularly relevant for the economic system as a whole. At this level, one is also bound to face explicitly the processes at work towards the fulfilment or non-fulfilment of the effective demand macro-economic condition. This is an extremely important aspect, which Ricardo was not able to grasp. He left it out of all his arguments, by a convenient, and rather cavalier, reliance on the optimistic view of Jean-Baptiste Say, as to the impossibility of overall 'market gluts'. But since Keynes (1936), we have become more aware of these problems, and the present theoretical scheme brings them out into the open.

This means that, in the practice of any actual economic system, to have recourse to taxation or to public debt at a certain moment in time is not a decision that may be taken independently of the actual conditions of effective demand in the economic system as a whole. When there were tendencies to a deficient overall effective demand, i.e. to under-fulfilment of macro-economic condition (IV.10.5), recourse to taxation could further depress overall demand and therefore bring about unemployment and under-utilization of existing productive capacity. In these cases, further taxation may bring about, as we have seen, net losses of consumption goods for the community as a whole (consumption goods which could have been, but were not, produced, and therefore are lost for ever, owing to lack of effective demand). It might thus become appropriate to decide against further taxation and in favour of increasing indebtedness, even with a budget deficit and monetary financing, if necessary.

On the contrary, when there were tendencies toward an excess of overall effective demand, i.e. to over-fulfilment of macro-economic condition

[9] In practice, it is precisely with reference to the inter-personal distribution of the taxation burden that most of the conflicts blow up, when a choice is to be made between taxation and increasing public indebtedness. Present taxation requires an immediate decision on how to distribute the tax burden. Public debt puts off to a future date the decision of how to allot to the various private citizens a tax burden which, in terms of overall foregone personal consumption, they have as a whole already undergone now.

(IV.10.5), public expenditure backed by public debt, and even worse by monetary financing, would not generate any further physical production but could only engender further (inflationary) pressures on the general price level, with all consequences inherent thereto. In such circumstances, it appears more appropriate to decide in favour of taxation.

The conclusion is, therefore, that a 'Ricardian neutrality' of the two methods of financing increases in public expenditure may be considered as placed in the background, in ideal conditions, and with reference to the public and private sectors each considered as a whole. Against this background neutrality, one must set the many specific features of the actual situation of each economic system – most importantly, the overall level of effective demand – as well as considerations of equity, concerning inter-personal income distributions, and redistributions, that are bound to take place, following upon the specific characteristics of the tax system and the distortions caused by deviations of the actual rates of interest from their 'natural' levels.

VII On the evolving structure of long-term development

1. Foreword

It would seem logical at this point that we should go into an investigation of the evolution of the physical production structure of the economic system through time. But this would open up an immense field of inquiry, at a stage – that of the minimal production model – which would no longer be sufficient to the purpose.

In the previous pages, we have quite extensively dealt with the evolution of the price system. The vertically integrated character of the present analysis has helped us through an almost self-contained treatment of the structural movements of prices. But as soon as we come to physical quantities, vertically integrated analysis can help only partially, i.e., only with reference to the evolving production structure of final consumption goods; and this is not enough. We have come to the point, mentioned towards the end of chapter I, where vertically integrated analysis and inter-industry analysis should be merged and used in a complementary way in order to proceed in a satisfactory manner. In simple terms, at this point it seems unreasonable that we should pretend to go satisfactorily into an analysis of the evolution of the physical production structure, without first enlarging the minimal model of a pure labour economy and extending it to the treatment of capital accumulation and natural resources. But this would take us well beyond the purpose of the present work.[1]

It may be useful nevertheless to push our curiosity beyond the present stage. In this brief chapter, an attempt will be made at taking a bird's eye view of the fields of investigation that open up. Though what follows will be little more than a few hints at an enormous work that has to be done, nevertheless some remarks will be made with reference first to technical

[1] I hope of course to come back to all this in following works. Let me mention in any case that research in this direction is not lacking. See, for example, Baranzini and Scazzieri (1990).

progress; secondly to the mechanisms *inside* any economic system that are responsible for shaping the evolution of its production structure, at least from the (vertically integrated) point of view of final consumption; and then to the topical subject of the fluctuations that are associated with economic growth. Finally, a few speculative remarks will be added on the eventual destiny of industrial societies.

The purpose, it should be stressed, is simply that of showing where and how these topics fit into, or link up with, the present analytical scheme, or how they represent a natural development thereof.

2. The puzzling sources of technical progress

Strictly speaking, an investigation on the sources of technical progress falls outside economic analysis proper. Yet there are so many questions an economist, *qua* economist, is bound to ponder on.

Where does technical progress come from? What is its source? How are economic systems induced to take advantage of it? And why is it that some countries took advantage of it earlier than others? Why are most countries still so far behind? By which factors have they been blocked? And again, how is it that some countries, after lagging behind, have then caught up so quickly and are now themselves among the leaders? Will it be possible for other countries to do the same? How?

These and similar questions are really fascinating. They are precisely the type of questions that have constantly struck and puzzled the imagination of the most perceptive minds among economists. At the time of the industrial revolution, Adam Smith himself quite consciously, in his search for 'the nature and causes of the wealth of nations', singled out, 'the skill, dexterity and judgment with which ... labour is generally applied' (Smith, 1904 [1776], p. 1) – in modern terminology: the way in which technical progress is generally set to fruition in production activity – as the major cause of 'the wealth of nations'.

After Smith, economists have unfortunately shown less and less interest, with only a few exceptions, in the rôle played by technical progress. We must come to our own days to find a resurgence of this interest, though this is taking place mainly outside mainstream economics.[2]

In the minimal model presented in this work, the process through which technical progress is generated has been kept in the background and taken

---

[2] Suffice it to mention here the setting up recently of associations for evolutionary economics, both in Europe and in the United States. For a survey of bibliographical references, one can see Dosi *et al.* (1988). But it is interesting to record the very recent tendency to pay more and more attention to technical change even within the aggregate models of mainstream economics (see chapter I, footnote 6).

as given from outside. However, it has been taken not as a set of data, but as a *process*. This has required specific hypotheses on the movements of technical knowledge through time; a procedure which has been sufficient to bring to the surface extremely important, in fact crucial, implications, as has been seen.

The present theoretical scheme, therefore, presupposes, and takes as complementary, the investigations that philosophers, historians, engineers, scientists, and indeed economists, may all carry out, to unveil the sources of technical progress. All these investigations fit in quite naturally and their obvious place appears to be behind the movements of productivity coefficients through time, on which the previously investigated relations have been built.[3]

3. Consumption decisions in a dynamic context

We have noticed already, in our previous analysis, the great need for a theory of consumers' decisions, both private and public, in a dynamic context.

As has been stressed at the beginning of chapter IV, the theory of consumers' behaviour which is offered us by the textbooks of current mainstream economics is insufficient and inadequate for dynamic purposes. We had therefore to introduce a few general hypotheses in order to carry out our analysis. More specifically, we had to introduce a nucleus of broad commonsense empirical uniformities, which have simply been limited to: inequalities $r_i(t) \neq r_k(t)$, and $r_i(t) \neq \rho_i(t)$, for all $i,k = 1, 2, \ldots, m(t)$, $i \neq k$; a growing number $m(t)$ of goods and services as time goes on; the diminution, even to zero, and on certain occasions even to negative values, of the r_i's, as per-capita income increases; which means the inevitable final saturation of consumption, at least with regard to certain goods. As has been seen, this nucleus of empirical uniformities, simple and obvious as they are, have been shown to entail dynamic consequences of paramount importance.

Fortunately, for the purpose of developing a reasonable theory of consumption decisions in a dynamic context, we already have many important fragments.

To begin with, the classical economists did sense the importance of knowing the direction of the evolution of consumers' demand, and made the well-known distinction between necessaries, demanded by the poor, and luxuries, demanded by the rich (who have already reached a saturated

---

[3] This is also the point where attempts could be inserted to 'endogenize' technical change. The model is left open in this direction, also because these investigations could not but rely on the characteristics of specific institutional set-ups.

demand for necessaries). At the middle of the nineteenth century – as already recalled in chapter IV – Ernst Engel, the Saxon statistician, observed a fundamental statistical uniformity, namely that demand for food generally decreases as a proportion of total expenditure, as wages increase. In our own time, the statisticians and the econometricians who have been looking into time series concerning the evolution of consumption have felt the need to work out mathematical functions having the shape which we have already had occasion to illustrate graphically in chapter IV, to fit data referring to expenditure on consumption goods as a function of per-capita incomes.

Yet one must admit that all these remarkable hints and observed statistical findings, though coming indeed from the observation of a too overwhelming reality, have yet to be systematically and satisfactorily fitted into a comprehensive theory of consumers' behaviour in a dynamic context.

In the works from which the present investigation originates[4] the opportunity has been taken to sketch out a whole series of hints at such a theory. Among the characteristics that have been brought into relief, the following may be mentioned:

  (i) the inherent hierarchical ranking of most human needs;

 (ii) their tendency to saturation as incomes increase;

(iii) the widening of discretionary margins, and contextually the necessity of learning in consumption activity, when incomes increase;

(iv) the unnecessary narrowness of confining the concept of rationality to the process of utility maximization; and hence the necessity of widening such concept to include learning processes, especially in an environmental context in which events are subject to technological breakthroughs;

 (v) the inevitable asymmetry between consumption decisions concerning already known goods, for which consumption patterns have already settled through experience, and consumption decisions concerning goods that are consumed for the first time (either because a lower income did not afford their consumption before, or because they are newly invented);

(vi) the increasing proportion of consumption goods that require a process of preliminary training and learning, in order to be enjoyed.

All these are, of course, only fragments; but the considerable implications that have already been shown to follow from them prove that they are essential. For too long economic theorists have concentrated simply on the

---

[4] Especially Pasinetti (1981).

consistency of consumers' choice, at a given point in time, with given (and immutable) endowments, with perfectly known alternatives among which to decide. In a dynamic context, this is no longer enough.[5] It becomes necessary to go much deeper, or rather it becomes necessary to go *behind* the movements that are taking place in the consumers' endowments, knowledge, learning, and information gathering. It may in fact become necessary to investigate in some detail the inherent characteristics of human needs, about which we do have a lot of information, and about which to pretend to remain 'agnostic' would simply be self-defeating.[6]

4. Social choice theory – public goods and public services

It has long since become quite evident that consumer decisions theory cannot be exclusively individual. The demand for consumption goods comes from *all* members of the community, but the incomes that provide the source of such demand only flow to those members of the community who participate in the production process. In any community there must therefore be some channels through which the incomes, which flow only to some, provide the consumption that is needed by all.

In our societies there are normally two major channels of this type: families, or, as we may say here, households; and the community as a whole, or, as we may say for brevity using an all-embracing term, the government – be it national, regional or local.

As to the families, the strictly individualistic character of traditional consumer theory has rather discouraged so far the putting together of a theoretical framework concerning the consumption decisions of a household, as such. But the directions sketched out at the end of the previous section clearly indicate that a lot can be done to take advantage of the information we already have on needs and decisions of the households, provided we go below the surface, into the characteristics that we know to be typical of the needs of families throughout their various stages of change and growth over time – a very wide field of investigation indeed to pursue.

---

[5] It is reassuring to find that this has been realized even by authors who are working within the confines of mainstream economics. Very significant examples seem to be the works on endogenous change of consumers' preferences, such as von Weizsäcker (1971) and Pollak (1978).

[6] A separate, but obviously connected, field of theoretical investigations is the one concerning consumers' decisions on how to distribute consumption over their lifetime, as the flows of personal incomes and the needs of personal, or family, consumption do not exactly coincide in time. On this respect, it may be interesting to note that the elaborations concerning life-cycle theories of personal consumption and savings (as those of Modigliani and Brumberg (1955)) are perfectly insertable into the present theoretical scheme, which actually seems to offer, for such elaborations, a simpler and more appropriate context than that of traditional pure utility analysis. A confirmation may be seen in Baranzini (1991).

As to the collective institutions, the emergence of the community as a whole, as a decision-making unit with reference to overall needs and requirements (at various levels, national and local), and the necessity of providing public goods and services; all this requires typical economic investigations concerning the public sector.

The relevant elaborations we have inherited from current economic theory on this subject come from two distinct and quite separate sources. One source is social choice theory – roughly, considering collective choice as expressing an aggregation of individual preferences. The other source is the theory of public finance, which takes its starting point from the opposite end, i.e. from the necessity of charging taxes, in order to raise the funds necessary for public expenditure. Indeed, one cannot underestimate the importance of this field of investigation. In modern States, the community as a whole has taken charge of the provision, in more and more selected and differentiated ways, of many goods and services (public goods and public services). This refers not merely to a few fundamental public needs, such as justice and defence, of which all communities have taken charge since time immemorial. In the course of time, the community as a whole has taken up wider and wider responsibilities, such as caring for the weak, the handicapped, the old, besides taking substantial engagements in the fields of health, education, protection of the environment. This has happened to various degrees and extents in different places, and at different times. But this is precisely the point. It has happened to various degrees, according to the level of development of the society concerned, and especially of its per-capita incomes, besides what is due to tradition, experience, climate, tastes, and so on. What an enormous and largely unexplored field of research!

It should be quite clear that, in a dynamic context, the two sources of theoretical concepts just mentioned cannot be kept separate from each other. Social choice theory has nowadays become a most sophisticated set of concepts, but has at the same time reached a rather unsatisfactory state. Arrow's (1951) remarkable 'impossibility theorem' has put the whole field in a sort of state of frustration. It has already been pointed out that a fruitful way out may come from an enlargement of the whole framework of reference.[7] The direction the present analysis indicates is that, in a dynamic context, the process of enlargement must go a long way indeed. We can no longer simply accept that the options that are open to the individuals and to the community are given and known, as if the problem were simply one of

---

[7] The contributions of Amartya Sen, for example, are going in this direction. It is interesting that, starting from the realization that the traditional approach simply comes down, in many circumstances, to analysing the behaviour of 'rational fools', his proposal is essentially that of widening the conceptual framework (see Sen, 1977, 1985).

choice among them. By going behind them, one may indeed go in depth and investigate how they are constructed. This is the point where social choice theory merges with the theory of public finance, requiring investigations on the size of the funds to be raised for public expenditure, and on the methods to be used; i.e. through taxation (as well as which type of taxation), and/or through public indebtedness.

The very moment these investigations are carried out, they will inevitably entail the emergence of some sort of collective correspondent to the individuals' 'Engel curves', as it is quite clear that, in matters of public expenditure, criteria of priority, and therefore of hierarchical sequences in expenditure, become absolutely essential.

Some public-finance economists have even proposed a sort of 'law', in purely aggregate terms – the so called 'Wagner Law', named after the German economist who stated it in the last century. Wagner simply pointed out, from purely empirical observation, that in all industrializing countries, especially in Western Europe, a persistent tendency was under way of 'increasing expansion of public, and particularly state, activities', as a proportion of total economic activity.[8]

What one may surmise on this regard, from the present theoretical scheme, is that in the first phases of industrialization there may well be a strongly increasing demand for intervention on the part of the public sector, due to the needs of homogenization of the whole economic system, imposed by the requirements of fulfilling macro-economic condition (IV.10.5). But this tendency cannot go on indefinitely. There may well be a critical proportion beyond which the inefficiencies associated with increasing public bureaucracy bring in other elements counter-balancing the 'Wagner' tendency, and contributing to stabilizing the proportion between public and private activity. But these are precisely the problems that are wide open for investigation.

But most of all, what seems to be lacking at present, in the economic literature of public finance, is a solid set of theoretical elaborations concerning the types, priorities, and above all composition of public expenditure. Public finance theorists have carried out remarkably detailed theoretical work on the side of public taxation, but on the whole surprisingly little theoretical work on the side of public expenditure. Present elaborations hardly go beyond propositions concerning aggregate magnitudes, while desperate need for guidance is felt precisely on the matter of *composition* of public expenditure.

Suffice it to underline here how enormously relevant all these investigations may turn out to be, and how important it is that they should go deeply

---

[8] This empirical 'law' was originally formulated in Wagner (1883). See also, for an English translation of some of Wagner's elaborations, Wagner (1958), wherefrom the quotation comes.

behind the changing economic structure, for an understanding of the actual physical evolution of industrial economic systems.

5. On the evolving structure of production in the industrial economies

The study of the evolution through time of the structure of economic systems should obviously be a basic area of economic investigation and research. Very surprisingly, in the current state of economic theory, this area of research looks almost an empty chapter. Yet this is in sharp contrast with the early economists' original intentions.

It may be interesting to recall that Keynes himself used to make strong complaints about the ease with which economic theory had suddenly abandoned any investigation of overall effective demand and output.[9] But Keynes' complaint would be far more strongly justified if it were to be referred, not simply to overall effective demand and output at a certain point in time, but most of all to the whole evolution of demand and output in time, both in its overall volume and in its structure.

Preoccupations about these subjects were at the heart of classical economic analysis; but were later left to recede into the background. By the end of the nineteenth century, they had almost completely disappeared from economic discussions.

It is indeed very surprising that, ever since, so little interest should have been shown in trying to explain how the structure of production is evolving as an effect of industrialization. At first sight, the lack of theoretical concepts concerning the structural dynamics of production is something that appears incredible. And what is most puzzling is that, when theoretical economists have been compelled, by their own elaborations, to make specific assumptions on the evolution of the production structure in time, they have simply supposed, with apparent uncritical attitude, that production of all commodities expands proportionally. Yet we have all the evidence, and over the past few decades we also have had massive empirical findings, that leave absolutely no doubt to the contrary (recall the arguments and evidence mentioned in chapter I).

The generality of structural dynamics is so overwhelming as to be unquestionable. Indeed, very few economic phenomena are such as to allow us to draw, with a degree of reliability which practically amounts to

---

[9] The much quoted passage on this regard is contained in a letter of Keynes to Harrod, which reads:

> To me, the most extraordinary thing, regarded historically, is the complete disappearance of the theory of demand and supply for output as a whole, i.e. the theory of employment, *after* it had been for a quarter of a century the most discussed thing in economics (Keynes, 1973, p. 85).

certainty, assertions of such a general character as those concerning the continuous variation of the structure of production, as income increases. One might well be tempted to say that to have been unable to absorb into economic theory these widely diffused features of economic systems must be reckoned as one of the most serious failures of the whole modern theory of economic growth.

Let me therefore underline that the purpose of the present work goes precisely in the direction of providing theoretical background and stimulating further theoretical work to overcome these failures and to begin to fill in what has been defined above as an empty chapter. It has been argued insistently that the explanation of the sources of the structural dynamics of production must be sought in the *evolving structure of demand*.

The lack of and insufficiencies in the development of a satisfactory theory of consumption demand, both at the level of the single individual and at the level of society as a whole, within a context of technical change and increasing incomes, must be considered as the major factor responsible for the underdevelopment of this whole area of economic theoretical research.

We shall not overcome these serious deficiencies until the proper work on theory of demand is carried out.

6. Fluctuations as a consequence of economic growth

Another aspect of the above-mentioned need for research work on the evolution of production is represented by the unsatisfactory state of the theory of business fluctuations.

On this subject, unlike what has happened for long-term trends, many models of the trade cycle have been proposed between the two world wars and after the Second World War. Yet, all of them are in terms of aggregate economic magnitudes.

Of course, all economists who have been careful to observe the movements of economic systems through time have realized that the time movements of global economic magnitudes is typically fluctuating. But something puzzling has happened. Both the macro-economic models of equilibrium growth and the macro-economic models of the trade cycle have relied on exactly the same logical tool (the multiplier–accelerator dynamic mechanism), ending up alternatively either with a theory of smooth growth (which excludes fluctuations) or with a theory of economic fluctuations (which excludes smooth growth), this depending on the ranges of variation into which the various parameters have been supposed to fall.[10] It is in fact

---

[10] Elsewhere I have had the opportunity of pointing out this intrinsic limitation of the interpretations of cycles based on the multiplier–accelerator mechanism, due precisely to inability to deal with structural dynamics (see Pasinetti, 1960).

curious that this incompatibility of growth and fluctuations in macro-economic models should be kept so generally quiet.[11]

By contrast, the interesting hints at the rôle of structural change have come from non-mathematical economists. For example, Joseph Schumpeter (1934, 1939) did grasp the really profound idea of an inherent link between growth and fluctuations. Industrial activity does not simply grow; it fluctuates in time; and it fluctuates because it grows. It is important to notice that it would be impossible to take advantage of this remarkable Schumpeterian intuition within the macro-economic models of the trade cycle, old or new. Even less would it be possible to take advantage of it in the proportional growth models.[12]

The present theoretical scheme, at its present minimal stage, cannot obviously be used for a satisfactory theory of business cycles. One would have first to enlarge it to the introduction of capital goods and investment decisions. Yet, even at its present stage, the theoretical scheme already has something to contribute which seems to me of great importance.

We can see very clearly that, in a hypothetical economic system in which there were a perfectly proportional dynamics (of the type that has been explored in chapter III), there would practically be no dynamic problem to be solved. This is evinced by the fact that macro-economic condition (IV.10.5), once satisfied at any given point in time, would remain satisfied for all time. But the very moment technical progress is introduced, and a structural dynamics necessarily follows, all the coefficients entering that macro-economic condition change as time goes on; and a particular solution to that macro-economic condition will have to be sought for each specific point in time.

This is the source of all dynamic difficulties that emerge in a structurally changing, growing, economy. The suspicion quite obviously emerges that the source of the economic fluctuations should be looked for precisely here.

Without going into the details of this fascinating field of investigation, it will simply be recalled that a whole series of results on these problems have already been presented in the work from which the present one has originated.[13] There they are presented within an analytical context which is of course wider than the present one, i.e. in an analytical context of an

---

[11] There has recently been a revival of interest in trade cycle theory, and in two different directions. On the one side, there has been an application of mathematical models taken from fields outside economics, such as biology or meteorology (see, for example, Goodwin, 1987, 1990). On the other side there has been the tendency to define equilibrium position of 'representative' individuals facing external 'shocks' (see Lucas, 1987). Both approaches continue to ignore any change in the structure.

[12] Paolo Sylos Labini is one of the very few economists who have perceived the inherent incompatibility between macro-economic analysis and business cycles. (His latest views are in Sylos Labini, 1991.)   [13] See Pasinetti, 1981, chapter X.

economy in which there are capital goods (and thus two different types of demand – for consumption goods and for investment goods). But even within the present framework, where only demand for consumption is considered, the general flavour of the relevant arguments can be perceived quite distinctly.

With structural dynamics, the leading sectors and the contracting sectors will generally be different in temporal sequence. Therefore, economic fluctuations can never be a repetition of themselves. Each fluctuation is bound to be quantitatively, and most of all qualitatively, different from the previous ones, as it is bound to be characterized by different expansionary pressures, different importance of the various production branches, different successes, or failures, in the learning processes either in production and/or in consumption.

It should be noticed, incidentally, that these theoretical arguments lead one quite naturally to look for integrating and complementary research in the field of historical investigations.

7. Some speculations on the eventual destiny of industrial societies

A few remarks may be allowed at this point, on a more speculative level. Where are the industrial systems heading for? Will they continue to bring us benefits or will they get us into trouble, and eventually break down and end in chaos?

We may recall that these questions deeply troubled the economists of the classical period. Malthus and his followers feared growth of population as generating self-defeating effects, owing to decreasing returns to scale in agricultural production. Sismondi and others were impressed enough by the possibilities of production, but feared inability on the part of consumers to generate sufficient demand for consumption. These arguments and others were later and more powerfully developed by Marx, with catastrophic predictions for capitalist industrial societies.

In the course of the years, many of the original fears proved to be without foundation. But new fears have emerged and added up at a quickening pace: energy crises, upsetting technological breakthroughs, population explosions in the poor countries, insufficient awareness of the deterioration of the environment, etc.

In the past century, the dominant economics school tried to push the frightening questions aside, and took a hopeful general view, by relying on what became known as 'Say's Law', from the name of the famous French economist. Suffice it here to recall that the implication that everybody drew was that there could never be chronic unemployment of the existing resources, and in particular of labour, apart from temporary, short-lived, disruptions, when some unforeseen events take place, or some major mistakes are made.

Later on, dominant economics never went back to reconsider those problems. Say's Law was no longer explicitly mentioned. It was simply taken for granted. Within the bounds of the economic theory which became dominant (neo-classical theory), Say's Law does not make much sense: the problems to which it is addressed simply do not arise.

It was the great depression of the 1930s that opened up once again the discussions and reinvigorated old fears and doubts about the self-correcting abilities of the mechanisms operating in industrial economies. And it was Keynes who again brought Say's Law to the fore, but in order openly to put it under indictment. (We shall have the opportunity to come back to Say's Law in the following chapter on institutions.)

From the analysis which has been carried out in the previous pages, at the basic level of the fundamental (natural) relations, we have been able to unveil, simply by examining the requirements that must be satisfied in order that macro-economic condition (IV.10.5) may be fulfilled, a number of problems that the industrial societies must face in the long run. One way of synthesizing them may take the form of the following two propositions:

(i) as time goes on, there can be no reliance on any automatic fulfilment of the macroeconomic condition that would ensure the correct level of overall effective demand and hence full employment (except in completely unrealistic conditions such as those of proportional dynamics). On the contrary, the tendencies generated by the underlying structural dynamics lead unmistakably towards the breaking down of any such fulfilment, even starting from a position at which it had previously been achieved;

(ii) at the same time, one can see, in the industrial economic systems as such, no inherent impossibility of finding ways to counteract such tendencies so as to bring the above-mentioned macro-economic condition back towards fulfilment. The ways open to achieve this aim are manifold.

This seems to mean that the questions and fears that bothered the economists of under-consumption and of chronic depression are not imaginary; they are real. At the same time, there is no justification to speak of intrinsic impossibilities. An industrial economic system can indeed develop indefinitely. But such development is not automatic. It is subordinate to the solution of the problems that its structural dynamics is bringing about.

This is the point where the 'institutional problems' that any economic system must face become relevant.

VIII From the 'actual' towards the 'natural' economic system – the rôle of institutions

1. The 'institutional problem'

Any economic system, taken as a whole, must face an 'institutional problem'. In the previous chapters, the analysis has been concentrated on the theoretical scheme of what has been called the 'natural' economic system of a simple, pure labour, production economy. The natural economic system represents so to speak the framework skeleton of the present theoretical construction. It is a set of relations that possess characteristics of analytical relevance and logical consistency, with strong normative properties.

But the natural economic system does not come into existence automatically. For any actual economic system, the problem arises of inventing and setting up those organizational devices – in other words those 'institutions' – which put into motion processes actually able to bring the natural economic system into existence.

This is not an all-or-nothing undertaking. If not in an absolutely accurate and precise way, the natural economic system may be aimed at with a tolerable degree of approximation. This is not a once-for-all undertaking either, as it must take place continually, as time goes on. In a hypothetic perfectly stationary (or proportionally growing) economic system, the setting up of certain institutions rather than others would not really make much difference, except at the outset. The natural features would sooner or later be discovered. Then, once singled out and achieved, they would remain for ever. But when all coefficients of production and of demand vary continually, natural positions, even if achieved at a given point of time, are no longer so as time goes on. It becomes very important to single out those organizational devices that may continually search for, and lead to, the natural positions; and do so within relevant, and reasonably acceptable, spans of time.

This is what is called here 'the institutional problem'.

2. The non-existence, in the economic field, of 'natural' institutions

The institutional problem does not need to have a unique solution, nor does it emerge once for all. By being a problem of construction of organizational devices (the institutions) in order to achieve certain results (the natural economic system), it is obviously susceptible of being faced in different ways, from place to place, from time to time, and at the variation of many external circumstances, without mentioning that the organizational field is itself subject to continuous evolution and innovation.

Moreover, an economic system does not come about in a vacuum. It presupposes a complex network of political, juridical, and legal institutions. These institutions may have been shaped through different historical processes or according to different traditions in different countries, sometimes with even stronger requirements than those behind economic institutions. With this wider institutional framework, the economic institutions must merge and intermingle, while carrying out the task entrusted to them.

The classical economists of the end of the eighteenth century thought that, in the economic field, one could single out 'natural' institutions. They were too simplistic, or perhaps too ambitious. Historically this has been proved not to be so. Those that may be called the 'natural' features of an economic system remain at a deeper and more fundamental level. The organizational devices (what we here call the 'institutions') that may be able to lead to the actual realization of those natural features are indeed open to various solutions.

In the course of time, there have been many important institutions which have proved successful and which have been and still are in continuous evolution. The investigation of these institutions is an essential part of economic analysis. Obviously, in the present work, we cannot enter into this wide field of analysis in any detail; a task which will have to be pursued in a separate place, and after the minimal model here developed has been extended and completed. A number of hints will however be made in the present chapter, with reference to those institutions that have historically been so far the most widely adopted.

The purpose is that of showing explicitly that economic analysis does not end with the investigation of the natural economic system; and, moreover, that economic research on the appropriate institutions which are needed is a spontaneous follow-up of the previous analysis concerning the natural economic system.

3. The 'natural' magnitudes to be aimed at

Five categories of magnitudes have emerged from the present theoretical scheme as forming the 'natural' economic system:

(i) a set of commodity prices;
(ii) a set of commodity physical quantities;
(iii) a wage rate;
(iv) a physical quantity of employed labour;
(v) a rate of interest.

For all of these five categories of natural magnitudes, any actual economic system must face the problem of setting up the organizational devices (institutions) capable of aiming at their realization.

4. Fixing the prices – centralized methods and methods relying on competition and freedom of initiative

In logical order, the first institutional problem that emerges from the present theoretical scheme is that of the actual searching for the natural prices; for which, as we have seen, the criterion that has emerged is that of proportionality to physical quantities of labour. But how is this proportionality going to be achieved?

Historically, two institutional methods have from time to time been used in an alternative and/or a mixed way: the method of imposition of the prices by some kind of central ruler, and the method of their being left free to be determined by individual initiative and competition.

The centralized method has prevailed especially in closed economies and in times of emergency, and more recently in centrally planned economies; the free initiative method has worked best in times of great openness and relative calm. It must be added that these two methods have never been in operation in a completely separate way; they have always been mixed to different degrees, with the justification of trying to avoid the respective drawbacks.

The main drawbacks of the free initiative method emerge when the producers find themselves in some kind of privileged position (e.g. in monopolistic positions) and are able to exploit the counterpart. The main drawbacks of the centralized method arise from the bureaucratic apparatus that it requires and from the difficulties of preventing illegal transactions (the so called black markets), as well as from hindrances to diffusion of information.

It may be interesting to consider here, at least briefly, the free initiative method as, when it can be used, it works automatically and requires a minimum of background attention (essentially ensuring orderly transactions) from any central organization. This method has two components: the free initiative in production (freedom of choice of techniques and of their organization and improvement) and free competition among producers, in offering the products on a market at freely determined prices. These two aspects are complementary. When a certain technical process has proved to be more efficient than any other, in the sense of requiring a lower physical quantity of labour per unit produced, free competition 'compels' the producers to adopt it, lest they be eliminated from the market owing to the accumulation of losses with respect to the other producers who are adopting the efficient technical method. At the same time, freedom of initiative will induce all producers to look for better technical methods of production; for, to the extent that one producer succeeds in realizing savings of inputs per unit of product, he or she will be able also to obtain a temporary profit, at least until the other producers are also able to follow suit. When all producers have adopted the new method, the market price will in normal circumstances be brought to coincide with the actual cost, i.e. with the natural price, and all temporary profits will disappear.

Free initiative in production and free competition in marketing the products are therefore powerful institutional devices for the actual realization of efficient technical methods of production ('compulsion' to minimize costs) and for maintaining a process by which freely determined market prices are constantly tending towards the natural prices.

5. Market prices and the emergence of Schumpeterian profits (and losses)

There is an important practical consequence that follows immediately from the institutional mechanism of a free market price system. Technology determines costs, and in the end natural prices. But *actual* prices are allowed to be determined by competition in the market and the two will not in general coincide. This means that there will be deviations of actual, i.e., market, prices from natural prices, even when a mechanism is in operation by which these deviations are only temporary.

But this also means that some producers (the innovators) will enjoy temporary profits. Other producers (those who are not quick to adapt) may suffer temporary losses. We may call these temporary profits (and losses) 'Schumpeterian' profits (and losses), from the name of the economist who most vividly was able to focus our attention on them.

These temporary profits (and losses) do not belong to the natural economic system. In fact there exists no profit (or loss) in the natural economic system of a pure labour economy. They are introduced by the particular institutional mechanism (the competitive market mechanism) which is adopted for the determination of the actual prices. They can be considered as justified, and therefore 'physiological', to the extent that they fulfil the function of keeping up a reasonably speedy tendency to make the actual price structure tend towards the natural price structure, and to the extent that they stimulate the introduction of new techniques.[1]

---

[1] This is obviously the place where, in the present scheme, a vast field of investigation opens up on the activity of research and of development of new techniques at the level of the single production unit.

6. Discrepancies between effective demand and productive capacity

The second institutional problem that emerges from the present theoretical scheme, symmetrically to the one concerning the attainment of natural prices, is that of actually bringing the correct physical quantities into being. Here we know that the correct physical quantities are those that exactly match the effective consumer demand for them. But when technology and per-capita demand change as time goes on, then even if a perfect match between demand and productive capacity has been achieved at any given point in time, discrepancies are bound to emerge as time passes.

For any specific commodity, any producer, be it a single individual or a corporation or any sectoral or central planning board, faces the organizational problem of adapting productive capacity so as to match the corresponding expected demand by the consumers. This organizational problem is not solvable in any obvious way, even in as simple a scheme as the present one, where the provision of productive capacity is nothing but the provision of an adequate quantity of labour. In more complex models, with capital goods of any kind, the organizational problem is of course much more complex. In fact, a whole set of discussions might be opened at this point on the conditions under which single individuals or more complex production units acting competitively, or a planning board with an overall network of information may be the more appropriate channels for correctly estimating effective demand for the various commodities.

In any case, it seems rather inevitable, under any institutional system, that mistakes will be made, so that discrepancies will normally arise for the various commodities, between the effective demand for them and the corresponding available productive capacities. At any particular point in time, some commodities may turn out to be in excess demand, and some other commodities may turn out to be in deficient demand, with respect to the corresponding productive capacities.

The institutional problem that emerges in this respect is that of devising some organizational mechanism by which the discrepancies, when they arise, set into motion corrective tendencies operating towards their elimination (so that they may only be temporary).

7. A physical quantity self-adjusting mechanism with fixed prices

It is reasonable to expect that physical discrepancies between demand and productive capacity, by their mere existence, should set into motion a mechanism of self-correction. But the problem of a self-adjusting physical quantity mechanism is more complex than the corresponding problem of a self-adjusting price mechanism.

The simplest way to begin is to consider the response of a production system to the emergence of physical quantity discrepancies on the assumption that prices are kept pegged to their natural level, i.e. to the corresponding costs of production. (In the short run this practically means a fixed price structure.)

Let us therefore first make the assumption that, in some way and for some reason, prices are kept fixed at their natural level (i.e. at the cost level). When, in a particular sector, demand turns out to be lower than available productive capacity, the producer will be induced to produce an output which is equal to demand. There would be no point in producing more, if the product is not demanded, as the producer would otherwise suffer a corresponding loss. Thus when productive capacity is excessive, effective demand determines output in the actual system (and not only in the natural system). However, part of productive capacity, and of the labour force, will remain idle. The production unit will then be induced to get rid of idle capacity and idle labour. Thus, sectoral shrinkage of productive capacity and of sectoral employment, and therefore inducement to sack workers, is an automatic response in the (correct) direction, when demand falls short of productive capacity.

Conversely, when demand in a particular sector turns out to be higher than available productive capacity, the production unit will be physically constrained to produce that output which its available productive capacity makes possible, except for some opportunities, within certain limits and for temporary periods, to make some exceptional efforts to increase production out of existing productive capacity (e.g. with overtime, etc.). Thus the physical effect of an excess demand is not symmetrical to that of a deficient demand. In this case, output being physically constrained to productive capacity, excess demand will normally generate a queue of unsatisfied customers. To the extent that a queue of unsatisfied customers induces expansion of productive capacity, this response will also be in the correct direction, i.e. it will represent the other side of a quantity self-adjusting mechanism.

This is a field in which centrally planned economies should have cumulated a rich experience. Unfortunately, from what we know, they do not seem to have taken good advantage of such experience. What is rather surprising is that we have had very few contributions from economists in centrally planned economies that may help us toward understanding the working of the process of physical quantity self-adjustment at given prices.

In the competitive market economies, it is quite easy to realize that a more complex picture is bound to arise as soon as one goes on to allow prices to diverge from their 'natural' level.

8. Short-run physical quantity adjustments with flexible prices (a Marshallian market mechanism)

Competitive market economies are characterized by freedom in the actual determination of market prices, and this is an institutional mechanism that fulfils the function of making prices gravitate towards their natural level, as has been pointed out in sections 4 and 5 above. But if prices are left free to be determined on the market, they are bound to exert their influence on, and to interfere with, the mechanism of change of the physical quantities, which in the previous section was illustrated under the assumption of prices fixed at their natural level.

The economist who perhaps did most to theorize the operation of the market price mechanism, as traditionally conceived, in the field of physical quantity adjustment is Alfred Marshall (1920). As is well known, Marshall's claim has been that the competitive market price mechanism also has a rôle to play in the field of physical quantity adjustment. His contention has been that the free determination of prices on the market of industrial products will drive actual prices above their 'natural' (in his terminology 'normal') level, whenever demand is in excess of productive capacity; and will drive actual prices below that level when demand falls short of productive capacity. This generates discrepancies between actual (i.e. market) and natural (in Marshall's terminology 'normal') prices, i.e. generates profits or losses for the production units. Precisely these profits or losses will induce increases or decreases, respectively, in the corresponding productive capacities and thus bring about a process of self-adjustment in the physical quantities, a process which, while bringing productive capacity in line with demand, will at the same time whittle away the initial profits or losses, which again will emerge as short-run, i.e. temporary, profits or losses. These temporary profits or losses too – which we may call 'Marshallian' – do not belong to the natural economic system; but they acquire the justification of serving the institutional purpose of keeping in operation a self-adjusting mechanism for the physical quantities.

Thus, according to this (Marshallian) view, not only does the market-price mechanism fulfil the institutional function of bringing actual prices towards their natural level; it also fulfils the institutional function of bringing the actual productive capacities in line with the requirements of the physical production required by consumers (i.e. it also fulfils the institutional function of bringing into existence the 'natural' physical quantities).

9. More complex institutional arrangements for the realization of the 'natural' physical quantities

It is important to realize that the institutional task, that may be entrusted to the competitive market-price mechanism, of equilibrating the price structure, as investigated in sections 4 and 5 above, is quite distinct from the institutional task, considered in the previous section (though the latter may also be entrusted upon the competitive market-price mechanism) of equilibrating the physical quantities. And the two should not be confused with each other.

The conditions that may be favourable to one institutional task may not necessarily coincide with the conditions that are favourable to the other. More specifically, if the market-price mechanism were to turn out to be particularly appropriate for one of the two tasks, that does not mean that it would also be *ipso facto* equally appropriate for the other.

Now, there seems to be widespread consensus on the proposition that experience has shown the appropriateness of the competitive market-price mechanism to the task of inducing the actual prices (at least in a competitive context) to tend towards their 'natural' level. But the institutional problem of achieving the 'natural' physical quantities is a much more complex one. To this purpose, the conditions of, or the obstacles to, entry of new firms into existing markets have revealed themselves to be particularly relevant. It has often been observed in the practice of industrial systems that the competitive market-price mechanism may well be left aside, and not be used at all, even when it is freely available.

This is not the place to go into this matter in any detail, but it may be useful to mention that, in industrial economies, the phenomenon is quite widely observed of production units (especially, but not exclusively, when they are very large) deciding to keep prices constant and allowing queues of customers to build up, when demand exceeds productive capacity; and conversely of restricting production, and again keeping prices constant, while letting some productive capacity remain idle, when demand falls short of available productive capacity.[2] New theoretical investigations in this field have been abundant recently (think of the literature on the full-cost principle, on oligopoly, on 'contestable' markets, on game theoretic situations, on so called 'non-Walrasian' equilibria etc.). But more research is badly needed. What can be said here is that the 'production' approach proposed in the present work seems to be a most appropriate

---

[2] An additional problem in this connection is that of producers – especially when they are powerful – exerting pressures of various kinds (e.g. through misleading advertising) to distort consumers' tastes, and thus demand, in their favour. This is a typical field for 'economics and law plus social psychology' research.

theoretical framework in which this type of investigation may be fruitfully carried out.[3]

10. 'Natural' wage and full employment

The two next institutional tasks to be briefly considered are those concerning the realization of the 'natural' wage rate (in the price equation system) and the realization of the full employment of the available physical quantity of labour, in the physical quantity equation system.

Here again, it should be noted that these are two distinct institutional tasks; and moreover that they are quite distinct from the tasks (considered in the previous sections) of the realization of 'natural' commodity-prices and of the realization of 'natural' physical quantities of consumption goods.

We shall consider them in turn.

11. Aiming at the 'natural' wage

The natural wage rate emerges from the present theoretical scheme as an amount of purchasing power that gives command on a certain basket of physical goods and services. On average, this basket of goods and services is simply the total national product divided by the number of workers that have contributed to its production. Fundamentally, therefore, the natural wage rate is a *macro-economic* concept. Its basic nature is that of a personal share into the national product of the economic system as a whole. This conclusion has emerged very clearly from the present theoretical scheme (see chapters II and IV), referring to a pure labour economy. But it would not change in a more complicated model. If the scheme were to be extended to include capital goods and natural resources, the analysis would indeed become more complex. A further very important problem would appear (which is here absent); namely the problem of the distribution of the national income between wages, profits and rents. But this complication would not affect the macro-economic nature of the natural wage rate.

The question to be faced is: Can one conceive of an appropriate institutional mechanism to be adopted for aiming at the 'natural' wage rate?

Let us note straightaway that, if the natural wage rate is a macro-economic concept, it follows that its determination cannot but be one of

---

[3] It is interesting to find that, in the recent economic literature, research on adjustment processes, on both prices and physical quantities, *within* the classical, production, framework has begun to be carried out. See, as examples, Boggio (1985), Duménil and Lévy (1987, 1991), Kubin (1991).

those matters that are of concern for the economic system as a whole. But let us also note, at the same time, that the macro-economic nature of the wage rate and its being a matter of general concern does not necessarily mean that it should be decided by a central authority. Obviously, if an institutional mechanism were at hand that could lead the economic system automatically towards the natural wage, that would spare a lot of trouble.

On this respect, the first obvious question is whether the traditional competitive market-price mechanism could be used also for the search of the natural wage rate. This is what in fact has historically tended to happen. Does the present simple model help us in investigating this question?

We may imagine 'entrepreneurs' that organize the production process and 'workers' that are willing to offer their work. In widespread competitive conditions, entrepreneurs would hire workers any time they can charge commodity prices that more than cover the wage costs, so as to gain differential entrepreneurial profits, and workers would agree to work for those entrepreneurs that offer the highest wage rate. The conditions for the differential profits tending to zero (the 'work' of the entrepreneurs being itself remunerated as such),·and thus for the wage rate tending to reap the whole product, i.e. tending to its natural level, can now be seen in a particularly clear way. If entrepreneurship were a uniformly spread characteristic of all people, so that being an entrepreneur or being a worker were a perfectly indifferent alternative, workers becoming entrepreneurs with no obstacle or attrition (and vice versa), then all differential profits could only be temporary, and the actual wage rate would constantly tend to the natural wage rate. But any time entrepreneurship is not uniformly spread and there are more difficulties in the process of workers becoming entrepreneurs than vice versa, then the entrepreneurs are in a privileged position, i.e. are in a position that enables them to reap permanent differential profits. The divergence of the actual from the natural wage rate would therefore depend on the degree of 'monopoly', so to speak, conferred by the entrepreneurship characteristic.

Even in a simple pure labour economy, it is reasonable to expect that entrepreneurship is not a uniformly spread characteristic of people and therefore that there would inevitably appear a negative divergence of the actual from the natural wage rate, as an effect of a freely competitive market price mechanism applied to the actual determination of the wage rate. The divergences would clearly become the more pronounced the more complex the economic system becomes in the direction of introducing differences and asymmetries among people or various groups of people.

As is well known, the classical economists were the first to analyse situations of this type. They thought that people belong to distinctly different classes, between which mobility is difficult and slow because of inheritance, education and many other various factors. Clearly, with different and distinct classes that perform different rôles in the production activity, the competitive market-price mechanism would *not* be an appropriate institutional mechanism for guiding the economic system towards the realization of the natural wage.

In such a situation, the market-price mechanism would simply bring about competition among workers, and would in fact lead to another effect. Among the classical economists, it is Marx who most clearly perceived this other effect of the competitive market-price mechanism, as applied to labour. He gave the clearest picture of what may be considered as the other extreme (with respect to the one depicted above, when referring to a uniformly spread entrepreneurship in a pure labour economy) of the application of the market-price mechanism to the determination of the actual wage rate. As is well known, Marx (1867) thought that, in a society in which entrepreneurs form a quite distinct class (in his analysis, because they own the means of production), entrepreneurs and workers cannot mix; they are not interchangeable. If then labour is thrown on a market and is traded as any other commodity, then we can only expect the competitive market-price mechanism to perform its job with labour precisely in the same way as it does with any commodity: namely to drive the price of labour toward its cost of production. In the case of labour, the cost of production is the subsistence wage rate; this is what the competitive market-price mechanism would achieve. Therefore the entrepreneurs would reap whatever is above subsistence ('exploitation'). We should note the perfectly logical consistency of Marx's arguments.

In the practice of modern day industrial societies, the situation may be different from one country to another, but we may expect it to lie somewhere between the two extremes considered above. It is almost impossible to conceive of cases that are near that of uniformly spread entrepreneurship and of widespread interchangeability of the rôles of entrepreneurs and workers. We may exclude therefore the possibility of relying on the competitive market price mechanism in the search for the natural wage rate. But we may well exclude by now the other extreme as well, even though at some times or in certain places, reality may actually have approached it (think of the early years of industrialization or of some situations, even today, in very low income countries).

We may therefore begin here by drawing a negative conclusion. There is an institutional necessity, emerging quite clearly from the arguments carried out above, of preventing the economic system from falling into a situation in which the competitive market-price mechanism acts on the wage rate in the same way as its acts on the commodity prices.

The truth is that labour could be traded as any other commodity only in a slave society. In any modern economic system, labour is not a commodity, precisely because institutions have been set up that do not allow labour to be traded as a commodity.

To conclude, the competitive market-price mechanism appears *not* to be the appropriate institutional mechanism to search for the natural wage rate, precisely because of its main property, namely because it is the most appropriate mechanism for drawing the market prices towards the corresponding costs of production. In the case of wages, we do not want a wage rate reflecting the cost of production of labour. We want a wage rate that gives each worker his or her share of national income.

It is no chance therefore, nor is it a historical accident, that, in all industrialized countries, wage negotiations have moved far away from the very early attempt at adopting a competitive market mechanism, and have become more and more a matter of national concern, involving by now well-established institutions such as workers' trade unions, entrepreneurs' associations, and in many cases also appropriate government ministries.

12. Aiming at full employment – another genuinely macro-economic task

The other institutional task mentioned in section 10 above appears as symmetric to that of achieving the natural wage rate. It emerges from the physical quantity equation system and concerns the physical quantity of labour to be employed. Here the aim is clear: achieving the full utilization of available labour, i.e. full employment. The macro-economic nature of this problem needs no stressing. As we have seen, the full employment of existing labour requires the fulfilment of a necessary condition that concerns the whole economic system. This condition emerged originally in the form (II.2.5), in chapter II, and has been variously reformulated in the ensuing sections, until it has taken the form (IV.10.5) in chapter IV.

Unlike expressions (II.2.6) and (II.2.7), which represent *sectoral* solutions for physical quantities and for commodity prices, respectively, expression (IV.10.5) refers to the economic system as a whole: it represents a genuinely macro-economic condition (as was pointed out earlier in chapter II).

The importance of the fulfilment of this macro-economic condition has cropped up time and again in the previous analysis. In chapter IV, we saw how many complex problems of structural dynamics lie behind it. Our analysis has been carried out at the level of the basic forces that, by being at work in the background, are constantly moving the industrial economic systems. This means that macro-economic condition (IV.10.5) is continually being upset, and thus full employment is continually being disrupted. But we have also seen that the possibilities of bringing that macro-economic condition into fulfilment are nevertheless manifold, which by itself implies the opening up of a range of possibilities for macro-economic (i.e., social) choice.

It is precisely those (upsetting) movements at the more fundamental level and at the same time the manifold possibilities that are open to counteract them, which create, at the institutional level, the problem of setting up a mechanism that may permanently drive the (continually upset) economic system back to full employment. They create the institutional problem of constantly making the economic system aim at full employment. It is from this (institutional) point of view that we are now looking at the problem.

13. Can market clearance of the labour market be relied on?

It is reasonable to ask whether the usual and traditional institutional mechanism – the market-price mechanism – might also be helpful in performing the job of leading the economic system towards the fulfilment of macro-economic condition (IV.10.5).

Note that we have already seen (in section 11 above) that, in general, the market-price mechanism is not the appropriate institutional mechanism to search for the 'natural' wage rate. Yet, an analogy spontaneously comes to mind with the physical quantity equilibrating features that have been claimed for commodity market prices (see section 8 above). And the question is whether a 'market' wage rate, determined by demand and supply of labour, even if it is not the appropriate institutional mechanism to search for the 'natural' wage rate, might be instrumental in bringing demand and supply of labour into equality with each other. In this case, one could talk of a market-determined wage rate which, though not necessarily at the natural level, would however have the property of achieving equality of demand and supply of labour, thereby ensuring no involuntary unemployment.

The argument here rests on whether it is possible to conceive of a downward sloping overall demand function for labour and of an upward sloping overall supply function for labour, both having the market wage rate as their argument, so that the latter could settle where aggregate demand equals aggregate supply and the market for labour (as it is said) is being 'cleared'.

In fact this is the central problem faced by Keynes (1936), who, as is well known, challenged the traditional view that the market for labour is just one of the various markets, and can therefore always be cleared, as any other market, when it is allowed to work competitively and without interference.

Interestingly enough, we may look at Keynes' analysis on this respect as a continuation, with reference to the wage rate, of the same analytical task that Marshall undertook with reference to the commodity prices. We may say that both Marshall and Keynes have explored the possibility of using the market-price mechanism as an equilibrating device for the physical quantities of commodities and of labour, respectively (reaching, however, opposite conclusions). Let us follow Keynes' arguments for a moment.

As is well known, Keynes accepted the traditional proposition that each entrepreneur demands labour up to the point at which the market wage rate is equal to the marginal product of labour. Now, the marginal product of labour may not exist at all, as an autonomous concept. Here, however, if not the marginal product of labour, the average product of labour becomes relevant, as a technical and *micro*-economic concept. We must in any case accept that the physical productivity of labour, i.e. its average product, is a decisive element for the demand for labour of the single entrepreneur. We may even go one step further and accept the possibility of constructing a downward sloping labour demand function, for the single entrepreneur. However this requires it to be made compatible with the *macro*-economic nature of the wage rate; and this entails making a few very definite assumptions, two of which are crucial for our purposes.

First of all, in order to draw any single producer's demand function for labour, one must make the assumption of a given, fixed, structure of prices in the whole economic system. This is because the marginal, or average, product of labour, by being a micro-economic, physical, concept, is measured in terms of the good or service that is actually being produced, while the wage rate is, as has been pointed out above, a macro-economic concept, as it represents a basket of commodities which are produced in the whole economic system. Each producer cannot and does not pay the workers with the goods that are produced! He or she pays them with a wage rate, normally expressed in terms of a nominal unit, the real content of which is made up of all the goods each worker plans to buy. It follows that, to draw the producer demand function for labour, the assumption is necessary, as said above, of a given price structure in the economic system.

Secondly, the same demand function must be drawn on the assumption of the entrepreneur being able to evaluate the specific demand for the product that is going to be produced. In other words, we must imagine the entrepreneur evaluating the market demand for the product, the technology to which he or she has access and the price structure in the economic system, while taking the prevailing levels of pre-capita incomes as given. But in this way we arrive at a typical 'partial equilibrium' concept! It does not follow at all that, when we go on to consider the economic system as a whole, such demand functions can be aggregated. In fact, the case of labour and the wage rate is precisely a case in which they *cannot* be aggregated, because aggregation is going to destroy precisely the assumptions on which they are constructed: it certainly destroys the second assumption just mentioned; it may destroy the first assumption as well.

Here we can see becoming relevant precisely the intrinsic nature of the wage rate, which is not a concept to be likened to, or to be put on the same level as, any commodity price. The wage rate *appears* like a price of any commodity to the single entrepreneur, who will in fact treat it as any other price. But the wage rate has the other crucial aspect, from the point of view of the economic system as a whole: it represents per-capita income. And income is the basis for the provision of demand.

This means more precisely that, although it may be meaningful to conceive of a single entrepreneur increasing his or her demand for labour as against a decrease of the wage rate, it makes no sense to pretend that the overall demand for labour will increase if there is a fall in the wage rate at a given structure of prices. For, if the wage rate is cut, that means that incomes fall, and thus overall demand falls, which will affect the basis on which the original demand for labour was supposed to be based.

The important conclusion is – contrary to what Keynes conceded – that a downward sloping *aggregate* demand function for labour cannot be constructed.

Consider now the possibility of constructing a supply function for labour. As is well known, this is the part of traditional economic analysis that Keynes rejected completely, and rightly so. What one might think dependent on the magnitude of the wage rate, expressed in real terms, is the proportion of total time that each individual wishes to devote to a labour activity. The higher the real wage, the lower, one supposes, is the time that any person will in general like to devote to work (and the longer the time he or she will like to devote to leisure). But this is not always so (suffice it to mention the effects of different family sizes). Moreover the proportion of labour time to total time is a matter to be agreed upon at each stage of development by a sort of social norm, within which, then, all workers will ideally have to be fully employed. It is not very sensible therefore to draw an aggregate rising supply function of labour, or for that matter any backward leaning aggregate supply function for labour, except under very special or restrictive conditions; in fact so restrictive as to deprive such a supply function of any reasonable generality.

To conclude, the traditional economic analysis (which, it may be useful to recall, has its origin in the 'pure exchange' model) depicting a market for labour, with an overall demand function and an overall supply function for labour, where a flexible wage rate is supposed to act as a price that clears the market and thus always ensures full employment, or rather ensures the absence of voluntary unemployment, does not seem to make sense. To put it in other words, the market-price mechanism, if applied to the labour market, cannot ensure the clearing of such market. It cannot ensure full employment, simply because a labour market does not satisfy the basic conditions of a traditionally intended market, in which there is a market determined price that settles at the point where a downward sloping demand curve crosses an upward sloping supply curve, thus equating demand and supply. A market determined wage rate simply cannot do that.

But full employment is too important for the economic system as a whole. Keynes was therefore right in advocating, at the institutional level, the inclusion of full employment into the objectives of overall economic policy, in the sense that the community as a whole takes charge of it as a goal to be pursued with whatever measures of economic policy may be appropriate, whenever the spontaneous forces of interaction between employers and workers fail to bring it about.

14. Wage differentials as incentives to labour mobility – an efficiency-inducing use of the market-price mechanism

The conclusions just reached must not be intended as excluding entirely the use of the market-price mechanism from the field of wage determination. The arguments that have been developed above refer to the determination of the basic level of the wage rate and to the overall pursuit of a reasonably high level of employment in the economic system as a whole. But once these aims are being pursued on a national level, then, on single or sectoral markets, where the effects on the national scale are negligible, there is an important auxiliary function that market wage determination can fulfil. This does not regard the search for the natural wage rate, nor the pursuit of a clearing of the overall market for labour (which, as we have seen, the market-price mechanism cannot do), but it regards the rather different, but important, problem of quantity adjustments and adaptations.

More specifically, appropriate advantage may be taken of the incentive-generating characteristics of the market-price mechanism in dealing with the problem that always arises of inducing labourers to move across sectors. In this case, some market determined wage differentials may perform the function of inducing and favouring the labour mobility that is required by the structural dynamics that is due to take place (as we have seen earlier). After all, this represents another typical use of temporary, and/or limited, deviations of actual from natural levels to fulfil the institutional function of inducing actual physical magnitudes to tend towards their 'natural' norm.

In other words, useful wage negotiations, with due regard to labour requirements and labour availabilities, at the sectoral and even at the individual level, may be allowed to take place to suit intervened sectoral scarcities and redundances. These negotiations are of course useful as long as they affect, not the national average, but the *relative* wage rates, as between the various sectors or the various production units, even in the same branch, or the various individuals. They serve the purpose of giving incentives of various kind and especially incentives to the mobility of labour out of declining sectors and into expanding sectors. Their effects on the economic system as a whole (in terms of deviations from natural norms) must obviously be kept within tolerable limits. They would become of concern for the economic system as a whole at the very moment their effects on the whole wage level or on the wage structure were to become no longer negligible.

To conclude, what emerges as being needed in this field is a judicious use of the efficiency-inducing stimuli of the market-price mechanism, to help and speed up sectoral adjustments, within a general framework drawn from the overall requirements of full employment in the economic system as a whole.

15. Full employment in institutionally more primitive economic systems, and the relevance of 'Say's Law'

There is a question that might legitimately be asked at this point. After all, when one considers an economic system as a whole, all that is demanded comes from all that is received; overall demand and overall supply are not independent of each other. Should it not be the case that all aggregate magnitudes are after all bound to match simply as a matter of overall consistency?

This is in fact the remarkable intuition that Jean-Baptiste Say, the French economist, had at the beginning of the nineteenth century. As is well known, he stated a famous 'law' (which has since become known as Say's Law), according to which, except for temporary maladjustments, there can never be gluts on competitive markets, i.e., there can never be crises of over-production, or under-consumption (in our terms, macro-economic condition (IV.10.5) can never remain unfulfilled), because any production always generates a demand exactly equal to it.[4]

Say's Law was accepted by most economists without much elaboration or questioning. In fact, it had not undergone careful scrutiny until Keynes brought it back in order to question it.[5] The standard reference is by now

---

[4] More detailed references to Say's Law may be found in Pasinetti (1974) p. 30n.
[5] In the early nineteenth century, mainstream economists simply referred to Say's Law as something obvious (see for example how Ricardo refers to it – Ricardo (1951) [1817], e.g., pp. 290–1). There were of course also economists who tried to contend it, but without

Keynes' *General Theory*, but it is interesting to note that Keynes, in the works of preparation to his major work, was very worried and took great pain to examine Say's Law (Keynes, 1979). He pointed out that there are institutionally more primitive types of economic systems than our present ones, in which Say's Law by and large does hold. Let us briefly consider at least three such institutionally more primitive types of economic system.

(i) A barter economy. A barter economy is one in which physical goods are exchanged only against physical goods. In a barter economy, producers may of course make mistakes about the goods they produce, but a simple market-price mechanism may easily deal with these mistakes, by punishing with losses the producers who make them, thereby inducing self-adjusting corrections. The favourable feature of a barter economy, with respect to the requirement we are considering, is that any demand cannot but be demand for goods, and this translates itself into demand for the employment of the corresponding labour.

(ii) An economy with physical money. By this term we intend an economy in which a produced physical commodity is used as the medium of exchange, so that goods are exchanged with the physical good that is used as money, and vice versa. An economy of this type is in fact a particular case of a barter economy. The only difference is that there is a particular commodity which, by its characteristics, is able to facilitate all exchanges and is explicitly singled out as an intermediate item, accepted by everybody. The crucial feature to be noticed in this case is that, even those people who want to hold money *per se* in fact demand a physical commodity (the physical money), which has a cost of production in terms of labour, and therefore requires the employment of the corresponding labour.

(iii) A cooperative economy. A cooperative economy is intended here in a sense near the one used by Keynes (1979, pp. 76ff.). Such an economy is one in which all producers cooperate to induce full expenditure of all incomes, so that no produced commodity is left unsold. We might imagine that each worker receives for his services a production coupon (which is accepted by any producer) denominated, for example, in terms of physical quantities of labour. It is stipulated that all production coupons must be spent at the end of each production period, for they would have no validity beyond the production period for which they have been issued. Thus again total overall demand automatically absorbs an amount of goods that incorporate all the available labour (full employment).

success (Malthus (1820) was no doubt the most notable among them). Later on, with the emergence of Walrasian, and of neo-classical economics in general, Say's Law came to be confused with Walras' budget constraint equation, which, by being an accountancy equation, is always satisfied. (See also chapter II, footnote 6.)

We may note that in these three simple cases (roughly along the lines sketched out by Keynes), there is a need that the community as a whole has a minimum of organization so as to make it possible that all transactions take place in an orderly way. In the second case, there might also be a central monetary authority supervising a correct use of the commodity used as money. And in the third case a further need arises of a kind of central clearing house for all labour-denominated coupons. But the basic characteristic of all the three cases is that all incomes, by virtue of coming into existence, are necessarily spent in full to buy some goods, and since the value of the goods produced is equal to total incomes distributed, there can never be a difference between labour employed in the economic system and labour incorporated into the goods that are actually demanded.[6]

Therefore, in all three cases, the task does not appear to be too difficult to organize the economic system in such a way as to lead it always towards the point at which all available labour is fully employed. In other terms, to paraphrase Keynes' words, barring particular cases of miscalculations or unjustified obstinacy, in the three cases mentioned above, and in other similar ones, the avoidance of mismatches between overall available labour and overall actual employment should be within the reach of easily constructed automatically self-adjusting institutional arrangements. After all, this is what Say's Law was basically intended to convey. Involuntary unemployment could normally be avoided.

16. Paper money – a major institution of modern economic systems

Modern economic systems are no longer of a type nearly resembling any of those mentioned in the previous section. They are characterized by the circulation of paper money;[7] and have become monetary economies. This has made a crucial difference. Paper money, by becoming a major distinctive institution of modern economies, has in fact crucially modified their characteristics, as far as their possibilities of reacting to the continuous changes that are taking place behind the coefficients that enter macro-economic condition (IV.10.5) are concerned.

We are calling here monetary economies those economies in which the money unit is no longer a particular physical commodity (traditionally a precious metal), nor is it any longer effectively linked to any physical

---

[6] In more complex models, with capital goods, a further requirement would also have to be satisfied, namely, an overall productive capacity would have to be realized, which is congruent with the full employment of the available labour force.

[7] The term 'fiat money' is more generally used, as it includes all sorts of nominal money (bank deposits, bank cards, etc.). For simplicity's sake, I shall keep to the term 'paper money'. The crucial change for our purposes was after all the adoption of units which lost any intrinsic value.

commodity. It simply is represented by a document, or a symbol, with no intrinsic value and with no (or negligible) cost of production.

Thus a monetary economy is characterized by a very typical institution: the existence, alongside the flows of goods and services, of a stock quantity of money – an asset which we may call M – which is made up of symbolic notes on fiduciary circulation originally issued by a central bank. (We shall not enter any discussion here on whether a 'bank of issue' may not necessarily be a central bank. We shall take it for granted – especially after the problems that have emerged from our analysis of chapter V in connection with the movement of the general price level – that existence of a central bank has become necessary.)

Legally, money is a document representing a debt by the central bank, a debt, which, if claimed, the central bank may satisfy by simply issuing other paper notes of the same type. These paper notes have a nominal value, but have a legal and fiduciary basis – legal, because by law they must be accepted in settlement of debts; fiduciary, in the sense that people will hold them if they can rely on the expectation that the central bank behaves in such an appropriate way as not to depart unreasonably from at most an acceptable mild trend in the erosion of their purchasing power.

As is well known, the monetary unit, in general, is traditionally meant to fulfil three separate functions, namely those of: (i) *unit of account*; (ii) *medium of exchange* for all transactions; and (iii) *store of purchasing power*.

The first of these functions has already emerged, in our analysis, at the fundamental stage of the 'natural' economic relations, and has posed no particular problem. The second and third functions emerge explicitly now, as they are bound to be connected with the working of specific institutions, and especially with the working of systems with purely nominal money units. A full investigation of these functions of money can only take place at the institutional level. Here it is important to point out that it is the store-of-value function, entrusted on purely nominal money units, that makes the working and behaviour of a monetary production economy so different, in fact so crucially different, from those of a barter or of a cooperative economy.

17. Monetary production economies – the breaking down of 'Say's Law'

We are now able to return, with an enlarged and more comprehensive grasp, to the macro-economic problem of overall effective demand. As pointed out already, we have seen this problem emerge, in the previous chapters, straight from the structural dynamics that moves the industrial systems. Here we are looking at it from the side of the institutional tools that an economic system may bring into being to deal with it.

Which institutional devices may be set up? The answer that has been given in the foregoing pages is that this institutional problem could be solved in a reasonably easy way in more primitive economic systems, where – by inherent properties – income distribution almost automatically meant income expenditure. (Essentially, this is the message that Say's Law was intended to convey.)

But in monetary production economies, this is no longer so. Monetary production economies, by inherent institutional properties, do not impose on their members the total expenditure of the purchasing power that they receive. People are entitled to hold abstract purchasing power for later spending; or are enabled, through borrowing, to exert demand beyond the level of their potential production. It is precisely the *monetary* institutional characteristics of a production economy that empower them to do so. Thus, in monetary production economies, Say's Law no longer holds.[8]

It is important to stress that these intrinsic properties of monetary production economies have enormously increased and enriched the possibilities of choice – most of all, inter-temporal choice – of their single members. At the same time, they have made monetary production economies more vulnerable to intervening situations of lack of effective demand (with unemployment tendencies), or conversely of excess of effective demand (with inflationary pressures).[9]

---

[8] It is no doubt a merit of Keynes to have underlined, and to have brought attention to, this point. It was precisely the discovery of the crucial importance of this characteristic of the production monetary economies, shortly after publication of his *Treatise on Money* in 1930 that convinced him, quite dramatically, to abandon the line of thought behind that voluminous treatise, on which he had been working for almost ten years, and undertake the writing of a new book. Very significantly, he originally intended to give his new book the title *A Monetary Theory of Production* (Keynes, 1979). This title was not maintained in the subsequent drafts of the work, as Keynes became concerned with analysing in detail the functioning of a monetary economy in a somewhat more restricted way. Yet it undoubtedly represents much more vividly the general line of approach that Keynes was going over to; much better in fact, and more fundamentally, than the final title of his great work.

[9] These characteristics may be explored a little further. It is first of all interesting to note that, from the present theoretical scheme, something emerges that goes very near Say's Law, namely: whatever the amount of production that is undertaken, the current value of such production, at natural prices, is always exactly equal to the amount of personal incomes (in our simple case, to the amount of wages) that are distributed to the persons who have contributed to production. If Say's Law were simply to be understood in this sense, it would obviously be correct. But, of course, we know Keynes' argument is that, in this sense, it would only mean that *potential* total demand is always as high as total production. It would not necessarily mean that *effective* total demand coincides with it. This might nevertheless appear as an undue restriction to considering a specific point in time (Keynes' short-run analysis). Surely Say's Law was aimed at a wider (inter-temporal) framework.

Within the present structural dynamics framework, the arguments become much stronger, because attention is brought to bear on the *increases* that take place over time. An increase in production entails an increase, exactly equal to it, of personal income, and this means an increase of potential demand. But in this case one can see clearly that this does not mean an increase of effective demand, precisely because actual expenditure requires that new consumption decisions must be undertaken (as we have seen in section IV.15).

The institutional problem that arises is precisely that of actually *inducing* these new consumption decisions.

Can inducements be set up, at the institutional level, that may act to counterbalance the disequilibrating tendencies, that are constantly surging up from the structural dynamics background of monetary production economies?

We have seen that the market determination of the wage rate cannot be relied on for this purpose. But, at a strict institutional level, there still remains a further important variable to be considered. The time has come to turn to it.

18. Money and bonds

Paper money is not the only form of abstract purchasing power that people may hold. Paper money formally represents a debt by the issuing central bank. But if there are paper documents (i.e. documents without any intrinsic value) representing debts by a central bank, there may well be other paper documents representing debts by various people and organizations.

We have examined inter-personal debt/credit relations in chapter VI, and we have seen that, in connection with the wide possibilities that are open to single individuals and to groups of individuals and indeed to the community as a whole (through the government) to advance or postpone consumption in time, they bring into being financial assets and liabilities (both private and public).

This means that, in the economic system as a whole, side by side to the stock of paper money (M), a whole series of other inter-personal, or inter-group, debt/credit relations normally come into existence, which give rise to another stock of abstract purchasing power (call it B, for bonds). Therefore, it is the sum ($M + B$) that must be considered as the mass of purchasing power, which may at any moment be converted, or which people may try to convert, into demand for physical goods and services.

This obviously enlarges the set of circumstances that may lead to under- or over-fulfilment of macro-economic condition (IV.10.5), which, in this more complex context, comes to depend not only on the decisions to convert into effective demand (totally or partially) the purchasing power deriving from current incomes (and normally received in the form of money), but also on the decisions to convert into effective demand at least part of the purchasing power cumulated earlier, under the form of either money or bonds.

Problems will arise immediately concerning the decisions on the *composition* of the total stock of abstract purchasing power which is held, i.e. on the composition of the sum ($M + B$). Granted that people want to hold abstract purchasing power, and that both money and bonds represent abstract purchasing power, a series of problems to investigate concerns what will induce people to hold money or bonds.

Money and bonds have different characteristics. Money is perfectly liquid by definition but at the same time yields no nominal interest. Bonds on the other hand are less than perfectly liquid, as they always entail the risk of some capital loss if the holder happens to need to sell them at a time when their prices have fallen; but at the same time they always yield a rate of interest, which may be fixed either in nominal or in real terms.

We know, from our previous analysis, that the relations are more complex. Whatever the nominal rate of interest may be, there is a real rate of interest that is associated with *any* financial asset; and this is true also of money. Now the real rate of interest associated with paper money depends on the rate of change of the general level of prices: in chapter V we have shown it is equal to $-\sigma_M$, i.e. to minus the rate of inflation of the general price level. In other words, the real rate of interest associated with paper money is zero only when the rate of inflation is zero. When, as is more usually the case, inflation is positive, the real rate of interest associated with paper money is negative. (And it is positive when inflation is negative.)

This is not necessarily the case with bonds, for which the real rate of interest may well be fixed in such a way as to be independent of inflation – e.g. bonds indexed to the price level. Thus, while with bonds the real rate of interest may be fixed and the nominal rate of interest may be variable, with paper money it is the other way round. Paper money has a fixed nominal rate of interet (always zero) and a variable (with inflation) real rate of interest.

This means that the decisions on what proportion of total purchasing power to hold in the form of money or bonds will also depend on the rate of inflation, besides depending on people's preference for liquidity and on the rate of interest on bonds.

The point of view from which we are looking at these problems here is obviously that concerning how the introduction into our analysis of money and bonds is influencing the institutional task of aiming at the fulfilment of macro-economic condition (IV.10.5). The new relevant element that is being introduced at this stage is the determination of the *actual* rate of interest.

19. The actual versus the 'natural' rate of interest

We are thus back full circle to the 'natural' economic system. The natural rate of interest is the last of the natural concepts that have emerged from the present theoretical scheme. As with all the others, the question arises of what kind of institutions may be set up to bring it into being.

The terms of the questions are clearer here than with the other natural concepts. The natural rate of interest has emerged from the present theoretical scheme on strictly logical, and normative, ground: it has the property of ensuring an inter-temporal distribution of income that realizes proportionality to physical quantities of labour. There appears to be no obvious automatic institutional mechanism that may be said to perform the job of bringing it into actual realization.

More specifically, in this case, we can say straightaway that the market-price mechanism cannot perform this job. If, as it is generally claimed for a production system, the market-price mechanism has the property of making commodity prices tend to costs of production, then we must say that there is no cost of production to which the natural rate of interest may be related. Moreover, the difficulties with the market-price mechanism due to asymmetries connected with the one-directional character of time are well known. Simply, we must infer that the market-price mechanism does *not* appear to be the appropriate institutional mechanism for bringing the natural rate of interest into being.

Yet, we must also take note that, historically, the free market-price mechanism has been applied also to the actual determination of the rate of interest. More precisely, the usual market-price mechanism relying on demand and supply has indeed historically been allowed to operate on financial markets. It has actually been claimed that a market determined rate of interest, on financial markets, acts as a usual market price that brings demand and supply into equality, by equating the demand for loans and the supply of financial funds. This is an important claim, for our purposes, and must be examined seriously.

A market determined rate of interest, as has been concluded above, will not in general coincide with, or even tend to, the natural rate of interest (there is no reason to expect that it will). However, the deviations from the natural rate of interest might after all find a justification if it could be shown that the clearing of financial markets has an institutional function to perform.

We may look into this matter in further detail.

20. Can market clearance of financial markets set in a tendential fulfilment of 'Say's Law'?

It has been claimed that the clearing of financial markets – through the market determination of the rate of interest – fulfils a very important institutional function that goes well beyond the financial markets themselves, namely the institutional function of making total effective demand in the whole economic system automatically tend towards the amount of total production that is coming along. If this were so, we would be taken back to reconsider the possibility of at least some tendential satisfaction of Say's Law.

The argument may be put in the following way. The amount of purchasing power that is distributed through the price system is always equal to the value of total production, at current prices, as we have seen. But there are people who like to postpone some of their consumption and there are other people who want to bring it forward. This is how financial obligations (i.e. debt/credit obligations or bonds – either directly among individuals, or more likely, through financial intermediaries) come into being, as we have seen. Now, there can be little doubt that the willingness to postpone and to bring forward consumption is influenced, at least to a certain extent, by the rate of interest. The higher the rate of interest the greater, we might expect, is the inducement to postpone personal consumption, and vice versa. Now, a market determined rate of interest, by equating the demand and the supply of purchasing power, fulfils the function of equating the demand for advanced consumption by some individuals and the supply for deferred consumption by other individuals, thereby preventing imbalances between personal savings (for deferred consumption) and personal dissavings (for advanced consumption).

The argument can be extended to the working of secondary financial markets as well. People holding long-term bonds may change their personal plans, owing to unforeseen events, and suddenly wish to sell their bonds, thereby converting their purchasing power into present consumption. But symmetrically other people may well decide to postpone their consumption in time and buy them. When supply tends to overcome demand, the market price of bonds falls below their nominal price, which means that the rate of interest they yield will increase above their nominal rate of interest. The opposite will happen in the reverse situation. Again the movements of the market interest rate go in the correct direction, thus tending to equilibrate demand for advancing consumption with supply of postponing consumption. Again the equalization of the two goes in the direction of tending to avoid imbalances between savings and dissavings.

This appears therefore to be a very important function of the actual market determination of the rate of interest, through the clearance of financial markets, even if there is no reason to expect that the rate of interest so determined will in general tend to the normative ideal of a rate of interest at its 'natural' level. Again one might say that actual deviations from an ideal norm would find a justification at the institutional level, by the avoidance of actual imbalances on financial and, most importantly, on 'real' markets.

It may be noticed that this is a parallel claim to the one made for a market determined wage rate, examined in section 13 above. It is the two of them together that have provided the basis on which traditional economic theory has claimed an automatic tendency to the full employment of labour and to the full utilization of all resources (real and financial), in monetary economies.

21. Insufficiency of a demand and supply 'loanable funds' theory, and the rôle of monetary and fiscal policies

It may be noticed that the arguments presented in the previous section follow pretty closely the 'loanable fund' theory of the rate of interest of Robertsonian memory[10] – a theory which in the thirties was discredited by Keynes' work, but which has recently made a comeback into current economic literature.

Keynes' criticisms referred of course to an economy in which investment decisions play a crucial role. Our simple theoretical scheme considers a pure consumption economy; yet it may be even more useful in order to bring sharply into relief both the merits and the shortcomings of a loanable funds theory of the working of financial markets.

From our theoretical scheme, we know that the rate of interest can play no rôle in real inter-temporal transfers of consumption for the economic system as a whole, simply because overall consumption for the economic system as a whole cannot be transferred through time. However, any single individual can postpone personal consumption if other individuals are willing to do the opposite. Now, since personal savings and personal dissavings are responsive (and responsive in the correct direction) to variations in the market rate of interest, the question we must consider concerns the extent to which a market determination of the interest rate may be used as an institutional equilibrating device, when total consumption demand tends to outstrip, or to fall short of, the full-employment level set by macro-economic condition (V.10.5).

The basic problem here is that, in order to draw demand and supply functions of purchasing power for the single individuals, one must assume as given two variables of crucial importance for the economy as a whole, namely total national income and the general price level. These are in fact exactly the same variables (in addition to the structure of prices) that would have to be assumed as given in the case (considered in section 13 above) of the single entrepreneur's demand functions for labour. Unfortunately, all these crucial variables (total national income, structure of prices, the level

---

[10] See Robertson, 1940.

of prices) cannot be taken as given, when we consider the economic system as a whole.

The simplest way to put this point is to say that the supply of purchasing power by some individuals (personal savings) and the demand for purchasing power by other individuals (personal dissavings) depend on the real rate of interest, on personal and total incomes, and on the movement of the price level. All three variables are important. The demand and supply 'loanable funds' theory considers only one of them (the rate of interest).

This means that the equilibrating effects of changes in the rate of interest may well be working in periods in which, starting from a full employment situation, the expectations are rather tranquil, in the sense of there being reasonable expectations of general policies tending to maintain full employment and an acceptably stable level of prices.

A 'loanable fund' theory based on the equilibrating prerogatives of a market determined rate of interest seems therefore to have some function to perform in periods of relative calm and stability. This implicitly presupposes in fact an alert presence of both a central monetary authority, overlooking the orderly functioning of financial markets and a central fiscal authority, overlooking the maintenance of full employment.

A central monetary authority may exercise vigilance and control on the monetary and financial aggregates in relation to overall total demand. When overall effective demand tends to outstrip current production and pressure is exerted on the general price level, the central monetary authority will have to act with an appropriate monetary and credit policy to curb the disequilibrating tendencies that are under way. This may well be done also by manoeuvring the rates of interest, but also by acting in various ways on total credit, or by influencing any channel through which money gets into circulation, or through a combination of all these and other measures.

This seems the appropriate point to underline the fact that the use of the interest rate as an instrument of monetary policy carries with it intrinsic limits. The 'natural' rate of interest, as has emerged from the previous analysis, is after all always there to mark a normative rule. One cannot imagine outrageously large deviations from it. If the financial market situation were such as to require (on the basis of demand and supply alone) large excesses of the actual over the natural rate of interest, equity considerations might advise to correct the imbalance by other means. We might say that deviations from the natural rate of interest may be justified for the sake of equilibrating demand and supply of loanable funds if these are temporary and if they are not too large. For these deviations do entail distortions in inter-temporal income distribution. These distortions may not be socially acceptable beyond certain limits. After all, historically, ethical and social considerations have always put a bound on the magnitude of the rates of interest (the usury laws of the past are only the most conspicuous example).

Interventions by the fiscal authority become more likely in the opposite situation, as regards overall effective demand. The two macro-economic disequilibrium situations have many asymmetrical features, as has been pointed out repeatedly. When overall effective demand tends to be too feeble, the rate of interest encounters a lower bound: it cannot go below zero, in nominal terms (though it may become negative in real terms, but only with inflation). The economic system may well find itself in a slump situation, without any possibility of being helped by any policy aiming at cutting the rate of interest, if this has already reached its bottom limit.[11] The central monetary authority can do very little in this case: monetary policy becomes impotent. This is when direct interventions by a central fiscal authority (through fiscal policy measures) become the reasonable option to take.

22. Financial institutions and the risks of financial instability

Before closing the discussion on financial markets, it is worth stressing at least briefly some important consequences of the wide possibilities that have become open to single individuals to bring forward or postpone personal consumption, by exchanging among themselves debt/credit obligations; and indeed of the wide possibilities that have become open to the government, acting on behalf of the community as a whole, to proceed to public dissavings, by borrowing or by deficit spending. It appears quite obvious in this respect that the carrying out of debt/credit operations concerning millions of individuals, in order to take place in an orderly way, requires the setting up of institutions with the task of financial intermediation (financial intermediaries).

It is a typical feature of advanced economic systems that there will normally be in circulation a stock of paper money, issued by the central bank, side by side with a multiform stock of other credit documents and bonds, issued by various financial institutions. Money and other near-money documents may bear no nominal rate of interest (though they always entail some real, normally negative, rate of interest); bonds will normally bear, in various forms, nominal (and *a fortiori* real) rates of interest.

It is well to be aware that the existence of monetary and financial assets – besides having enormously widened the possibilities of choice open to the

---

[11] This is the situation that has become known, since Keynes, by the name of the 'liquidity trap'. Recent attempts at reviving the pre-Keynesian view that a re-equilibrating effect (called the Pigou effect) might be obtained by an overall fall of the general price level clearly appear to be inconsistent in a production theoretical framework.

single members of a modern society – also carries with it a set of risks. Financial assets do represent purchasing power for the individuals who hold them, but only on the condition that this purchasing power is not exercised; or more precisely it is exercised, within each period of time, within the bounds set by macro-economic condition (IV.10.5). Any attempt, for example owing to any sudden wave of panic even if completely unjustified, to convert all, or even part of this purchasing power into actual purchases of goods and services would be self-defeating; it would be physically impossible and would only cause hyper-inflation and financial chaos.

Thus, the existence of monetary and financial assets is always associated with the risk of financial instability.

This obviously requires the setting up of norms and rules of behaviour. It also requires vigilance, control, and supervision over financial intermediaries, which is yet another institutional task normally entrusted to the central bank.

23. A programme for research, and a challenge for action

In bringing to an end this long chapter, at least two main points may briefly be touched upon.

With reference to the economic institutions to be set up for realizing the 'natural' economic system, we have paid some attention to the competitive market-price mechanism. This institutional mechanism has evolved over centuries with (good and bad) experience. It has been refined continually to meet changing circumstances and still remains, without any doubt, the most powerful of all automatically working institutional mechanisms that have been discovered so far in the economic sphere. When an institutional mechanism of this type emerges, that works in an automatic way, one must take it very seriously. Most of all, one must be very cautious against cries to dismiss it, if well defined alternatives are not available. Clearly, the merits of the market-price mechanism must not be under-estimated.

But these merits must not be over-estimated either. In a production economic system, we have seen that the market-price mechanism, when applied to the actual determination of the economic variables, cannot work equally well for all of them. Therefore, it cannot be applied uncritically; it cannot be thought of as the only institutional mechanism to be used for a satisfactory determination of all economic variables.[12]

---

[12] From this point of view, the 'pure exchange model' appears quite differently. It appears as an analytical construction in which all assumptions are made to shape the economic problems in such a way as to reduce them to problems that may optimally be solved with the application of the market-price mechanism.

By being typically micro-economic, the market-price mechanism performs at its best as an efficiency-stimulating mechanism that leads the actual commodity prices toward the corresponding costs of production, and induces the producers to look for ever better technical methods. It may have a function to perform also in the field of physical quantity adjustments, though in a less decisive way, as we have seen. At the same time, we cannot expect the market-price mechanism to solve for us the macro-economic problems of searching for the natural wage rate and of ensuring full employment, though it may be judiciously used to promote an efficient mobility of labour among the production sectors. Neither can we expect from the market-price mechanism a search for the natural rate of interest, which is a typically normative concept. Yet it can be used, again in a judicious way, to contrast disequilibrating tendencies in the financial markets.

A confirmation thereby emerges of the necessity of setting up some major coordinating institutions, at the level of the economic system as a whole – a necessity that emerges both in the field of fiscal policy and in the field of monetary policy.

In fact, one of the great challenges for economists in the near future appears precisely that of finding ways to reconcile and render complementary the automatic stimuli coming from the competitive market-price mechanism with the necessary requirements for overall policies concerning the economic system as a whole.

A second point that may be briefly touched upon concerns a few further reflections on the significance of the 'natural' economic system. The obvious question is: What is the justification of the approach proposed here, which aims at starting from a deeper, 'natural', level, with respect to the approach of dominant economics, which begins directly from the working of the market-price mechanism, i.e. from a successful institutional mechanism?

The answer that emerges in this connection points at the informative richness of an economic analysis that goes deep into examining the determinants of the economic magnitudes that characterize the industrial economic systems. This is a call which the classical economists felt very strongly and which later on was left aside, as economists preferred the less engaging, but inevitably more superficial, attitude of simply observing what is showing up in the actual markets. We may recall that the classical economists always underlined the necessity of penetrating below the surface of the immediately observable economic phenomena, into the more fundamental forces that move them. The 'pure production' model which has been constructed here brings us back to the classical preoccupations. And it evinces a twofold kind of analytical fecundity.

At the logical level, it has brought out a clear distinction between what, in an economic system, is fundamental, and is thus imbibed with normative connotations, and what is institutional, and is thus instrumental to the task of bringing the fundamental features into existence. The same economic variables may actually come under scrutiny at both levels of investigation, but in a quite different manner: at the *natural* level as ideal positions to be achieved; at the *institutional* level as actual positions that are in practice realizable, through particular institutional mechanisms; the latter having to be compared with the former, and to be gauged according to the speed with which they tend towards the former.

At a more substantial level, the same approach has brought us discoveries of its own. It has led us to the analysis of the structural dynamics that is set into being by the fundamental forces that are at work, and that could not be perceived from the superficial observation of the actual market evidence. It further conveys important knowledge and a whole set of information about the industrial economic systems, which, by their own inherent characteristics, are shown to be moving all the time; and to be unable to stay put. A structural dynamics analysis uncovers multiform aspects about how they move, and about the directions in which they move, which is crucially relevant for institutional purposes. As we have seen, even simple pieces of information about the direction in which they move have surprisingly relevant implications on the characteristics, and on the requirements, of the institutional mechanisms to be set up in order to react and adapt.

A vast programme of research is thereby opening up. But there also emerges a wide programme for action. Not only is there an 'institutional problem' to be solved; there also is a challenge for 'institutional action' to be met.

IX Boundedness of economic systems, and international economic relations

1. Multiplicity of economic systems

The analysis of the foregoing chapters refers to a single economic system. But we know that in reality there are many economic systems. Why?

Traditional economic theory has never given, and in fact is unable to give, an answer to this question.[1] As traditionally considered, an economic system is, one might say, open-ended; it offers no reason why it should not be extended to the whole world.

Of course there may be many explanatory circumstances from outside economics. Historical, political, religious, cultural, ethnic factors weigh heavily on the formation of separate political entities, which then necessarily make up separate economic systems. But common sense warns us that it is not reasonable to think that economic factors should be completely extraneous.

The theoretical (production) scheme presented here contains an important explanation of why each economic system is necessarily bounded; and therefore, indirectly, of the fragmentation of the world into a multiplicity of economic systems.

Once again the source of the explanation is to be found in macro-economic condition (IV.10.5) – the 'necessary' condition for economically significant equilibrium solutions. As has been pointed out, this condition concerns and connects the entire economic system to which it refers. Hence it makes of it a unitary entity, and at the same time separates it from all other economic systems. In other words, macro-economic condition (IV.10.5) requires a *delimitation* of the economic system to which it refers;

---

[1] Perhaps one of the few economists who perceived the intrinsically bounded character of the emerging industrial economies, in the nineteenth century, was Friedrich List (see List (1841), especially his Preface, where he criticizes dominant economics for considering nothing in between the single individual and the whole world). By lacking a formal theoretical scheme, he ended up with rather distasteful conclusions (German nationalism).

for two reasons, which correspond to its two (symmetric) aspects. On the one side, it requires a delimitation of the labourers who are entitled to the 'natural' wage rate, and thus to the growing productivity benefits, of the economic system. On the other (physical quantity) side, it makes (full employment) responsibilities emerge towards these people, i.e. towards a specific community. All this means that a (production) economic system cannot be open-ended; it must be bounded.

Of course, the fact that an economic system is intrinsically bounded does not necessarily mean that it is, or should be, closed. Or rather, it does not mean that it should be closed in all respects. The relevant question that immediately arises precisely concerns the extent to which an economic system is closed and the extent to which it may be opened.

Here again, exogenous factors can have a great influence on closing an economic system. Exogenous conditions of a political character can without any doubt close certain economic systems towards the outside world (think of autarchic policies). But, from our point of view, the question must be posited in the opposite way: in the *absence* of external impositions of any kind, what are the economic characteristics that are at the basis of the closures of economic systems, and what are the economic characteristics that allow the openings?

As may immediately be perceived, the economic variables of our natural economic system that are easiest to open towards the similar variables of other economic systems are the commodity prices and the physical quantities produced. (There can be no surprise therefore if traditional economics has almost exclusively concentrated on international trade of the commodities susceptible to being exported and imported.) Mobility of commodities from one economic system to another does not interfere with any process concerning the fulfilment of macro-economic condition (IV.10.5), and its implications for the community as a whole. Or, more precisely, fulfilment of this macro-economic condition is compatible with perfect mobility of commodities from one economic system to another.

The situation is radically different for labour.[2] The mobility of labour is in fact required, inside each economic system, like the mobility of commodities. But, unlike the mobility of commodities, the mobility of labour from one economic system to another generates a series of problems. It interferes with the processes that may be set up to maintain full employment, and it interferes with the process of distribution of the benefits of technical progress performed by the natural wage rate (see section IV.9). Looking at it from another point of view, the fulfilment of macro-economic

---

[2] The proposition, earlier stated, that in a production economic system commodities and labour belong to two different conceptual categories altogether could not be better illustrated than by these relations.

condition (IV.10.5) is incompatible with indiscriminate and free mobility of labour in and/or out of the economic system to which it refers.

The ultimate source of the boundedness of any economic system is indeed precisely here: it is the size of its labour force.

Of course, in reality, there may be many obstacles to the mobility of labour also within each economic system. But the crucial point is that macro-economic condition (IV.10.5) requires a tendency toward internal mobility, because of the already examined requirements of structural dynamics. Conversely, in reality, even among various economic systems, migrations of people always tend to occur and, in effect, do continue to occur. But the crucial point is that their interfering with the measures necessary for the fulfilment of the mentioned macro-economic condition make their regulation inevitable.

The result is inescapable: fulfilment of macro-economic condition (IV.10.5) inevitably imposes a regulation of international flows of labour.

It must also be underlined, in spite of the tendencies not to admit it,[3] that territorial mobility of the labour factors is of enormous importance. Labour enjoys very little international mobility because its mobility would be too upsetting!

To conclude and summarize, the industrial economic systems require at least a tendential fulfilment of macro-economic condition (IV.10.5). This implies that they require macro-economic coordination, in order to safeguard both full employment and the productivity–growth benefits for their citizens. Such a macro-economic condition thus necessarily delimits the community of labourers towards whom an overall responsibility is taken up. It necessarily follows that any inflow of labourers from outside must come under some regulation concerning the fulfilment of that macro-economic condition.

In this framework, the emerging on the international scene of a plurality of economic systems, coinciding with corresponding political entities, appears as entirely normal and in fact as a necessary consequence of the responsibilities which, in each economic system, are bound to arise towards a well defined community considered as a whole.

In the following pages we shall go on to consider relations among different economic systems (international relations). For the sake of simplicity, we shall make no distinction between internal and external causes of delimitation. We shall take the terms 'economic systems', 'countries',

---

[3] It is significant to note that the rôle of regulations concerning labour migrations has always been played down. Traditional economic theorists have (perhaps unconsciously) always tried to make international mobility of labour appear irrelevant, or at least not important. (We shall return to this matter in section 11.)

'states', as if they always coincided. Furthermore, for the sake of analytic clarity, we shall adopt the supposition that, within each economic system, both commodities and labour enjoy perfect mobility, and that institutional devices are at work that tendentially bring the various economic magnitudes towards their 'natural' levels. On the other hand, betwen one economic system and another, we shall suppose that labour is characterized by immobility. As far as commodities are concerned, specific hypotheses concerning their international mobility will be made from case to case.

2. International comparisons at the same (identical) price structure

We may begin our analysis with some comparisons at a given moment in time, and we may start with an extremely simplified and analytically significant, though purely hypothetical, case.

Let us suppose that there are two countries (i.e. two economic systems) which we may call A (for advanced) and U (for underdeveloped). Technical knowledge of the average person is such that per-capita productivity in country A is ten times greater than in country U, for each single consumption good, so that the structure of costs (in spite of their absolute levels being different) is exactly the same in both countries.

Suppose moreover, again for the sake of simplicity, that in both countries the medium of exchange (money) is anchored to gold, so that the exchange rate of the two currencies is fixed by the ratio of gold contents of the two monetary units. At this rate of exchange, both currencies have exactly the same purchasing power, in both countries, in terms of any physical commodity. However, since all commodities (gold included) can be produced in A with one-tenth of the labour they require in U, the amount of physical production per worker, and therefore the amount of real per-capita income (i.e. of purchasing power) at the disposal of the average person is ten times greater in A than in U.

By applying our previous analysis, we can say immediately that the relative prices of commodities – or, more specifically, all commodity prices in terms of gold – are exactly the same in both countries, but the wage rate, and per-capita incomes, in terms of real purchasing power, are dramatically different.

The first important thing that this hypothetical case shows is that, across countries, the principle of embodied (or for that matter commanded) labour as a regulator of commodity prices no longer holds. In our case, all prices, in terms of gold, or in terms of any arbitrarily chosen physical commodity, are exactly the same in both countries; and they would clearly remain the same if exchange was allowed across borders. But the embodied labour that each price represents in the two countries is dramatically different: in U it is ten times greater than in A. This means that relative quantities of embodied labour will continue to regulate relative commodity prices *within* the boundaries of each country, but not across borders. A bushel of wheat is a bushel of wheat, wherever it is produced. Nobody would be prepared to give ten bushels of wheat produced in A in exchange for one bushel of wheat produced in U, simply because these two quantities have been produced with the same quantity of labour.

These propositions crudely evince the fact that, when communities are separated into different economic systems, any exchange across borders cannot but take place on the basis of *physical commodity comparisons*. To look at the matter in another way, international exchanges are bound to be 'unequal', if assessed in terms of embodied labour. It is physical comparison that is bound to prevail in international relations. More precisely, it is the comparison of physical commodities that determines how many units of embodied labour of one country exchanges for one unit of embodied labour of another country.[4]

3. Different relevance, for advanced and for less developed countries, of the disparities in technical knowledge

An interesting, and important, feature of the simple case discussed in the previous section is that it brings to the fore, clearly and without any complication, the primary factor accounting for the different wealth of the two countries considered, A and U; namely, the level of labour productivity.

An immediate consequence is that we can also single out immediately the primary source of gains from possible international economic relations; namely, the improvement and diffusion of technical knowledge.

There is a third aspect, which will here be taken up immediately. If we try to evaluate the importance of this primary source of international gains, we discover a quite asymmetrical picture.

In general, economic inquiries into international relations have been prompted by this simple question: granted that various countries with different characteristics exist side by side with one another, are there ways in which one country may take advantage from the existence of the others, without the others being put at any disadvantage? Now, it becomes quite clear, in our hypothetical case, that this question has a different answer,

---

[4] It should be noted that an explanation is provided here (based on disparities of technical knowledge) of the international 'unequal exchange' in terms of labour. This explanation is simpler, and at the same time more fundamental, than the one (in terms of 'international exploitation') provided by the author who originally introduced this expression (Emmanuel, 1972).

according to whether it is posited from the point of view of country A or from the point of view of country U.

Consider first the position of country A – the industrially advanced country. From the standpoint of this country, the situation appears entirely uninteresting. There is nothing that country A can learn from country U. Moreover no gain (but actually losses) would accrue to people migrating from A to U. The price structure is exactly the same across the borders, so that there would be no gain whatever from any exchange of commodites, i.e. absolutely no gain from international trade (except in times of temporary shortage).[5]

But the situation appears quite different from the standpoint of country U, the less advanced country. Of course, for country U too, as much as for country A, there is no possibility of obtaining any gain from international trade (as the structure of costs and prices has been supposed to be the same in both countries). However, for country U, this aspect of the situation only emerges as a very minor part of the whole picture.

4. Learning of technical knowledge as the primary source of international economic benefits

Let us now consider the situation from the point of view of country U. First of all, the movements of population become relevant. From a strictly individual point of view, workers from country U would gain substantially if they could move to country A, where the per-capita incomes (and per-capita wages) are ten times as large. There is, therefore, for single individuals, a strong inducement to emigrate to country A, an inducement that will especially apply to the more educated and more skilled part of the U population (as they will normally encounter fewer difficulties in being accepted in country A). This is obviously a great danger for country U as a whole. A 'brain drain', as it has become known, though advantageous to the single individuals concerned, is harmful to country U taken as a whole, as it lowers the average stock of knowledge of its people, while its needs would lie in precisely the opposite direction. In any case, the single individuals of the industrially advanced country, especially the less educated and less skilled ones, fearing competition for jobs, are likely to

---

[5] These considerations may also contribute to explain why, in economic analysis, there has always been a tendency to attribute so little importance to what here appears instead as the principal source of international benefits (the level of technical knowledge).

It is a fact that the foundations of the theory of international trade have been laid by economists who lived in the economically advanced countries. Quite understandably, their attention has been attracted by those problems – and by those ways of obtaining gains from international relations – that were relevant for the countries in which they lived. And for these countries, the backwardness of knowledge in other countries was irrelevant.

exert strong pressure for the introduction of limitations to immigration. There arises therefore a convergence of interests: the community as a whole in the U country (except in cases of great demographic abundance) will favour disincentives to emigration (especially with regards to its well-gifted members), and the community as a whole in the A country will tend to induce disincentives to immigration.

Hereafter we shall proceed (simply as a question of practical relevance, and without implying any moral approval) on the assumption that migration of people from country to country is negligible.

Yet, even if migration were forbidden altogether, people in country U have at their disposal a most fundamental way of taking advantage of the existence of country A, and of increasing their wealth. They can *learn* the methods of production which are being used already in country A. For country U as a whole this is the most important of all available means of augmenting the national wealth. Just because methods of production are in operation already in A, it is actually possible in U (simply by learning to do what other people do already) to improve productivity at such a rate of change as could never be achieved in A. In other words, it is actually possible for U to grow at a faster rate than A. There can be no doubt that, for country U, international learning represents the major source of international gains.

It must be added that, in general, for any country – whether industrially advanced or underdeveloped, whether in practice it can take advantage from international learning or no advantage at all – any increase in knowledge represents a gain for the country *unconditionally*, i.e. without any requirement or proviso at all being satisfied first. (It will be seen in a moment that this is not true of other sources of international gains.) In this sense, international learning can indeed be said to represent the primary source of international gains.

5. The hierarchical order of the expansion of demand as a rigid constraint on international learning

The possibility of international learning just considered is not as wide as it might appear at first sight. For although accumulated technical knowledge may cover a wide range of fields, and although it may be to a large extent freely available, the part of this technical knowledge which an underdeveloped country can draw from, at any particular point of time, is only a small fraction of the total.

This point is important and deserves to be stressed. In our case, the simplifying assumption has been made that relative prices are the same in both countries. But nothing has been said about the structure of production. Now, even if relative prices are the same, the structures of production and of employment cannot be the same in A and U, if there is a tenfold difference in real per-capita incomes. The physical quantity of each single commodity to be produced is determined by demand, as was seen earlier (chapters II and IV), but we have also seen (in chapters IV and VII) that the inherent patterns of human needs and preferences give rise to entirely different compositions of consumer demand, and therefore to different structures of production and employment, at the various levels of real per-capita income.

In our case, where real per-capita income in A is supposed to be ten times larger than in U, the structures of production and employment must be very different indeed. If, for example, annual per-capita incomes are on average of the order of $1,500 in country U, and of the order of $15,000 in country A, demand in U will amost entirely be concentrated on food, while, in A, demand for food will represent only a small part of total income. And since productivity in U is one-tenth of what it is in A, most probably a proportion of the order of, let us say, 70 per cent of the labour force of U will have to be concentrated in agriculture, while in A this branch of production, though giving a higher physical output, will only account for, let us say, roughly 5 per cent of total employment.

Most likely, almost all types of commodities which are produced in U will also be produced in A, but not all types of commodities which are made in A – in fact only a small fraction of them, let us say only one-fifth of them – will also be produced in U. Thus, production in A is much more differentiated and concerned with a much wider range and variety of commodities than in U. Which of all these commodities produced in A will also be produced in U clearly depends on the needs of the U-consumers at their lower level of per-capita incomes. But the point is that whatever the choices of the U-consumers, the number of types of commodities demanded by them can only be a small fraction of the number of types of commodities which are produced in A.

Of course, as time and economic growth go on, country U will be able to enlarge the variety of its production. But this process will have to follow a very strict order. At any given point of time, producers in U are not free to pick up any type of commodity they like from among the four-fifths of all types which are not produced. They will have to start production only of those commodities for which demand is expanding. Our simple case brings out this phenomenon very sharply and without secondary complications, owing to the assumption of precisely the same commodity prices in both countries and thus of no need for international trade. There is a very definite order in which the various production processes can be introduced in U, strictly fixed by the hierarchical order in which demand for each commodity is expanding, as incomes are increasing.

But a fixed order in which the production process can be enlarged also represents a fixed order in which the various methods of production can be *learnt*. Thus, however large the stock of accumulated technical knowledge may be in *A*, country *U* can only take advantage of that small part of it which refers to the few products for which demand is expanding and for those commodities (in our case only one-fifth of the total) which are produced already. This also means that people in *U* are not free to draw as they please from the existing pool of technical knowledge, however freely available it may be. They have to follow a very definite order. And if they do not follow this order, their increase in technical knowledge will simply have no effect on their incomes at all. To give an example, if any increment of productivity, and thus of per-capita income, that takes place in *U* translates itself into more demand for food, the learning activity will have to be concentrated on increasing productivity in food production. It would be no use to learn how to make, let us say, refrigerators, because very few people would want them. Demand for refrigerators will come later on, but only at higher levels of income, which will never be reached if productivity is not increased in food production to begin with.

There is a stringent conclusion that follows. If country *U* is incapable of learning in the particular fifth of the total field of technical knowledge for which it can provide demand, it will never grow at all, whatever its possibilities of learning may be in the other four-fifths. This other vast four-fifths of the total field of technical knowledge may well be freely available and easy to acquire but will remain, for the time being, entirely irrelevant. (As far as the possibilities of increasing production are concerned, it is as if it did not exist.)[6]

These are, of course, severe restrictions indeed to the process of international learning. And they are the stricter, in each particular country, the lower its level of per-capita income. For any underdeveloped country, therefore, a process of growth of per-capita income also represents a way of widening continually the field in which advantage can be taken of the stock of technical knowledge that has accumulated in the outside world.

6. Some important practical implications

We may draw immediately at least three implications of great practical relevance.

The first implication is that international comparisons of aggregate magnitudes are misleading. Clearly, the aggregate economic magnitudes of

---

[6] These propositions follow logically, and in fact rather crudely, from the present arguments, owing to the strict assumption of complete absence of comparative cost advantages. When these initial assumptions are relaxed, as will be done in the following pages (see sections 6, 7, 10) the present propositions will also have to be modified accordingly.

the various countries (their national products, consumptions, investments, etc.) become less and less comparable the greater are the disparities in their per-capita incomes. This circumstance is of course rather well known; yet it is seldom kept in mind in international comparisons of national incomes. One normally forgets that the average billion dollars of, let us say, India's gross national product is, in real terms, i.e. in terms of its physical composition, something almost entirely different from the average billion dollars of, let us say, the United States' gross national product. One may have a second look at the statistical tables of chapter I, which, even in their crude classification of national products in three broad categories (agriculture, industry and services), already evince how dramatically different the compositions are.

The second implication may be stated as follows: the rather widespread view that low-income countries enjoy comparative cost advantages in agricultural production – a view drawn too hastily and uncritically from the fact that, in underdeveloped countries, the great majority of people are working in agriculture – is false.

The example of the foregoing pages has been constructed deliberately on the assumption that prices – and costs for the production of all commodities – are exactly the same in country A and in country U; in other words on the assumption that there is absolutely no comparative cost advantage, for any production for any country. Yet, in country U (the low per-capita income country) almost all active population will normally be concentrated in agriculture. (See, with reference to this, statistical table 2 in chapter I, from where one can see that in India agricultural employment was 71 per cent of the total in 1981.) By contrast, in country A, the agricultural employment will presumably amount to a very small part of total employment (from the same statistical table one can see that in the United States such percentage was 2 per cent of total employment in 1981. Notice the order of magnitude of the difference: from 71 to 2!).

The explanation is of course much simpler and much more fundamental. Productivity in U is so low that the great majority of people can afford no time to produce anything else but the very basic goods necessary to their survival (which, of course, come from agricultural activity).

There is a third implication, which may turn out to be even more important, for practical purposes, than the two previously mentioned ones. Precisely the constraints on the internal market demand which, in the low-income countries, render technical learning useless in the productive processes of those goods which are demanded only at higher per-capita incomes (four-fifths of the total, in the example of the previous chapter) may exert an extraordinarily powerful inducement towards the undertaking of international trade. To the extent that the low-income countries succeed in finding markets abroad, they will be in a position to extend their learning (and thus their ability for production) to all that range of goods which are demanded at higher incomes – something they could not do if they were to rely exclusively on internal markets.

This source of stimulus to production for export, and to learning, represents an explanation of international trade which paradoxically has been ignored by all traditional economic literature, both classical and neo-classical, and which may on the other hand turn out in many cases to be by far more relevant than the one (based on comparative costs) so far considered in all treatises of international trade.

7. Disparaties of comparative costs – a secondary source of international economic benefits

The powerful inducement to international trade which has emerged from the arguments just stated is intimately linked with a change in the structure of costs.

We have so far carried out our analysis on the (unrealistic) assumption that the two countries A and U, which we have considered, have the same structure of costs (and prices). But this assumption has been made only for analytical purposes. We may now drop such a simplifying assumption.

In practice, relative costs cannot be the same in all countries. Particular geographical positions, traditionally cultivated skills, climates, endowments of natural resources, and many other factors may put some countries in a better position than others to produce certain commodities. In some countries certain particular commodities may not be producible at all. Other, important, reasons are connected with the different stages of economic development. There are certain products and services for which productivity can be increased only at a much smaller rate than for the average of all other commodities. Thus, within each economic system, the costs of these commodities and services inevitably become greater and greater, relative to the costs of all the others, as economics growth continues. Similarly, there are certain products for which learning can proceed at an extraordinarily high pace (and this is particularly relevant in less developed countries, which can absorb know-how from abroad). Furthermore, especially in manufactures, there are products which can be made at low costs only on a large scale, or only with the complicated complementary organization of many other branches of production. Between countries which are of different size, or which are at different stages of economic development, these differences in relative costs may reach quite striking proportions.

Let us therefore now enlarge our analysis to the case in which the two countries we are investigating, A and U, have different structures of costs (and prices). We shall suppose that average overall productivity and thus also the real wage rate are, as before, ten times greater in A than in U. But sectoral productivities in the two countries are now supposed to differ according to a much wider range: in some sectors productivity may be, let us say, twice as great in A as in U, and in others it may be up to twenty times as great. Since, within the same country, the wage rate is uniform *ex hypothesi* over all sectors, relative prices will now differ in the two countries. We may still suppose, for simplicity's sake, that the two monetary units are linked to gold and that productivity in the gold producing industry is equal to the average, i.e. it is ten times greater in A than in U.

Then, we can say unambiguously that those goods for which differences in productivity are smaller than tenfold will have a lower price in U than in A and those goods for which differences in productivity are greater than tenfold will have a lower price in A than in U.

As opposed to the previous case, this is a case in which, if international trade were allowed, goods would be induced to move across borders. People in A would buy goods of the first type in U, where they are cheaper; and similarly people in U would buy goods of the second type in A. Country U would be induced to specialize in producing, and then exporting, the first type of commodities; and country A would be induced to specialize in producing, and then exporting, the second type of commodities.

It is here that an important asymmetry arises between the two countries. While in country A the range of producible goods will remain roughly unchanged, in country U such a range is susceptible to an enormous widening. It is here that the possibilities mentioned in the previous section become relevant. As pointed out above, what becomes extremely important is that the possibilities of learning for country U undergo an enormous widening, with respect to what they would be if the country were to be confined exclusively to its internal market.

At this point the question arises: should international trade be allowed? Are movements of commodities across borders going to be beneficial to the two countries? The question has become relevant, at last, for *both* countries. However, the degree of relevance of the answer continues to be different for the two countries and to reveal many asymmetries.

First of all, it must be pointed out that the answer has become a conditional one. International trade is going to be beneficial to both countries, provided that two conditions are satisfied.

The first condition (well known from traditional analysis) is that the trading countries actually be able to specialize in production, in the sense of being able to transfer the factors of production from the less to the more favoured branches of production, without suffering a drop in the level of employment. During this process, if production were disrupted, and labour remained idle, the country as a whole would lose the physical amount of commodities which would have been produced by the unemployed labourers, had they not remained unemployed. These might well be temporary losses only, and when the chances for a quick re-absorption of unemployment are reasonable, a country may well accept some short-run disruption in view of the longer-run advantages. Yet the short-run losses have to be taken into account. There is, moreover, an important aspect of this proviso to be reckoned with, which again is particularly relevant for any country (most likely the underdeveloped country) which had unemployment to start with. In this case, clearly, the importation of any commodity which, by having a lower price than that possible at home, induces disruption and further local unemployment (which would not otherwise take place) entails – to the extent that it is not compensated (or is only partly compensated) by re-absorption in those sectors that have succeeded to increase production for export – a net loss for the country. For, although some particular people (those who buy the imported commodity and at the same time do not lose their jobs) might well gain by paying the lower international price, the workers who would otherwise produce that commodity remain unemployed and produce nothing. So the country as a whole would suffer a net loss which is represented by the amount of those physical goods which are given in exchange for the imported commodity.

The second condition is of a more dynamic nature, and (unlike the first one) has been neglected by traditional theory. The condition is that, at the particular point in time when exchanges take place, the existing structure of costs be the best one which can be obtained for the time being. For if this were not so, i.e. if it were easy to learn quickly (let us say, from abroad) how to bring costs (and prices) down to the international level, then it would obviously be more advantageous for each country to bring about increases in productivity and produce the commodities concerned at home. This proviso is worth stressing because it is likely to be overlooked, owing to the fact that it normally will not be relevant for the advanced countries. Yet, it is obviously extremely important for the underdeveloped countries. It is only when all possible efforts to increase learning have been made (i.e. all possible efforts have been made to take advantage of the primary source of international gains) that an underdeveloped country can hope to obtain further gains from international trade. In other words, possible benefits from international trade are subordinated to the benefits from international learning.

In this sense, international trade, aimed at taking advantage of differences in comparative costs, emerges as a subordinate source (subject to the conditions that employment be safeguarded and that all efforts be made for international learning) and therefore as a secondary source of international gains.

8. Static and dynamic aspects of the principle of comparative cost advantages

When the two conditions stated above are both satisfied, i.e. when employment is being safeguarded (or unemployment is prevented from increasing) and when all possible efforts have been made to improve productivity, international trade will clearly bring real gains to both countries.

Country A, by being induced to concentrate on producing (for both countries) those commodities for which it has been able to secure the higher levels of productivity, rather than those for which its productivity lead is less pronounced, will be able to increase for both countries the physical quantity of those commodities in which it specializes. And similarly, country U, by being induced to concentrate on producing (for both countries) those commodities for which it least lags behind A, will similarly be able to increase for both countries the physical quantities produced of these commodities.

These propositions apply, of course, only to those commodities which can be traded internationally. There are many other commodities which cannot move outside the country where they are produced and for which nothing at all will happen. Most services, after all, come into this category; they cannot be exported separately from the people who provide them. Many other commodities, moreover, are so quickly perishable as to be subject to limited geographical mobility. Even for those commodities that can move, trade will only be induced by those differences in comparative costs that are large enough to cover the costs of transport, storage, and risk insurance.

However, for those commodities which can move internationally and for which the comparative cost differences are larger than transport, storage, and risk insurance costs, trade will take place and will generate international specialization, with a consequent increase of production of the physical quantities available for both countries. It is precisely this increase of production of the physical quantities of commodities that become available for *both* countries that represents a net gain from the international trade of those products for which comparative costs are different in the various countries.

As the reader will realize, this is nothing but the well-known 'principle of comparative cost advantage', of which David Ricardo gave a celebrated and perhaps yet unsurpassed exposition in his *Principles* (Ricardo, 1951 [1817]), more than one and a half centuries ago.

With respect to this principle, the novel feature that emerges from the present analysis is that the principle itself has not only a static aspect (consisting in taking advantage of existing differences in costs), but also, so to speak, a dynamic aspect, consisting in the possible acquisition of technical knowledge from abroad.[7]

There certainly are comparative cost advantages which derive from the climatic and natural characteristics of each particular country. But there are other comparative cost advantages which may be *acquired* through learning technical methods already in operation abroad. The comparative advantages that are susceptible of being acquired through learning from abroad are crucially relevant for the economically less developed countries, as has been stressed at the end of section 6.

9. Updating previous results to account for differences in price structures

We are now able to introduce the necessary modifications to the statements of section 2, consequent upon the enlargement of the theoretical framework to include differences in the price structures of the countries considered.

If the currencies of both countries are anchored to gold (as we have supposed so far), the rate of exchange between the two currencies again coincides with the ratio of gold contents of the two monetary units. But, in order to assess their purchasing power, a distinction must now be made between the goods that are traded internationally and those that are not.

For those commodities which cannot move, and hence are not internationally traded, prices remain different in the two countries. Therefore, if assessed in terms of any one of these commodities, the purchasing power of either currency will be different in the two countries. With reference to any specific commodity, their purchasing power will be higher (or lower) in that country where the commodity is produced at a comparative cost advantage (or disadvantage).

But for those commodities which can move and are internationally traded, relative prices in A and U become the same. In terms of these commodities, the purchasing power of either currency becomes the same in both countries. If, contrary to what was supposed above, the disparity of

---

[7] Even in the simplest of all cases, in which the opening up of international trade compels the firms that operate at a comparative cost disadvantage to face the prospect of closing down, some firms may respond with exceptional efforts to the challenge, and learn quickly how to bring costs down, at least to the international level, in which case they would put themselves back into the category of those firms whose production is not affected. This means that, even in branches of industry which, on the whole, are compelled to close down, some firms might still be able to survive owing to quick acquisition of new technical knowledge.

the labour productivities in the sectors producing the numéraire commodity ('gold') were to be different from the average disparity of productivities, the only consequence would be that the numéraire commodity would be produced in only one of the two countries.

The terms of the problems do not change if we go on to consider a regime of nominal monetary units (rather than monetary units linked to gold). In this case, the term of reference becomes the whole set of internationally traded commodities. In terms of these commodities, the two nominal monetary units will tend, in the absence of specific obstacles, toward a purchasing power that is the same in both countries, and thus generate a rate of exchange which reflects, for both countries, the parity of purchasing powers (but only in terms, note, of those commodities that are internationally traded).

Thus, for those commodities that are internationally traded, the results of our analysis of section 2 continue to hold. Relative prices are determined by the relative amount of embodied labour *within* each country. But the same physical quantity of any internationally traded commodity, evaluated at the current (common) price, expressed in either currency, represents a different quantity of embodied labour in the two countries; the physical quantity of labour required in A and in U, to produce the same commodity, being different.

The general proposition is that relative prices of internationally traded commodities are determined by relative amounts of embodied labour inside each of the trading countries. But the absolute quantities of embodied labour will be different from country to country so that exchanges of commodities across countries will be 'unequal' in terms of labour, as was seen already in section 2.

The only complication, with respect to the simpler case of section 2, is that some (internationally traded) commodities may not be produced any more in one of the two countries. For these commodities the quantities of embodied labour must be intended as the quantities of labour embodied in those commodities that are given in exchange. Therefore, for these commodities, relative amounts of embodied labour can be arrived at through an intermediate comparison – i.e. through the relative price with respect to one of those (internationally traded) commodities which are produced in *both* countries.

10. The benefits of international trade

Summarizing the results of the previous three sections, we may say that there are two distinct channels through which each country can obtain benefits from international trade.

A first channel is that of specialization in the productive branches in which the country is enjoying comparative cost advantages. This is the traditionally explored channel, which emerges as relevant for all countries, provided that the two provisos mentioned in section 7 are satisfied.

A second, and distinct, channel is that of learning new techniques in those production branches that cannot rely (or could only partially rely) on internal demand (mainly because of low incomes), but that can find demand abroad. This second channel, which has been ignored by traditional economic theory, is of paramount importance especially for those countries which are economically less developed. For these countries, it may well surge to a position of far greater relevance than the first (traditionally more explored) channel, with which it may in any case jointly operate.

11. What international trade cannot do

It clearly emerges, from the foregoing analysis, that international trade represents, for any economic system, an important means to overcome the constraints of boundedness imposed by the fulfilment of macro-economic condition (IV.10.5). But it also emerges equally clearly that international trade cannot but be only one of such means; in certain circumstances, not even the most important.

Before going further, it may be useful to turn round our comparisons and remind ourselves, briefly and synthetically, of what international trade *cannot* do.

International trade, of course, brings about the equalization of the prices of those goods and services that can move from one country to another (taking costs of transport, storage, and insurance into account). But international trade cannot equalize the prices of those goods and services that do not move. In some countries, such goods and services may well reach a considerable proportion of the entire national output.

Moreover, and most of all, international trade cannot equalize the price of the primary production factor *par excellence* – labour – when international labour mobility is not allowed. This proposition is of enormous practical relevance. It is, in effect, surprising that theoretical economists should have generally kept so quiet on this problem.

Perhaps, an undeclared 'hope' (at times maybe a subconscious hope) has always been that of finding justifications for asserting that, after all, the non-mobility of production factors, and in particular of labour, is immaterial.[8] Unfortunately, this is not so. As the present simple theoretical

---

[8] The analytic efforts of economists have always tried to do the impossible in this direction. Commodities can easily be transported from one country to another. On the contrary, natural resources are fixed where nature placed them and factors of production can

scheme shows very clearly, non-mobility of labour, when associated with differentiated levels of technical knowledge, and thus of productivity, inevitably brings about international disparities of wage rates (and thus of per-capita incomes), which may well reach enormous proportions, and which are at the roots of inevitable international 'unequal' exchanges in terms of labour.

The extremely simple manner with which it is possible to make these statements here is of course due to assuming labour as the only factor of production. But their validity is quite general, when technical knowledge is different from country to country.[9]

The conclusion may be stated as an addition to the list of what international trade cannot do: international trade cannot be a substitute for the international mobility of labour.[10]

12. Movements through time – the substantial closure of economic systems with regard to productivity growth

Our analysis has essentially been carried out so far on comparisons of different economic systems (for simplicity's sake reduced to two, A and U) at a given point in time. And we have found that there are two sources of benefits from international economic relations: there is a primary source (learning of technical knowledge from abroad), and there is a secondary

certainly move, but only partially and with difficulty. The purpose, or better to say, the 'hope', has always been that of finding justifications for saying that the impossibility of moving resources and the difficulty of moving production factors could be compensated by the movements of commodities. The hope, in other words, has always been that international trade could be a substitute for the movement of persons, of resources and of production factors in general. The most typical expression of this 'hope' is perhaps represented by the well known 'theorem of factor price equalization' stated by Samuelson (1948), within the so-called Heckscher–Ohlin model. According to this theorem, under ideal conditions of international trade, with extreme, i.e. infinite, possibilities of substitution (among factors in production, and among goods in consumption), not only the prices of commodities, but also the prices of the factors of production reach full equalizatrion in the end. Such a theorem, if it were relevant in practice, would justify by itself complete opposition to international mobility of labour and no concern for inequalities in natural resource endowments.

The theorem is, alas, crucially dependent on the assumption of identical production functions, i.e. identical technical knowledge, in all countries.

[9] In effect, the just-mentioned factor price equalization theorem (see footnote 8) ceases to be valid for much less than non-uniformity of technical knowledge in the various countries. The theorem is built on assumptions that are so extreme (infinite possibility of substitution among the production factors, with production functions which, besides being identical in the various countries, are of 'well-behaved' neo-classical type) as to be, in practice, impossible of realization. It is enough (even within neo-classical theory) to have a less-than-infinite possibility of substitution, i.e. to have even only partial complementarity among the factors of production, to restrict the application of the theorem so severely as to make it practically irrelevant.

[10] The list is not exhaustive. It refers to the aspects considered so far. An even more important addition will be made in the following section.

source (international trade, itself acting through two channels: specialization in those fields where comparative costs are advantageous, and access to production sectors – and related possibilities of learning – which would otherwise be closed, owing to insufficiency of internal demand). We are now in a position to go on to investigate the effects of *movements* through time.

Returning to the two countries of our comparison, A and U, let us suppose that in both countries there is technical progress, but at the same time that the two price structures, which are supposed to be different, remain unchanged as time goes on. This means supposing that, in each country, technical progress occurs at a rate which is exactly the same in all sectors, even if it may be different from the rate of technical progress in the other country.

This is a strong assumption; it is made only for the analytic purpose of separating the effects of technical progress from those of the variation of comparative costs. For the moment, therefore, the supposition is that the comparative costs remain unchanged through time, in both countries, while at the same time each country enjoys those increases in productivity which it is able to generate from within.

In this way, *ex-hypothesi*, the conditions under which international trade is taking place remain invariant through time. If the two countries under consideration have already developed that specialization which allows them to take advantage of the benefits deriving from the disparities in comparative costs, this situation will remain invariant through time, since *ex-hypothesi* comparative costs remain unchanged. In other words, with regard to international trade deriving from disparities in comparative costs, there will not occur *any* increase of benefits in either of the two countries.[11]

At the same time, however – and this is the phenomenon to be stressed – in each of the two countries a process of increase in production is under way owing to internal increases in productivity.

It is now important to ponder for a moment on the meaning and implications of this process. It means that all the increases in productivity that take place in country A remain in country A and all the increases in productivity that take place in country U remain in country U. International trade, even though it takes place freely and even though it takes advantage of all the benefits deriving from the differences in the comparative costs, does not have any possibility of transferring the increases of

---

[11] Of course, even if comparative costs remain unchanged, there may be *indirect* beneficial effects from trade. The mobility of goods can also be an indirect means of spreading technical know-how (which we have, however, here excluded *ex-hypothesi*, at least as an additional factor). Moreover, if in one of the two countries there is unemployment (which, here again, we exclude *ex-hypothesi*) there might be indirect benefits due to an increase in external demand.

productivity from one country to another. If, to make an extreme, though not that unrealistic, hypothesis, the rate of technical progress were positive in country A and were zero in country U, we would be observing, with the elapsing of time, a process of a continuous growth in real per-capita incomes in country A, and absolutely stationary real per-capita incomes in country U, even though international trade is completely free between the two countries.

The practical significance of this conclusion is enormous. It explains the reason why, in the course of the last two centuries, throughout the world there have come into existence – and continue to persist and in certain cases to widen – such disparities in the real per-capita incomes of various countries, which are so extraordinarily wide (for a quick idea of the differences involved, see again table 1 of chapter I).

In other words, the important result that emerges from the present analysis is that *economic systems are substantially closed with regard to increases in productivity*.

The benefits from productivity increases inevitably remain within the country where they take place. Normally, they are transferred backwards, to the inhabitants of the country under consideration, through increases in their real per-capita incomes (namely through increases in the remunerations of the factors of production; in our simple scheme, wages). This process has of course been widely observed in the real world, and in the economic literature it has also been interpreted as a consequence of the oligopolistic behaviour of the large corporations (see, for example, Prebisch, 1959). But the present theoretical scheme, by going to a deeper level, makes it emerge as something much more fundamental. Even if we were to imagine a perfectly competitive mechanism that would compel firms to lower the prices of their products (instead of letting wages increase), our theoretical scheme tells us that this would be exactly compensated by the variation of the rate of exchange, thereby leaving the real position of the various countries unaltered. The result follows from a very basic process, which from our analysis has emerged as associated with the income distribution rôle played, within each economic system, by the uniform growth of the wage rate (see section IV.9).

No mobility of commodities, i.e. no international trade, can, as such, transfer the gains of productivity from one country to another. Indeed, no mobility of commodities will ever be a substitute for the mobility of technical knowledge.

In a way which may seem paradoxical, but which in the present theoretical scheme emerges in all its logical stringency from macroeconomic condition (IV.10.5), the boundedness of each economic system also appears as a basic institutional device, that allows the members of the community of any economic system not to disperse – or, from another point of view, to keep and distribute among themselves, not allowing any escape of – the productivity increases which, as a community, they have been able to achieve.

13. Changes in the terms of trade and leakages of the gains of productivity

In the previous section, the hypothesis has been made of constancy through time of the price structures of the two countries under consideration. This is roughly equivalent to making the hypothesis of constancy through time of their terms of trade. The purpose of such hypothesis is analytical; it has been made in order to separate the effects of technical progress from the effects of changes in comparative costs. In the real world, of course, the two effects are connected: technical progress *generates* changes in comparative costs, and therefore in relative prices.

If we therefore go on now explicitly to consider changes in relative prices, we also come to face, with the passing of time, possible changes of the terms of trade, i.e., defining them explicitly, of the ratio between the weighted average of import prices and the weighted average of export prices. Of course, despite the variation of all relative prices, it might just happen that on average, the terms of trade remain constant through time, in which case the conclusion of the preceding section would remain valid (complete closure of economic systems with regard to the benefits deriving from increases in productivity), even if now with reference to the *average* of the increases in productivity.

But in general, when all the relative prices vary, the terms of trade will also tend to vary. In this case, the country that experiences an improvement in its terms of trade (a decrease in the ratio specified above) will absorb part of the increases in productivity that occur in the country with which it trades. But, symmetrically, the opposite also occurs – the other country will lose a corresponding part of its increases in productivity to the first country.

This outcome appears as an exception to the rule stated in the previous section (complete closure of the trading countries with regard to the benefits deriving from increases in productivity). Nevertheless, this exception does not change the principle or general rule, since – whatever the leakages of productivity gains from one country to another – *all* the gains enjoyed through this means by one country are exactly compensated by the losses suffered by the other country (or countries). In other words, international trade as such, in the aggregate, cannot add anything to the gains that come from the increases in productivity. For all the trading countries considered together, the changes of the terms of trade exactly compensate one another and cannot bring any net benefit at all.

It is also to be noted that, from the general rule, appropriately modified by what has just been said about the changes of the terms of trade, it does not follow at all that the leakages of increases-in-productivity benefits should necessarily go from the rich country to the poor country. They might well go the opposite way.

I have had the opportunity to investigate these problems elsewhere, showing that the changes in the terms of trade depend on the comparative speed with which, in each country, productivity proceeds in the industries specializing in exports, with respect to productivity in the other industries (and I have called it the 'general principle of comparative productivity change advantage').[12]

This means for example that, when in a poor country most of the efforts to increase productivity are concentrated in the export industries, while the rest of the country is stagnant – a situation which is by no means unrealistic – this country might well suffer a drain of its productivity gains towards the outside world (owing to the worsening of its terms of trade). In other words, the poor country, besides being unable to take part in the increases of productivity that occur in the rich countries, might well lose to the rich countries even part of those productivity gains that it is able to obtain domestically.

14. Necessity of reconsidering the problem of international economic relations

The outcomes of the analysis of the foregoing pages leave very little space (in fact, on average, no space at all) for any participation of the poor countries in the increases of productivity that occur in the rich countries. But precisely for this reason, they bring sharply to our attention the need for a reconsideration of the entire problem of international economic relations.

For more than two centuries, both theoretical and applied economists, facing the closures that were appearing between the various economic systems, have thought they could attribute most of the blame to lack of international trade and have put all their trust, as to the possibilities of opening up the various countries, precisely on the international mobility of commodities.

To avoid any misunderstanding, let us first of all stress the point that international trade has an objective basis of enormous importance and

---

[12] In Pasinetti, 1981, pp. 263–6.

great relevance. International trade allows each economic system to maintain its identity and its autonomy and at the same time to acquire benefits by taking advantage of the favourable differences in relative costs (through specialization) and by the opening up of new outlets (especially important for poor countries).

But let us also honestly recognize that international trade does not impede the fragmentation of the world into a plurality of economic-geographic areas. Above all, it does not impede a process by which the rich countries get richer and richer, and the poor countries are left further and further behind.

After two centuries of industrialization, the disparities in the 'wealth of nations' have grown to frightening proportions. The magnitudes of such disparities have already become abhorrent to any feeling of human solidarity. And there is the grave danger that the relentless thrust of non-converging movements may make the situation worse, or even explosive.

The present theoretical scheme is inviting us, first of all, to abandon illusions. International mobility of commodities is not enough. International trade cannot be a substitute for the mobility of labour. Above all, international trade cannot be a substitute for the mobility of technical knowledge.

15. International mobility of labour

We may begin by considering briefly what prospects there are for international mobility of labour.

In general, when economic conditions are the same, most people (except for a small minority) tend to look for their jobs and their livings within the space and the ethnic/demographic group where they have grown up. But when economic disparities are severe, the pressures increase (despite the many difficulties of adaptation to alien environments) to emigrate towards economic systems with higher per-capita incomes and more opportunities. As has been pointed out in section 4, emigration from poor countries to rich countries gives single individuals the benefits of being inserted into economic systems with higher wages (and therefore higher per-capita incomes). But in the receiving country, even under the most favourable conditions, there are strict limits to the amount of immigration which can be accepted. The novelty of the present theoretical scheme is that it brings to light a solid explanation of the widespread opposition to indiscriminate immigration – the requirements of fulfilling macro-economic condition (IV.10.5). This macro-economic condition has revealed itself more and more insistently in the course of the present analysis as a focal point, as the centre of the identity of each economic system. It is precisely the requirement of satisfying this condition that engenders a responsibility of the community, taken as a whole, towards the single individuals, and makes possible – through the pursuit of full employment and of uniformity of wage increases – that homogenizing process which permits the distribution to all members of the community concerned of the increases in productivity that the economic system as a whole is able to achieve.

The consequences are very important. Macro-economic condition (IV.10.5) imposes first of all some regulatory measures for migrations – in practice, it implies the impossibility of a perfect international mobility of labour. Furthermore, it realizes the closure of each economic system with regard to the distribution of the benefits deriving from productivity increases. The distribution of the productivity gains go to benefit those components of the economic system to which the macro-economic condition refers. Those who are outside are excluded. This is in fact, as has been observed, the major factor behind the formation of a plurality of economic systems.

It is vital to realize that, as long as economic disparities persist, these tendencies can only partially be opposed. It is of course possible, and no doubt reasonable, to ask the rich countries to be willing to insert a certain amount of immigration from the poor countries into their programmes, thereby allowing benefits to flow to a certain number of immigrant persons. But it is quite clear that these kinds of measures can never by themselves solve the economic problems of poor countries. Pushed to the extreme, an exclusive reliance on immigration/emigration would end up in absurdity. (By a *reductio ad absurdum* argument, it would lead to a concentration of the entire world population in the now rich countries and to the de-population of the rest of the world!)

There is another channel that, at first sight, might seem to help; i.e. keeping all people in the geographic areas where they are, and at the same time gradually extending the boundaries of the rich countries, which would gradually swallow up the poor countries (and thus extend to the poor economic systems the benefits of belonging to developed economic systems). It does not take long reflection, however, to become aware of the impossibility of proposing such a measure. One may actually say that such a would-be solution has already been tried in the past and has produced the disastrous results of colonialism. One cannot of course exclude that the extension of boundaries, i.e. in practice the annexation of a poor to a rich economic system, may be successful in certain circumstances, but this cannot evidently be the general case. It may be conceived in those situations where there already exist profound ethnic–religious–linguistic identities, that spontaneously push towards the annexation. (The most striking example is perhaps the recent unification of Germany; another case, a little less clear-cut, is that of the unification of Italy in the second half of the nineteenth century.)

Paradoxically, the ideal conditions for a completely free international mobility of labour turn out to be those that come about among economic systems that have reached more or less the same level of development and thus of per-capita incomes. In these cases, adaptation difficulties are minor, discrimination becomes less likely, and above all the migratory flows become numerically less conspicuous. Moreover, such flows may go both ways!

The conclusion is important and should not be underestimated.

International mobility of labour is not immaterial – it matters a lot. But it is not possible to rely on international mobility of labour to eliminate the economic disparities among the various nations. Precisely the opposite seems to be the case. It seems that it would first be necessary to eliminate the international economic disparities, before we may be able to bring about the favourable conditions for a completely free international mobility of labour.

16. International mobility of information and of technical knowledge

We may now go on to examine the prospects for international mobility of technical knowledge. In fact, there does not seem to be any other option; but this option is of crucial importance.

The increases in productivity that are realized within each economic system are kept inside the system that produces them, as we have seen. But technical knowledge, which is the source of such productivity increases, can go everywhere. The often-mentioned macro-economic condition (IV.10.5), which makes indiscriminate mobility of labour impossible, is on the contrary in no way in contrast with international mobility of information and of technical knowledge.

In this regard, international mobility of technical knowledge shares many of the favourable characteristics of the international mobility of commodities. Both of them preserve the identity and autonomy of each economic system. Neither of them interferes with – on the contrary both are perfectly compatible with – the fulfilment of macro-condition (IV.10.5).

But international mobility of knowledge has so many further, and widely more favourable, characteristics. While mobility of commodities as such has no effect on the improvement of production activity, leaving the internal processes of productivity growth unchanged, and thereby being unable to cause any international transfer of the benefits deriving from such processes, mobility of technical knowledge can generate increases in productivity everywhere. The implications are of the utmost importance.

The acquisition of technical knowledge by poor economic systems, i.e. international mobility of information and of technical knowledge, represents the fundamental factor, in truth the crucial factor, that may put the poor countries on the way first of all to set a check to the widening, and later on to actually head towards the elimination, of the huge disparities in per-capita incomes that are nowadays observed throughout the world.

It should be stressed that a speeding up of the growth of productivity, and thus of per-capita incomes, depends on the speeding up of learning, independently of anything else, and thus also independently of whether or not there is any international trade.

But, as we have seen in sections 5–10 above, because in low-income countries internal demand is in practice necessarily limited to the realm of necessary goods, international trade, by widening considerably the possibilities of production, can also widen considerably the possibilities of both individual and social learning. Therefore it becomes important for the low-income countries, as a matter of strategy, to choose specialization in export production in those fields where they can achieve higher rates of growth of productivity than their competitors. I have had occasion to deal with this problem elsewhere and I have called the aforementioned strategy the '(special) principle of comparative productivity-change advantage'.[13] Huge amounts of research work would seem to be particularly required in this field. The purpose in view is ambitious, and yet not impossible: the pursuit of the widely invoked convergence of poor economic systems towards the level of per-capita incomes enjoyed at present by the economically advanced countries.

It may be useful to stress again that international mobility of knowledge does not exclude any of the other measures reviewed above, which thereby retain all their properties and become complementary. International mobility of commodities, besides widening the possibilities of learning, brings about *once-for-all* increases of incomes, due to the difference in the comparative costs. International mobility of people, to the extent that it takes place, can benefit those who can move. Yet neither of them, as we have seen, can bring a decisive solution to the problem of the world economic disparities.

International mobility of knowledge can.

Above all, the mobility of technical knowledge possesses a characteristic

[13] See Pasinetti, 1981, pp. 268ff. I have called this principle 'special' to distinguish it from the 'general' principle of comparative productivity-change advantage, which refers to the economic system as a whole, in its attempts at improving, or at not worsening, its terms of trade. The reference is in footnote 12 above.

which, if it were not so obvious, it would be spontaneous to define as 'prodigious', especially with regard to the characteristic canons of traditional economic theory, all focussed on scarcity. Mobility of technical knowledge leaves intact the consistence and characteristics of the source from which it comes!

As opposed to material goods – i.e. commodities, natural resources, and productive factors – whose possession by any individual is exclusive, knowledge is not susceptible of exclusive possession: it can be communicated to everybody. More precisely, the transfer of material goods also implies the transfer of their possession, which passes on to the person who receives them and ceases for the person who gives them. Communication of knowledge enriches those who receive it, without depriving the persons who give it (the process of communication of knowledge may even in certain cases stimulate an increase in the original knowledge). Knowledge remains at its origin, as it is, undiminished and intact, even if it is diffused conceptually and spatially.

Rather than a 'transfer' (as must be said of commodities) it becomes more appropriate to talk of 'diffusion'.

The diffusion of technical knowledge can indeed benefit all those who receive it, without taking anything away from those who communicate it. This is indeed its most 'revolutionary' characteristic. It is reasonable to expect that it is also bound to be revolutionary in the methods of research it requires.

Perhaps, the imperviousness of traditional economic theory to the treatment of technical progress may have something to do with precisely this. At the very basis of traditional economics, as is well known, there is the notion of scarcity of material goods; a notion that no longer makes sense with regard to knowledge.

From yet another point of view, with respect to the one taken at the very beginning (in chapter I), the structural dynamics analysis here pursued points decisively towards the need for the development of imaginative and new analytical tools.

17. The 'causes' and the 'nature' of the wealth of nations

A few final reflections may be added, after singling out and bringing into relief the acquisition of technical knowledge as the primary source of the wealth of nations.

Adam Smith, two centuries ago, in proposing for our attention precisely the 'nature and causes of the wealth of nations' as the principal object of political economy, merged together, perhaps naïvely, two very different questions; and – with regard to their complexity – inverted their order.

He singled out the 'causes' of the wealth of a nation, in remarkably simple manner, on the very first page of his major work, as has been pointed out already (section VII.2). In his words, they lie in 'the skill, dexterity and judgment with which its labour is generally applied' (Smith, 1904 [1776], p. 1).[14]

But the nature of the wealth of modern nations has revealed itself to be extraordinarily complex. The industrial era has brought us a type of wealth of a nature profoundly different from that which characterized the preceding periods. If, in pre-industrial societies, the wealth of a nation was founded principally upon the endowments of material resources inherited from the outside world and/or accumulated in the past, in industrial societies the wealth of a nation is founded principally on the technical (and therefore 'immaterial') knowledge that its inhabitants have been able to acquire. These are two quite different types of wealth: they interpenetrate and reinforce each other, and add up, but their relative importance has been progressively changing and is continually changing in time, with extremely wide implications.

Material resources (on which the 'old' kind of wealth was based) are physically definable, and have a one-to-one association with specific individuals. They represent, in a certain sense, an individualistic type of wealth. Their possession by certain individuals excludes possession by other individuals.

The immaterial technical knowledge (on which the 'new' type of wealth is based) can be transferred from one individual to other individuals – in principle, to all other individuals – without being lost by those who originally had it. Its nature is no longer exclusively individualistic.[15]

Furthermore, the productivity of the single individuals, which springs from it, does increase because of the improvement of individual knowledge (communicable to others), but also presupposes to be inserted into a whole

---

[14] The crucial point that needed to be picked up from Smith – and that was generally missed in the following literature, even when knowledge came to be discussed explicitly – is that 'skill, dexterity and judgment' can be *learnt*. Take, for example, von Hayek's well known essays on knowledge and economics (Hayek, 1937, 1945). He discusses at length how the knowledge of the single individuals is communicated through the market mechanism; but knowledge itself is taken as something given.

One can find some follow-up to Smith's lead, on the other hand, in the intuitive remarks of some non-orthodox economists. Take, as an another example, Friedrich List's concept of *Productionkräfte* ('productive forces' (List, 1841, chapter 12)), which has generally been taken as a hopelessly vague idea. Schumpeter (1954), perhaps rather ungenerously, called it 'not much more than a label for an unsolved problem' (p. 505). List himself did not help by his (misplaced) attempts to associate his distinction between (inherited) wealth and causes of wealth, with the Smithian distinction between causes and nature of wealth. Yet, if we now look at List's 'productive forces' as an urge to adopt ever better production techniques, we see the concept regaining quite a lot of meaningful content.

[15] In this regard see also Pasinetti, 1977, pp. 1–4, and 1981, pp. 274–6.

framework which relies, so to speak, on a 'social' organization. It requires division of labour, specialization and willingness to improve knowledge by single individuals, combined with an organization, and the assuming of responsibilities, on the part of the community as a whole.

The importance of the stimuli to the single individual (and the importance of the role of individual freedom of initiative) can hardly be stressed. But at the same time the necessity of overall coordination plays a crucial rôle and should not be under-estimated. The nature of the wealth of an industrial nation is, at the same time, individualistic and social.

This aspect of the matter entails consequences of paramount importance for international relations, because, on the one hand, it entails the formation of a network of interdependent relations within each economic system, and on the other hand it delimits it with regard to other economic systems.

In the present theoretical scheme, the social, and at the same time delimiting, requirement finds its analytic expression in the macro-economic condition for effective demand and full employment. As has been seen, this brings with it the consequence of circumscribing the demographic and spatial size of the group of individuals, one might say of the 'social unit', within which the production process (representing the up-to-date material consequence of the evolutionary process of acquisition of technical knowledge) is carried out. Knowledge, in and of itself, can be diffused and learnt, but the increases in productivities that the social unit derives from it do not seep through to the outside – they are kept within the economic system in which they are realized.

One might instinctively rebel against this characteristic, but one must finally recognize and accept it, as it is inherent in the social organization of the production process that characterizes all industrial economic systems.

It is *knowledge* that is not confined to those limits; knowledge can go anywhere and be acquired everywhere. It is therefore at the stage of the transmission and diffusion and acquisition of knowledge that the relations among nations must find their focal point. Those nations that remain behind have to speed up (and indeed must be helped to speed up) their processes of individual and social *learning*. It is no use to rely on the increases of productivity which take place abroad, since the associated benefits do not spill over the borders; they are intrinsically bound to remain where they have taken place.

It is knowledge that has to be captured. It is the acquisition of knowledge that eventually makes the wealth of a nation.

References

Aitchison, J. and Brown, J. A. C. (1957), *The Lognormal Distribution*, Cambridge University Press, Cambridge

Arrow, Kenneth J. (1951), *Social Choice and Individual Values*, John Wiley and Sons, New York

(1962), 'The Economic Implications of Learning by Doing', *Review of Economic Studies*, 29, 155–73

Baranzini, Mauro (1991), *A Theory of Wealth Distribution and Accumulation*, Clarendon Press, Oxford

Baranzini, Mauro and Scazzieri, Roberto (1990), 'Economic Structure: Analytical Perspectives', in M. Baranzini and R. Scazzieri (eds.), *The Economic Theory of Structure and Change*, Cambridge University Press, Cambridge, pp. 227–333

Barro, Robert J. (1974), 'Are Government Bonds Net Wealth?', *Journal of Political Economy*, 82, 1095–17

Baumol, William J. (1967), 'Macroeconomics of Unbalanced Growth: The Anatomy of Urban Crisis', *American Economic Review*, LVII, 415–26

Boggio, Luciano (1985), 'On the Stability of Production Prices', *Metroeconomica*, XXXVII, 241–67

Britto, Ronald (1973), 'Some Recent Developments in the Theory of Economic Growth: An Interpretation', *Journal of Economic Literature*, XI, 1343–66

Chenery, Hollis and Srinivasan, T. N. (eds.) (1988), *Handbook of Development Economics* (2 vols.), North Holland, Amsterdam

Clark, Colin (1940), *The Conditions of Economic Progress* (1st edn 1940; 2nd edn 1951; 3rd edn 1957), Macmillan, London

Domar, Evsey (1946), 'Capital Expansion, Rate of Growth and Employment', *Econometrica*, 14, 137–47

Dosi, Giovanni; Freeman, Christopher; Nelson, Richard; Silverberg, Gerald; and Soete, Luc (1988), *Technical Change and Economic Theory*, Pinter Publishers, London and New York

Duménil, Gérard and Lévy, Dominique (1987), 'La concurrence capitaliste: un processus dynamique', in J. P. Fitoussi and P. A. Muet (eds.), *Macrodynamique et déséquilibres*, Economica, Paris

(1991), 'Micro Adjustment toward Long-Term Equilibrium', *Journal of Economic Theory*, 53, 369–95

Einaudi, Luigi (1937), 'The Medieval Practice of Managed Currency', in A. D. Gayer (ed.), *The Lessons of Monetary Experience – Essays in honour of Irving Fisher*, Rinehart & Co., New York (reprinted by Kelley, New York, 1970) pp. 259–68

Emmanuel, Arghiri (1972), *Unequal Exchange – A Study of the Imperialism of Trade*, Monthly Review Press, NLB, London

Engel, Ernst (1857), 'Die Productions- und Consumtions-verhältnisse des Königreichs Sachsen', *Zeitschrift der Statistischen Bureaus des Königlich Sächsischen Ministeriums des Innern*, Nos 8 and 9 (22 November) pp. 153–84; (republished in *Bulletin de l'Institut International de Statistique*, IX (1895))

Furtado, Celso (1967), *Teoria e política do desenvolvimento econômico*, Companhia Editora Nacional, São Paulo

Goodwin, Richard M. (1987), 'Macro-dynamics', in R. M. Goodwin and L. F. Punzo *The Dynamics of a Capitalist Economy*, Polity Press, Cambridge
(1990), *Chaotic Economic Dynamics*, Clarendon Press, Oxford

Haavelmo, Trygve (1954), *A Study in the Theory of Economic Evolution*, North-Holland, Amsterdam

Hagemann, Harald (1990), 'The Structural Theory of Economic Growth', in M. Baranzini and R. Scazzieri (eds.), *The Economic Theory of Structure and Change*, Cambridge University Press, Cambridge, pp. 144–71

Hahn, Frank H. and Matthews, R. C. O. (1964), 'The Theory of Economic Growth: a Survey', *Economic Journal*, 74, 779–902

Harms, B. (1926), 'Strukturwandlungen der deutschen Volkswirtschaft', *Weltwirtschaftliches Archiv*, XXIV, 259–73

Harrod, Roy F. (1939), 'An Essay in Dynamic Theory', *Economic Journal*, 49, 14–33
(1948), *Towards a Dynamic Economics*, Macmillan, London

Hayek, Friedrich A. (1937), 'Economics and Knowledge', *Economica*, 4, 33–54
(1945), 'The Use of Knowledge in Society', *American Economic Review*, 35, 519–30

Hicks, John R. (1965), *Capital and Growth*, Clarendon Press, Oxford
(1973), *Capital and Time*, Clarendon Press, Oxford

Homer, Sidney (1963), *A History of Interest Rates*, Rutgers University Press, New Brunswick, N.J.

Houthakker, H. S. (1957), 'An International Comparison of Household Expenditure Patterns, Commemorating the Centenary of Engel's Law', *Econometrica*, 25, 532–51

Houthakker, H. S. and Taylor, Lester D. (1970), *Consumer Demand in the United States: Analysis and Projections* (2nd edn), Harvard University Press, Cambridge, Mass.

Kaldor, Nicholas (1961), 'Capital Accumulation and Economic Growth' in F. A. Lutz and D. C. Hague (eds.), *The Theory of Capital* (Proceedings of a Conference of the IEA), Macmillan, London, pp. 177–222

Keynes, John Maynard (1936), *The General Theory of Employment, Interest and Money*, Macmillan, London
(1973), *The Collected Writings of John Maynard Keynes*, XIII: *The General*

Theory and After: *Preparation*, Macmillan, London

(1979), *The Collected Writings of John Maynard Keynes*, XXIX: *The General Theory and After*: *A Supplement*, Macmillan, London

Kubin, Ingrid (1991), *Market Prices and Natural Prices*, Peter Lang, Frankfurt

Kuznets, Simon (1966), *Modern Economic Growth – Rate, Structure, and Spread*, Yale University Press, London

(1973), 'Modern Economic Growth: Findings and Reflections' (Nobel Memorial Lecture), *American Economic Review*, 63, 247–58

Leontief, Wassily W. (1936), 'Quantitative Input–Output Relations in the Economic System of the United States', *Review of Economics and Statistics*, VIII, 105–25

(1951) [1941], *The Structure of American Economy, 1919–1939*, (1st edn 1941, 2nd edn 1951), Oxford University Press, New York

Lewis, W. Arthur (1954), 'Economic Development with Unlimited Supply of Labour', *Manchester School of Economic and Social Studies*, 22, 139–91

List, Friedrich (1841), *Das nationale System der politischen Öconomie*, J. G. Cotta'scher Verlag, Stuttgart and Tübingen (translated into English as *The National System of Political Economy*, Longmans, Green and Co., London, 1885)

Lowe, Adolph (1955), 'Structural Analysis of Real Capital Formation', in Moses Abramovitz (ed.), *Capital Formation and Economic Growth*, Princeton University Press, Princeton, N.J., pp. 581–634

Lucas, Robert E. Jr. (1987), *Models of Business Cycles*, Basil Blackwell, Oxford

Malthus, Thomas R. (1820), *Principles of Political Economy*, J. Murray, London (and following edition and translations)

Marshall, Alfred (1920), *Principles of Economics*, (8th edn) Macmillan, London

Marx, Karl (1867, 1885, 1894), *Das Kapital*, vols. I (1867), II (1885), III (1894), O. Meissner, Hamburg (and following editions and translations)

Modigliani, Franco and Brumberg, Richard (1955), 'Utility Analysis and the Consumption Function: An Interpretation of Cross-Section Data', in Kenneth K. Kurihara (ed.), *Post-Keynesian Economics*, George Allen and Unwin, London, pp. 388–436

Noonan, John T. Jr. (1957), *The Scholastic Analysis of Usury*, Harvard University Press, Cambridge, Mass.

Nurkse, Ragnar (1935), 'The Schematic Representation of the Structure of Production', *Review of Economic Studies*, 2, 232–44

(1953), *Problems of Capital Formation in Underdeveloped Countries*, Basil Blackwell, Oxford

Pasinetti, Luigi L. (1960), 'Cyclical Fluctuations and Economic Growth', *Oxford Economic Papers*, New Series, 12, 215–41 (reprinted in Pasinetti (1974)).

(1962), *A Multisectoral Model of Economic Growth*, unpublished Ph.D dissertation, University of Cambridge

(1963), *A Multisectoral Model of Economic Growth*, King's College, Cambridge

(1965), 'A New Theoretical Approach to the Problems of Economic Growth', *Pontificiae Academiae Scientiarum Scripta Varia*, 28, Vatican City, pp. 571–677.

(1973), 'The Notion of Vertical Integration in Economic Analysis', *Metro-economica*, XXV, 1–29 (reprinted in Luigi L. Pasinetti (ed.), *Essays in the Theory of Joint Production*, Macmillan, London, 1980, pp. 16–43)

(1974), *Growth and Income Distribution – Essays in Economic Theory*, Cambridge University Press, Cambridge

(1977), *Lectures on the Theory of Production*, Columbia University Press, New York, and Macmillan, London

(1980–81), 'The Rate of Interest and Income Distribution in a Pure Labour Economy', *Journal of Post-Keynesian Economics*, 2, 170–82

(1981), *Structural Change and Economic Growth: A Theoretical Essay on the Dynamics of the Wealth of Nations*, Cambridge University Press, Cambridge

(1986), 'Theory of Value – A Source of Alternative Paradigms in Economic Analysis', in Mauro Baranzini and Roberto Scazzieri (eds.), *Foundations of Economics – Structure of Inquiry and Economic Theory*, Basil Blackwell, Oxford, pp. 409–31

(1988), 'Growing Sub-systems, Vertically Hyper-integrated Sectors and the Labour Theory of Value', *Cambridge Journal of Economics*, 12, 125–34

Pasinetti, Luigi L. (with Roberto Scazzieri) (1987), 'Structural Economic Dynamics', an entry of: *The New Palgrave. A Dictionary of Economics*, Macmillan, London, IV, pp. 525–8

Perroux, François (1939), *Cours d'économie politique*, (2nd edn), Les Editions Domat-Montchretien, Paris

Pollak, Robert A. (1978), 'Endogenous Tastes in Demand and Welfare Analysis', *American Economic Review*, Papers and Proceedings, May, 68, 374–9

Prebisch, Raul (1959), 'Commercial Policy in the Underdeveloped Countries', *American Economic Review*, Papers and Proceedings, May, 49, 251–73

Ricardo, David (1951) [1817], 'Principles of Political Economy and Taxation', in Piero Sraffa (ed.), *Works and Correspondence of David Ricardo*, I, Cambridge University Press, Cambridge

(1951) [1820], 'Funding Systems', in Piero Sraffa (ed.), *Works and Correspondence of David Ricardo*, IV, Cambridge University Press, Cambridge

Robertson, Dennis H. (1940), 'Mr Keynes and the Rate of Interest', Lectures given at LSE in 1939, in *Essays in Monetary Theory*, Staples Press, London, pp. 1–38

Romer, Paul M. (1990), 'Endogenous Technological Change', *Journal of Political Economy* 98, (5, pt 2), S71–S102

Rosenstein-Rodan, Paul (1943), 'Problems of Industrialization in Eastern and South-Eastern Europe', *Economic Journal*, 53, 202–11

Rostow, W. W. (1960), *The Stages of Economic Growth – A non-Communist Manifesto*, Cambridge University Press, Cambridge

Samuelson, Paul A. (1948), 'International Trade and the Equalization of Factor Prices', *Economic Journal*, 58, 163–84

Schumpeter, Joseph A. (1934), *The Theory of Economic Development*, Harvard University Press, Cambridge, Mass.

(1939), *Business Cycles – A Theoretical, Historical, and Statistical Analysis of the Capitalist Process* (2 vols.), McGraw-Hill, New York

(1954), *History of Economic Analysis*, Oxford University Press, New York

Sen, Amartya K. (1977), 'Rational Fools', *Philosophy and Public Affairs*, 6, 317–44
 (1985), *Commodities and Capabilities*, North Holland, Amsterdam
Smith, Adam (1904) [1776], *An Inquiry into the Nature and Causes of the Wealth of Nations*, edited by Edwin Cannan (2 vols.), Methuen, London
Solow, Robert M. (1988), 'Growth Theory and After' (Nobel Memorial Lecture), *American Economic Review*, 78, 307–17
Sraffa, Piero (1960), *Production of Commodities by Means of Commodities – Prelude to a Critique of Economic Theory*, Cambridge University Press, Cambridge
Streeten, Paul (1959), 'Unbalanced Growth', *Oxford Economic Papers*, New Series, 11, 167–90
Sylos Labini, Paolo (1991), 'The Changing Character of the So-called Business Cycle', *Atlantic Economic Journal*, XIX (3), 1–14
Syrquin, Moshe (1988), 'Patterns of Structural Change', in Chenery and Srinivasan (eds.) (1988), I, pp. 203–73
Tinbergen, Jan (1952), 'De quelques problèmes posés par le concept de structure économique', *Revue d'économie politique*, 1, 27–46
von Neumann, John (1937), 'Über ein ökonomisches Gleichungssystem und eine Verallgemeinerung der Brouwerschen Fixpunktsatzes', in *Ergebnisse eines mathematischen Kolloquiums*, Vienna, VIII, pp. 73–83; English translation: 'A Model of General Equilibrium', *Review of Economic Studies*, 33 (1945–46), 1–9
von Weizsäcker, Carl Christian (1971), 'Notes on Endogenous Change of Tastes', *Journal of Economic Theory*, 3, 345–72
Wagner, Adolf (1883), *Finanzwissenschaft* (3rd edn), C. F. Winter, Leipzig
 (1958) [1883], 'Three Extracts on Public Finance', in Richard A. Musgrave and Alan T. Peacock (eds.), *Classics in the Theory of Public Finance*, Macmillan, London, pp. 1–15
World Bank for Reconstruction and Development, *World Development Report*, various years, Oxford University Press, Oxford, and New York

Index